FORGOTTEN CUCHAREÑOS
of the
LOWER VALLEY

FORGOTTEN CUCHAREÑOS of the LOWER VALLEY

VIRGINIA SANCHEZ

THE History PRESS

Published by The History Press
Charleston, SC 29403
www.historypress.net

Front cover image: Adobe home of a Hispanic family in Cucharas. *Courtesy of Helen Cisneros Vigil Family.*
Back cover images: Carmel Bustos (groom), Rafaelita Ruybali (bride), Teofilo Bustos and Maria Virginia Lucero. *Courtesy of the Bustos Family.*

First published 2010
Second printing 2014

Manufactured in the United States

ISBN 978.1.60949.134.5

Sanchez, Virginia.
Forgotten Cuchareños of the lower valley / Virginia Sanchez.
p. cm.
Includes bibliographical references and index.
ISBN 978-1-60949-134-5
1. Hispanic Americans--Colorado--Cuchara--History. 2. Pioneers--Colorado--Cuchara--History. 3. Hispanic Americans--Colorado--Cuchara--Biography 4. Pioneers--Colorado--Cuchara--Biography 5. Frontier and pioneer life--Colorado--Cuchara. 6. Cuchara (Colo.)--History. 7. Cuchara (Colo.)--Biography 8. Cuchara Region (Colo.)--History. 9. Huerfano County (Colo.)--History. I. Title.
F784.C9S26 2010
978.8'51--dc22
2010044997

Contents

Preface

The United States created the Territory of New Mexico in 1850. At the time, the southern half of present-day Colorado, extending as far north as the Arkansas River, laid within New Mexico Territory. In 1861, the United States created the Territory of Colorado from land that lay within parts of Kansas, Nebraska, Utah and New Mexico Territories. Of the seventeen counties established by the Colorado Territorial Legislature that same year, five retained the Spanish names commonly used by the early settlers. The three large counties located in southern Colorado, whose populations were predominantly Spanish speaking, were named *Huérfano*, Guadalupe (later *Conejos*) and *Costilla*. Huerfano County was named for the orphan butte that stands today on the east side of Interstate 25, north of the town of Walsenburg. The other two counties located in central Colorado were named *El Paso* (the Pass) and *Pueblo* (town). Several counties established after 1861 also retained their Spanish names.

A lot of changes occurred when an influx of Anglos moved into the Lower Cuchara Valley of Huerfano County. Although Hispanos were the majority Spanish-speaking population, English became the dominant business language. Eastern correspondents and authors traveled through the area and wrote about the habits, food and customs of the Hispanos and Native Americans. Some of the earliest accounts of Cucharas were documented by John H. Beadle, Helen Hunt Jackson and Louis Bernhardt Sporleder. Beadle, a western correspondent for the *Cincinnati Commercial*, wrote of his travels through the territories, which included Colorado and New Mexico.

In his book, *The Undeveloped West or Five Years in the Territories*, Beadle compared the Southwest to the eastern United States. He was highly critical of Hispano homes, culture, spirituality and their "dark features." Helen Hunt Jackson published stories about her travels in her book, *Bits of Travel at Home*. She was the wife of a prominent citizen of Colorado Springs and secretary-treasurer of the Denver & Rio Grande (D&RG) Railroad. Her accounts were also laced with critical opinions. The third author, Louis B. Sporleder, arrived in southern Colorado and wrote about the early settlers and Native Americans.

In addition, newspapers printed articles to attract Anglo businessmen and farmers. Editors of local and regional English-language newspapers from Denver, Colorado Springs, Pueblo, Walsenburg and *Trinidad* (Trinity) worked with the D&RG to promote land in Cucharas and attract Anglo businessmen and farmers. These newspapers advertised that land was under ditch and cultivated predominantly by Mexicans willing to sell.[1] Spanish-language newspapers, such as the *Anunciador*, *El Progreso* and *La Opinión Pública*, would have been wonderful resources of the types of news reported to Hispanic readers; unfortunately, no back issues of these newspapers exist today.[2]

In this book, I use the term Anglo rather than whites or European Americans to refer to people of British descent, native English speakers from the eastern part of the United States and non-native English speakers who were not American Indian. Because the people from Cucharas—the Cuchareños—were no longer Mexican citizens after the United States' war with Mexico, I use the term Hispano to refer to the Spanish-speaking settlers of southern Colorado and northern New Mexico. In addition to scant published accounts, I analyzed maps, acequia ledgers, water decrees and oral histories to document the history of the Cuchareños. Church and civil records often used various spellings of certain surnames, such as Ballejos, Ruibal or Ruival and Valdes. I chose to use the spelling used in most records. Spanish-given names do not appear with accents, and place names are located in Colorado unless stated otherwise. Detailed information in the endnotes is intended to assist historical and family researchers. Because I could not include detailed information about all subjects I introduce, readers should consult primary sources and history books about those subjects.

The Cuchara Valley is divided into the upper valley and the lower valley. The Upper Cuchara Valley is the area close to and south of the town of La Veta, which is higher in elevation. The Lower Cuchara Valley is that area near and east of present-day Walsenburg. How *Cucharas* (spoons) and the Cuchara Valley got their names remains a mystery. It may simply be that the area resembled a large stirring spoon or ladle. In 1872, John H. Beadle described the lower valley as the "beautiful circular valley." The community of Cucharas lay within Townships 27 and 28 South, Ranges 65 and 66, 6th prime meridian. Within this 144-square-mile area once lay the Cucharas plaza, a stage station, four schools, seven acequias, a chapel and a *penitente* (religious fraternal) meetinghouse, the railroad town of Cucharas City and the D&RG railyard. Although Cucharas no longer exists, the descriptions in this book provide a historic context of all that once appeared on its landscape. This book introduces the Hispano settlers who first came into the Lower Cuchara Valley as early as 1862 and discusses the impact of culture and conflict brought about by change. Each chapter introduces new historical information about Cucharas and the Cuchareños. This information tells about the various ways Hispano culture, tradition and norms came in conflict with newcomers' views about religion, sacrifice, water use, class and ethnicity. Like movements on a chess board, events in play ultimately changed the social and political status of the Cuchareños.

Acknowledgements

I have always been fascinated by the history of the Southwest, specifically the history of New Mexico and southern Colorado. Research for this book began after my mother-in-law, Stella Hernandez, showed me an acequia ledger of an irrigation ditch located in Cucharas, Huerfano County. I learned that this Cucharas was not the same Cucharas on today's Interstate 25 sign near Walsenburg that directs travelers west. It is not the Cucharas Camp (est. 1906) located southeast of La Veta. In fact, this Cucharas no longer exists. The ledger started me on a wonderful historical journey to Cucharas.

I am very thankful to Richard Bustos, Marvin Davis and Marjorie Tatman who took me on entertaining and informative field trips. I also thank historical archaeologist Richard F. Carrillo, who met me in Cucharas to conduct field site reviews. He was a wealth of information. The following willingly shared photos and family histories: Anita Archuleta, Jean Barela, JoAnn Beadeaux, Richard Bustos, Marvin Davis, Conrad Lucero, Janice Martinez, Patricia Martinez, Tom Rogers, Donald Romero, Virginia Smith, Ida Valdez, Ronald Wadsack Jr., Cecilia Weber and Sister Rene Weeks. I also thank Monsignor Howard Delaney for allowing me to use a photo from his book, *All Our Yesterdays*, and for allowing me to borrow his interview tapes.

A special thank-you goes to the staff at the Office of the Colorado Water Engineer and Doug Brgosh, Joe Flory, Steve Kastner and Keith Kepler of the Colorado Division of Water. I also acknowledge the following for assisting me during my research: Kenton Forrest of the Colorado Railroad Museum; staff members of the Hart Library and Office of Historical and Archaeological Preservation of the Colorado Historical Society; staff members of the Denver Public Library Western History and Genealogy Department; Celinda R. Kaelin of the Pikes Peak Historical Society; Noreen Riffe of the Pueblo City-County Library District; Dan Scurlock and the Office of Contract Archeology at the University of New Mexico; Colorado State archivist Terry Ketelsen; Andy Senti and Merica Block of the Colorado Office of the Bureau of Land Management; Lorraine Guerin of the Archdiocese of Pueblo; Mary Ann Trujillo of St. Mary's Church in Walsenburg; Lorraine Castro and Judy Benine of the Huerfano County Courthouse; Monica Kirby of the Spanish Peaks Library District; and Nancy Christofferson and Carolyn Newman of the Huerfano County Historical Society. Carolyn told me about the Huerfano County teacher rosters "Voices of the Past: Historical Study of Huerfano County, Teacher's Edition 1891–1950," and Monica helped me locate them. They both also told me about the 1979 Huerfano County Oral History Project funded by Colorado Humanities. I thank Maggie Coval of Colorado Humanities for her assistance regarding these oral histories and acknowledge Karen Mitchell for posting them online. These oral histories, and the oral histories of some Huerfano County descendants published in the various volumes of the *Pioneers of the Territory of Southern Colorado*, provided a personal context about the events that took place during their lives.

I am grateful for the work of those who painstakingly transcribed church records, specifically Theresa Pino, who transcribed Walsenburg Catholic Church baptism records; Eileen Bankson, who copied the early Walsenburg Catholic marriage records; and Maria Clara Martinez, who transcribed Catholic Church records from the parishes of Arroyo Hondo and Costilla, New Mexico. Maria Clara was always willing to discuss genealogy with me, and I thank her.

This book would not have been possible without the many friends who reviewed chapters and willingly listened whenever I found something new about Cucharas. I appreciate their friendship and thank them all. I had the wonderful pleasure of meeting many descendants of the Cuchareños who willingly shared their family stories and were interested in learning what I had discovered about the area. I apologize to those families not listed in this book. Although I tried to locate records about each family and share as much as possible about them, I could not locate and include them all. I also thank my family members for their support, and I am so grateful to my mother-in-law, Stella Hernandez, for introducing me to Cucharas.

Cucharas and Its Beginning

No permanent settlement existed in the Cuchara valley prior to 1859...the country had been used, off and on, for summer grazing.[3]
—Louis B. Sporleder

It is the people and events associated with Cucharas that make it a fascinating piece of Southwest history. About October 20, 1862, eight Hispanos drove their sheep into the Lower Cuchara Valley of Huerfano County and "wintered there for the first time." They were familiar with the area from prior buffalo hunting expeditions. They traveled together for safety and to protect their sheep from Indian raids. These eight men were Jose Rafael Esquibel; the Jaquez brothers, Jose Salome Jaquez, Jose Eusequio Jaquez and Juan Ignacio Jaquez; Jose Andres Ruibal (Roybal); Jose Mariano de Jesus Valdez; Jose Desiderio Valencia; and Antonio Jose Vallejos. Each had family links to the Arroyo Hondo area of northern New Mexico. Although more information about these men is presented in other chapters, here are some introductory facts.

Jose Rafael Esquibel and his brothers, Jose Ramon and Juan Esquibel, were among the second group of settlers who settled the plazas of San Pedro and San Pablo in the San Luis Valley of southern Colorado. They were known for raising prize horses. They later moved to *la Plaza de los Leones* (present-day Walsenburg) and became *politicos* (politicians or civil leaders). Jose Salome Jaquez was one of the original settlers of *San Luís de la Culebra* (San Luis).[4] Jose Mariano de Jesus Valdez permanently moved from Costilla

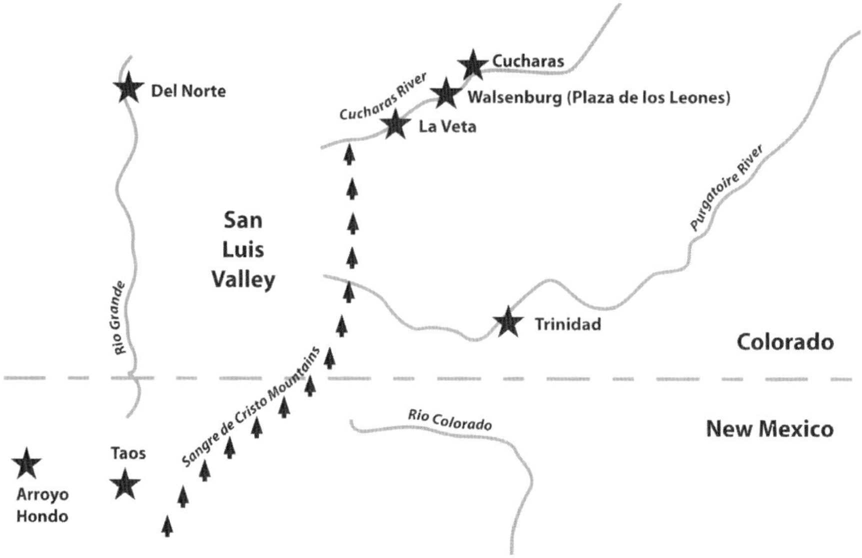

Area map of southern Colorado.

County in 1867. While living in New Mexico Territory, he held several "civil offices and was actively engaged in the Indian Wars." His family owned a share in the Valdez Land Grant at Abiquiu, New Mexico.[5] Presumably the share belonged to his grandfather, Juan Bautista Valdez.

When some of these eight men began moving their families into the lower valley, many transported their possessions "on two-wheeled carts drawn by two or four oxen."[6] They established their homes "in several places" along the Cucharas River. With them "in great numbers" came the "interesting" members of their families, Indian captives.[7] Between 1865 and 1869, more settlers arrived from Conejos and San Luis and from Abiquiu, Rio Colorado and Taos in New Mexico Territory.[8] By 1865, the population of the county was 371, of which 336 were Hispano. Some early historians recorded the *fandango* (a gathering where people come to dance) as the mode of entertainment and that the more "refined residents" owned a Colt army revolver and a good horse with saddle and bridle.[9] By 1866, the town of Badito was the county seat. Badito was located where several trails met at the Huerfano River.

Hispanos constructed their homes of adobe (bricks of dried mud, straw and lime). When these sun-dried bricks were ready, workers mortared and laid them to construct the walls. Adobe bricks, two to three feet thick, were energy efficient as they kept homes warm in the winter and cool in

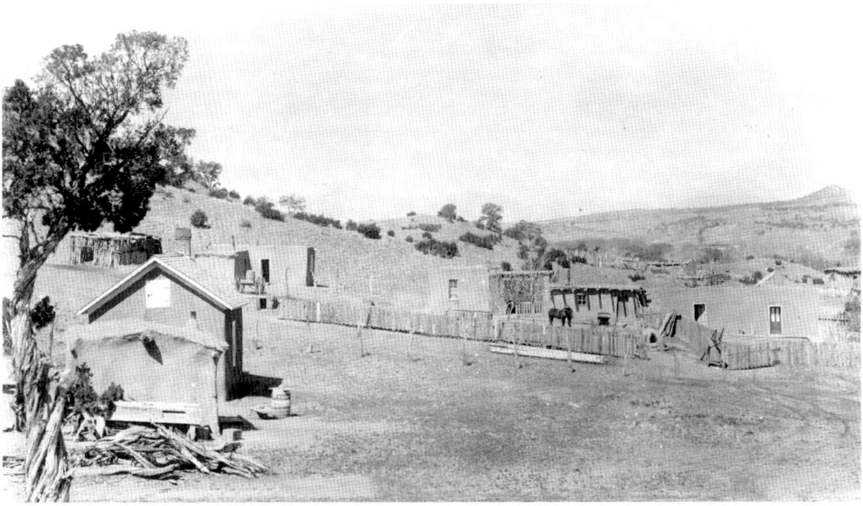

Mexican settlement near Walsenburg, 1888. *Courtesy of Colorado Historical Society, Denver & Rio Grande Collection, O.T. Davis, X-5436.*

the summer. This type of traditional New Mexican housing needed little resources and timber as *vigas* (pole support beams) supported the roofs. To accommodate a growing family, rooms could be easily added by cutting through the adobe from one room into the new addition.

Every year, women covered the exterior adobe with a mud and lime plaster to protect them from erosion. Years later, it was written that their homes "of a good color" were small, square, flat-roofed and "not more than six or seven feet high." Inside the "nicer homes," they covered the "hard, yet clean and smooth" hardened earthen floors with "bright" *jergas*.[10] Jerga was a type of coarsely woven, all-purpose cloth. It was used in men's trousers, "bagging material for wool and bulk products" and covers for windows and doors.[11] Folded mattresses, covered with "brightly colored blankets," served as seating areas.[12] They stored items in *nichos* (nooks cut into an interior wall), wooden trunks and chests. Handmade religious *santos* (carvings), crucifixes and *retablos* (paintings on wood) decorated the "rich-brown" walls.[13] Their homes had the traditional *fogón* (corner adobe fireplace). Rooms were lit by candles placed on an *araña* (wooden chandelier) that hung from the ceiling.[14]

These Cuchareños lived, acted and entertained themselves much the same as in other Hispanic communities of southern Colorado and northern New Mexico. Family members and neighbors shared cuts from butchered animals and assisted in the harvesting of crops. Their meals—mutton or game (antelope, deer, wild turkey or buffalo), corn, pinto beans, squash, eggs, goat's cheese and chile—were served on deep, tin plates. Hollowed-out horns or tortillas of wheat or cornmeal served as spoons. Beverages included coffee, *atole* (blue cornmeal with milk) and Mexican chocolate. Mexican chocolate was a popular drink; its taste and flavor were "incomparable." Hispanos purchased this chocolate from peddlers or traveling merchants coming north from El Paso, Texas, or Chihuahua, Mexico.[15] Because coffee was scarce, they served it only once a month.[16]

Their families enjoyed winter evenings sitting around the fireplace eating freshly roasted nuts from the plentiful piñon trees found around Cucharas. Families sang songs and played games by candlelight. They discouraged idleness and taught their children from an early age to work hard and to be responsible. Boys were courteous and tipped their hats. Children respected their elders and remained silent until spoken to.[17] Because little cash flowed throughout the territory, they bartered for goods and needed items.

THE CUCHARAS PLAZA

The Cucharas plaza, established in 1866, was situated along the north side of the Cucharas River and was only about eight miles northeast of *la Plaza de los Leones*. On June 8, 1891, Henry Daigre, of La Veta, purchased land on which the plaza lay. At the time, the "Town of Cuchara" was divided into four blocks. Blocks one and four had seven lots; blocks two and three had five lots. There were two cross streets. Bustos Street ran north and south and was fifty feet long. Valdes Street, which ran east and west, was eighty feet long. Valdes Street later became State Highway 10. Daigre claimed ownership of all lots but not the unpaved streets and alleys. Bustos Street was likely named for Jose Ramon Bustos, who was among the first settlers of Cucharas and whose sons were stocktenders for the Barlow and Sanderson Stagecoach Company. Valdes Street was likely named for Jose Leonides Valdez, a prominent sheepman, grocer and wheat farmer. By 1894, Valdez owned several lots. On December 18, he sold two lots to Bishop Nicholas Matz for one dollar.[18] Later the Cuchareños constructed a church on this land. By 1891, the majority of the remaining buildings lay in the southwest quadrant on block one along Valdes Street. These buildings included five houses, one barn and the Valdes store.[19]

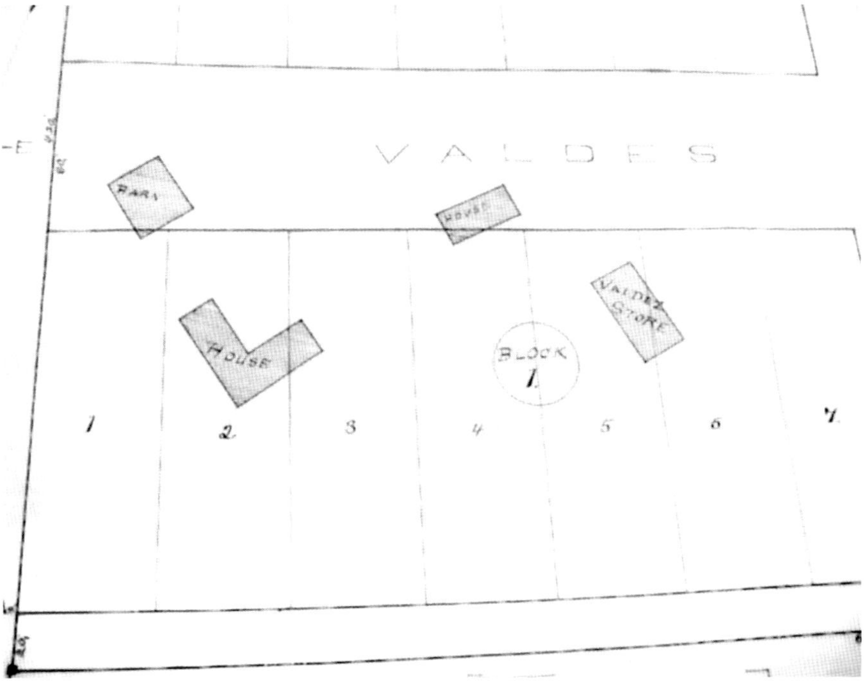

Cucharas Plaza, Valdez Store on Lots 5 and 6, Huerfano County Courthouse, Map of Town of Cuchara, Survey Plat, June 8, 1891. *Courtesy of the author.*

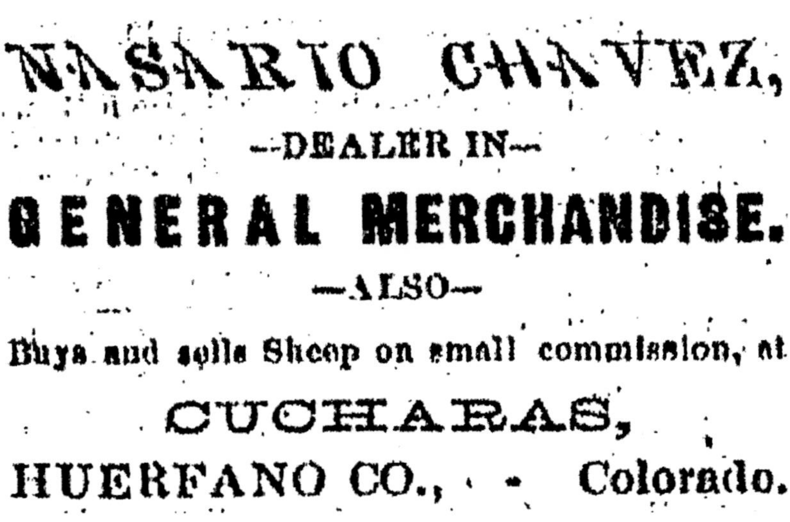

Chavez general merchandise advertisement. *Courtesy of* Trinidad Enterprise.

Colorado business directories for Cucharas listed Valdez & Chavez as grocers between 1884 and 1886 and L. Valdez and the Valdez Brothers as grocers from 1893 to 1896.[20] It is unclear whether these stores were at Cucharas or at the railroad town, Cucharas City. Valdez & Chavez grocers, which operated between 1884 and 1886, was owned by Jose Leonides Valdez and Nasario Chavez.[21] In 1873, Chavez advertised the purchase and sale of sheep on "small commission" (*partido*). That summer on July 24, Cucharas experienced a flood that spread over half a mile. Floodwaters nearly washed away adobe homes and detained the stagecoach for twelve hours. According to the *Pueblo Daily Chieftain*, Chavez lost "about $1,000 in houses, grain, merchandise, and wool." Two years later, he sold his property for $300. The sale was to secure a note to Gustave and Julius Louis Bartels, who owned general stores at Denver, Pueblo, Las Animas, San Antonio and Walsenburg.[22] By 1880, Chavez and his family lived in Trinidad where he worked as a store clerk.[23] The L. Valdez store, and the Valdez Brothers store that operated between 1893 and 1896, were owned by Jose Leonides Valdez and his younger brother, Antonio Domingo Valdez.

TAX ASSESSMENT

In 1869, Jose Anastacio de Jesus "J.A.J." Valdez was elected county assessor. As assessor, he was responsible for identifying, evaluating and assessing taxable property. Information produced (an assessment roll) determined the local property taxes for services, such as roads and bridges; teacher salaries, student desks, books, school building construction, heat and maintenance; and police and fire safety. With more than half of the county's population Spanish speakers, the county needed someone elected as county assessor who could speak Spanish and had an established rapport with Hispanos. In 1869, citizens of Huerfano County elected J.A.J. Valdez as their first official assessor.

J.A.J. Valdez was the son of Jose Mariano de Jesus Valdez, one of the eight men who wintered in the lower valley in 1862. He, his father and younger brother, Juan Bautista Valdez, taught school during their lifetimes. According to his father's obituary, published in the December 27, 1894 edition of the *Walsenburg World*, his father encouraged all of his children to "aspire to honored and useful lives." When J.A.J. was elected county assessor, county clerk John H. Brown gave him "legal-sized cap paper, an inkstand and a pen, [and] a copy of the 1863 [Colorado Territorial] Statutes." According

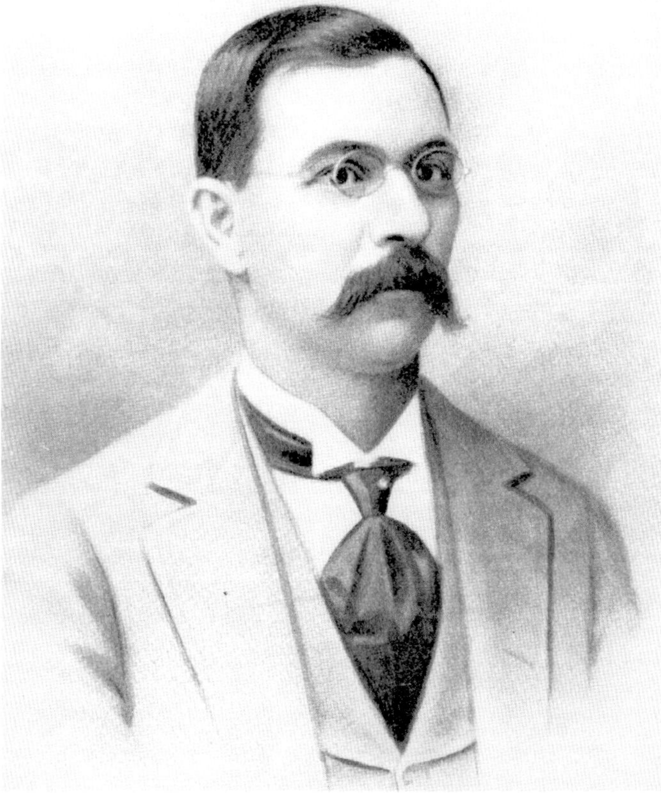

Honorable Jose Anastacio de Jesus "J.A.J." Valdez. *Courtesy of Denver Public Library Western History Collection.*

to a biography, at the time Valdez could barely read and write in English. As assessor, he visited every household in the county to identify, evaluate and assess taxable real estate, personal property and agricultural land. He met with county residents by day and prepared the tax schedules by night. Using the legal-sized paper he was given, he drew horizontal and vertical lines on each, and these became the assessment rolls he filed with the county clerk.

Although taxes were not new to Hispanos, they had difficulty paying them because little cash circulated at this time. While times were difficult, they favored taxes for public education.[24] County citizens trusted Valdez and elected him to a second term; he refused the nomination for a third.[25] He moved to Pueblo to attend an Episcopal school. Presumably he taught one Spanish class there but primarily studied English. During his stay in Pueblo, he resided at the residence of Judge Allen A. Bradford. During his free time, Valdez read the judge's law books. He returned to Huerfano County and went on to serve in other elected positions. He was elected to the House of

Representatives in the Colorado General Assembly in 1873. He served as county judge in 1881 and was elected county clerk in 1885. In 1888, he was admitted to the Colorado Legal Bar. He served as mayor of Walsenburg in 1886 and again in 1892.[26]

Sheep and Its Wool

The Cuchareños raised sheep for its meat and wool, which were important trade items on the frontier. In his younger years, second-generation Jose Anastacio de Jesus Valdez was responsible for his father's sheep. While herding sheep and goats, captive Indian boys could be heard playing reed flutes in a "tremulously sweet" minor key.[27] During winter months, families—including female Indian captives—kept busy carding (combing), dying, spinning and weaving wool. Hispanos used horizontal treadle looms while their Navajo captives used vertical looms. The treadle loom produced long narrow strips that could be sewn together or double woven as needed. The vertical loom produced a piece that was as wide as the two reinforced wooden supports. Clothing of the early Cuchareños was typical of southwestern pioneer fashion. Outdoors, men wore buckskin suits or a shorter version of the woven *sarape* or *tilma* (cloaks).[28] On their feet they wore *zapatos* or *chinelas* (leather shoes or buckskin slippers).[29] Men's shirts and women's skirts and blouses were made of *sabanilla*, a lighter and finer woven cloth.[30] Over their heads or on their shoulders, "women, young girls, and children wore bright [woolen] shawls."[31] Flannel, calico and cotton yard goods provided first by means of the Santa Fe Trail entered Hispano households when Hispanos worked as *fleteros* (freighters). Later, with the arrival of the railroad, commercially woven cloth came into use. Sewing machines soon followed and were in Hispano homes in 1890.

The Churro, a long-legged sheep that could withstand extreme climates, arrived in New Mexico with the first Spanish settlers in 1598. Its fine and long silky wool was ideal for weaving. Because its wool was practically greaseless, it needed less preparation.[32] From the wool, settlers wove *colchones* (mattress covers), *frazadas* (blankets), *sabanilla* for clothing, *mortajas* (burial shrouds), cloaks, saddle blankets and *jerga* for carpeting and sackcloth.[33] In 1859, sheep growers in New Mexico imported Merino rams and bred them with Churro ewes to produce larger sheep with more meat. No agricultural records were compiled to indicate how many pure Churro sheep were in the

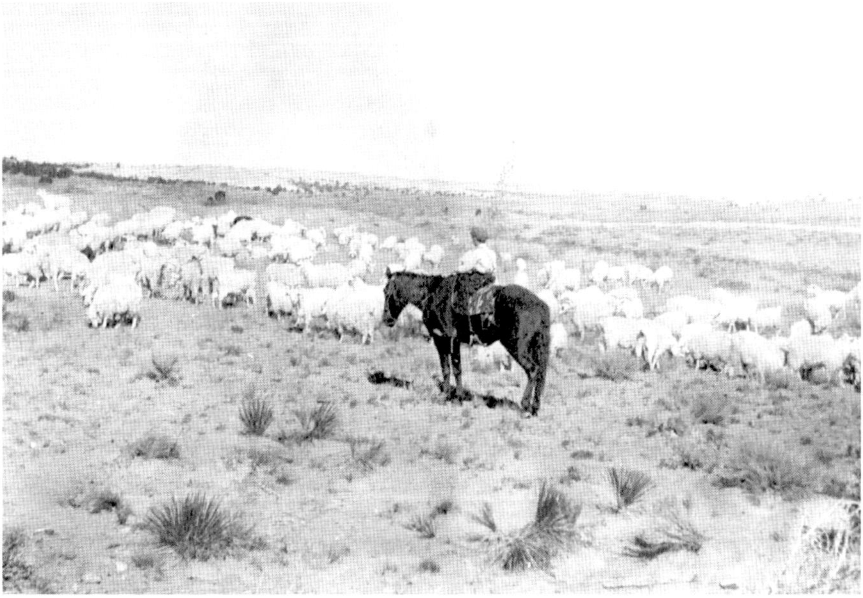

Young boy on horseback herding sheep and goats. *Courtesy of Las Animas Museum, La Plata County Historical Society.*

San Luis Valley. Wool produced from the mixed breed was harder to weave; its wool was shorter, kinky and had more grease content. Its wool was not as fine as the wool produced from the pure Churro. Lambs of these crossbred ewes became the foundation stock for many Colorado sheep raisers. Anglo sheep raisers preferred the purebred Merino or Rambouillet sheep. They referred to Churro sheep as an "unimproved," worthless breed.[34] The June 7, 1874 edition of the *Pueblo Daily Chieftain* reported, "In time, and not a long one we trust, the Mexican and his worthless stock will disappear from these beautiful and fertile mesas and valleys."

With the arrival of the D&RG at Cucharas in 1876, sheep and wool could now be easily transported. When a sheep was killed by a train or its employees, railroads compensated the owner based on the breed and quality of the sheep. "American" purebred sheep was worth $2.50 a head; the mixed Churro was worth $1.50 a head.[35] Until the D&RG reached Alamosa in 1878, Hispanos east of the Sangre de Cristo Mountains drove their sheep and freighted wool over La Veta Pass into Cucharas to load them onto trains at Cucharas City. By the 1880s, commercial sheep operators arrived with capital and improved livestock. Sheep ranges in southern Colorado quickly became dominated by Anglos who controlled the shipping of sheep and

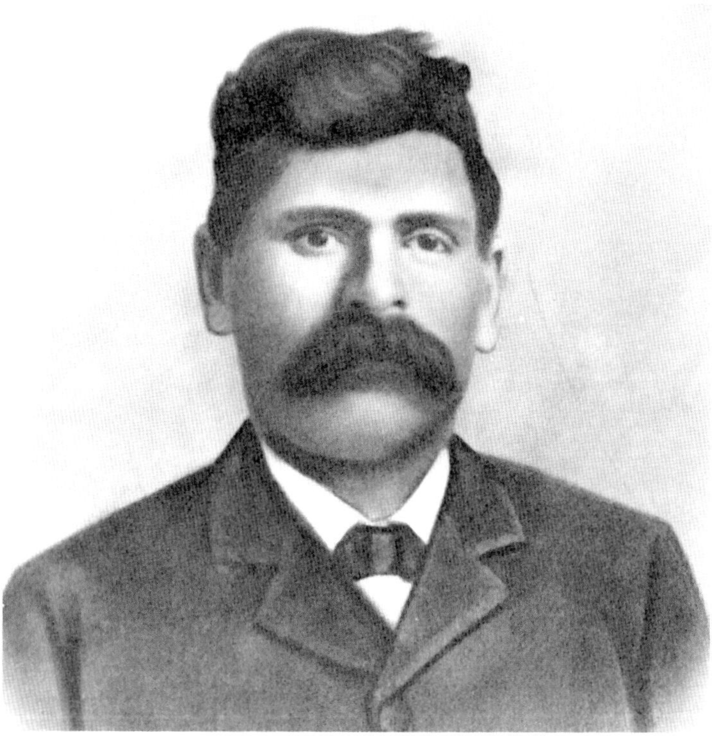

Juan Evaristo Gonzales. *Courtesy of Denver Public Library, Western History Collection, Sporleder Collection, WH916, Ph Bx 1.*

wool to markets in the Midwest and East.[36] By March 1893, twelve thousand head of sheep grazed on three-inch-tall grass at Cucharas.[37] By 1903, wool shipped to Boston, Massachusetts, came from Cucharas, Walsenburg, Del Norte, Antonito and Pagosa Springs.[38] Most Hispanos could not compete because they lacked what easterners called better breeds as well as their ample financial backing. The four Cuchareños able to retain a hold on the sheep market were Nasario Chavez, Jesus Maria Cisneros, Juan Evaristo Gonzales and Jose Leonides Valdez. Gonzales and Valdez were among the wealthiest men in Huerfano County.[39]

To build their flocks of sheep and herds of cattle, Hispanos, and later Anglos, participated in the *partido* system, a system similar to the shareholder system. In a sheep partido, a person obtained a starter flock by caring for the owner's sheep. The *partidario* (shareholder) was responsible for the loss of any of the owner's starter flock. At the end of the contract period, which lasted about three years, the partidario returned the original starter flock to its owner plus half of the flock's offspring. The partidario also paid the owner about two pounds of wool per sheep in the starter flock. In a cattle contract, the partidario returned the original starter herd plus half of the herd's calves and half of the profit from sales of the original starter herd.[40] Juan Evaristo Gonzales and Juan Benito Valdez were partidarios. Ute chief Ouray was in a goat partido with Gonzales,[41] and Captain Jose "Rafael" Sotero Chacon, who was now living in Trinidad, was in a cattle partido with Valdez. Valdez knew Captain Chacon during the Civil War. After his death in 1871, Chacon made arrangements with his family to obtain his equal share of fourteen cattle, including calves.[42]

Many workers were needed on a sheep ranch. Herders watched flocks of sheep on open pastures of fresh grass; shearers clipped, bundled and bagged wool clippings; and fleteros hauled the bagged clippings to the railroad depot. Shearing took place before lambing season, generally between March and June. In 1878, Colorado shearers earned four and one-half cents per sheep, without board, and a half cent more if they had to tie the clipped wool. A sheep yielded between three and one-half to five and one-quarter pounds of wool. Wool was such an important commodity that during shearing, children helped gather every last fluff. After shearers bagged the wool, fleteros hauled it to Cucharas City. There commission or forwarding houses sold or signed it over to an agent who handled its transport and marketing back East.[43] By December 5, 1878, the *Pueblo Chieftan* reported that commission houses earned between a 5 and 10 percent commission to store and sell wool. These houses were said to be in collusion with manufacturers and buyers to defraud wool producers. Fred Walsen owned a forwarding house. He operated a "mammoth business [selling goods] on space due to the scarcity of cash."[44] He rented space to Hispanos, but in lieu of cash, he took part of the proceeds from the sale of their wool.

Heinrich Anton Frederich "Fred" Walsen, of German descent, arrived in the United States in 1859 and was in the San Luis Valley by 1864. He was appointed the postmaster of San Luis in 1868 and applied for U.S. citizenship the following year.[45] Walsen followed the migration from the San Luis Valley and arrived in the Lower Cuchara Valley in 1870. He established his home at la Plaza de los Leones where he managed the Bartels general store.[46] La Plaza de los Leones, originally named for Miguel Antonio Leon, was the supply center and parent village of the many smaller settlements in the area. It later became known as Walsenburg, in honor of Fred Walsen.

The first longhorn cattle from Texas arrived in Huerfano County in 1870.[47] As the cattle market moved in, problems arose due to a free-range system based on the right of priority by possession. Sheep cropped grass too short, leaving little or none for their cattle. Trouble occurred when a sheepherder encountered Anglo cowboys herding cattle. Flocks herded by Hispanos and Native Americans were attacked and their sheep mutilated, poisoned or clubbed to death by cowboys. Even herders were not spared from the violence.[48] Second-generation Cuchareño Juan Vallejos had about one thousand head of sheep grazing in the Lower Huerfano Valley and Indians watching over his flocks. One time three boys "from the Lewis family" arrived on horseback and whipped his sheepherders with lariats "till they were raw." "[Vallejos] had to change sheepherders several times on account of they even [dragged] one." He instructed a sheepherder to return to the area and assured him he would be "looking out for him." When the Lewises arrived waving their lariats, Vallejos—who was "a little guy, but a good shot"—jumped out from behind some bushes of soapweed "with his 30-30 [rifle] blazing." He stopped them from injuring his sheepherder and made them drop their lariats and weapons, dismount and remove their boots. Vallejos then tied them up and made them walk home barefoot over dirt, cactus, grass and twigs. "That was the last whippin' [by] them Lewises.'"[49]

By 1900, Anglo settlement and cattle corporations absorbed much of the available range land. Hispanos now had to pay cash for national forest grazing permits or to lease privately held land. Cattlemen illegally fenced government land to reserve grass for their exclusive use during winter months. During the summer months, cattlemen turned their cattle out to graze on open range. The cattle ate all the grass and left nothing for the sheep of their less fortunate neighbors. Illegal and legal fencing continued to keep sheep out. In 1874, one hundred pounds of barbed wire cost $20.00; in 1885, the price was $4.20. (The Colorado Fuel and Iron Company at Pueblo began producing barbed wire in 1888.)[50] Stockmen who leased enclosed land to other cattlemen charged by the head. Farmers and ranchers unable to compete had no other recourse than to sell their land to big cattle companies at low prices.

The relationship between the cattlemen and the D&RG proved to be a long and profitable venture that stimulated growth in both industries. Cattlemen were on hand to supply beef for railroad workers, and the D&RG was available to transport cattle. Because the acreage allowed by government land laws was not enough to meet their needs, some cattlemen used fraudulent means and made false claims to obtain additional land and fence in large tracts of public domain lands along a river or stream. Some had their employees "put up a few boards" on a quarter section of land and file a homestead claim. When the required time passed, these employees swore they had lived on the claim as required by law. After obtaining the land patent, they deeded the land to their employer, either directly or through a third party.[51]

In 1876, cowboys drove five hundred head of two- and three-year-old steers from Texas to Cucharas for rail transport by the D&RG. At the time there was no stockyard or corral, so "they just turned them out four ways to the wind."[52] Fred Walsen and Alexander Levy, his future brother-in-law, were quite involved in the cattle business supplying beef for the D&RG.[53] Later many new cattlemen to Colorado were Texans who brought in and resupplied herds with Texas stock. In the 1880s, large cattle companies controlled much of Colorado. The Cleveland Cattle Company, financed by investors from England, had large interests in Huerfano County with two thousand and three thousand head of cattle.[54] The Prairie Cattle Company had a range of over 214 million acres between the Arkansas and Purgatoire Rivers. It became the largest cattle company in the history of Colorado.[55] Between 1884 and 1888, several lawsuits were filed through the U.S. Circuit Court in Denver against the Prairie Cattle Company for illegal fencing.[56]

Fred Walsen owned 18,000 sheep and 250 head of cattle. Four years later, Fred Walsen owned more than 6,000 sheep, ewes and lambs that had been "graded five years," bred with Merino sheep.[57]

Summary

The early Cuchareños established the same settlement patterns used by their ancestors in New Mexico. They congregated near the plaza for news and celebration. Like their Native American neighbors, they lived off the land. Their clothing came from animal skins and woven materials. Their food source came from seed and sheep.

As the D&RG cut through the Cucharas meadow, a continual influx of newcomers arrived to seek fame and fortune. Annual visits from county assessors occasionally resulted in changes in land ownership. Newspapers printed Anglo points of view and news only intended for their eyes. Conflicts arose between new Anglo cattlemen and established Hispano sheepmen, and occasional losses due to bad weather and disease plagued many in partido systems. As new Anglo-run stores provided new products, this cash-scrapped society relied on credit, and many ended up in debt.

Although they were criticized for their lack of better tools, their crops continued to produce.

The Cuchareños and their descendants were in for a lot of change. The impact of this change would continue to affect their homes, lifestyles, properties, crops and use of natural resources. As they faced obstacles regarding ethnicity, religion and the reduction of water, land and timber, they found solace in their religion and culture.

Conflict and Captivity

White people did not understand how to live with the Indians.[58]
—Louis B. Sporleder

Indian tribes of the Mouache Ute, Kiowa, Cheyenne and Arapaho Nations roamed land in present-day southern Colorado and northern New Mexico. The land of the Mouache band, one of seven bands of the Ute Nation, included the Rocky Mountain Front Range between Denver and Las Vegas, New Mexico. The land provided them with food and clothing from buffalo and other animals and tools and weapons from wood, stone and bone. To ensure it could replenish, Indians took no more than needed. Indian Nations acquired additional necessary items through trade with other Indians and Hispanos. Hispanos depended on trade with the Indians for goods such as hides and pottery. Many from the Mouache band of Ute Indians arrived each fall. There the women of their band picked ripe wild plums, *chaquaco* (elderberry), *capulín* (chockecherry) and grapes. They dried the fruit and then pounded it into powder (pemmican) that could be easily transported in leather pouches. Women in the band often added jerked (dried) strips of buffalo meat into soups seasoned with the fruit pemmican.[59] Indian camps were located at Cucharas, Badito, *Rito del Oso* (Bear Creek), Santa Clara, Rincón and Pass Creek.[60]

Anglos were unaccustomed to Indians traveling through the land and expecting gifts. The Cuchareños learned to accept unexpected visits from the Utes and often had extra bread or cornmeal available. In preparation

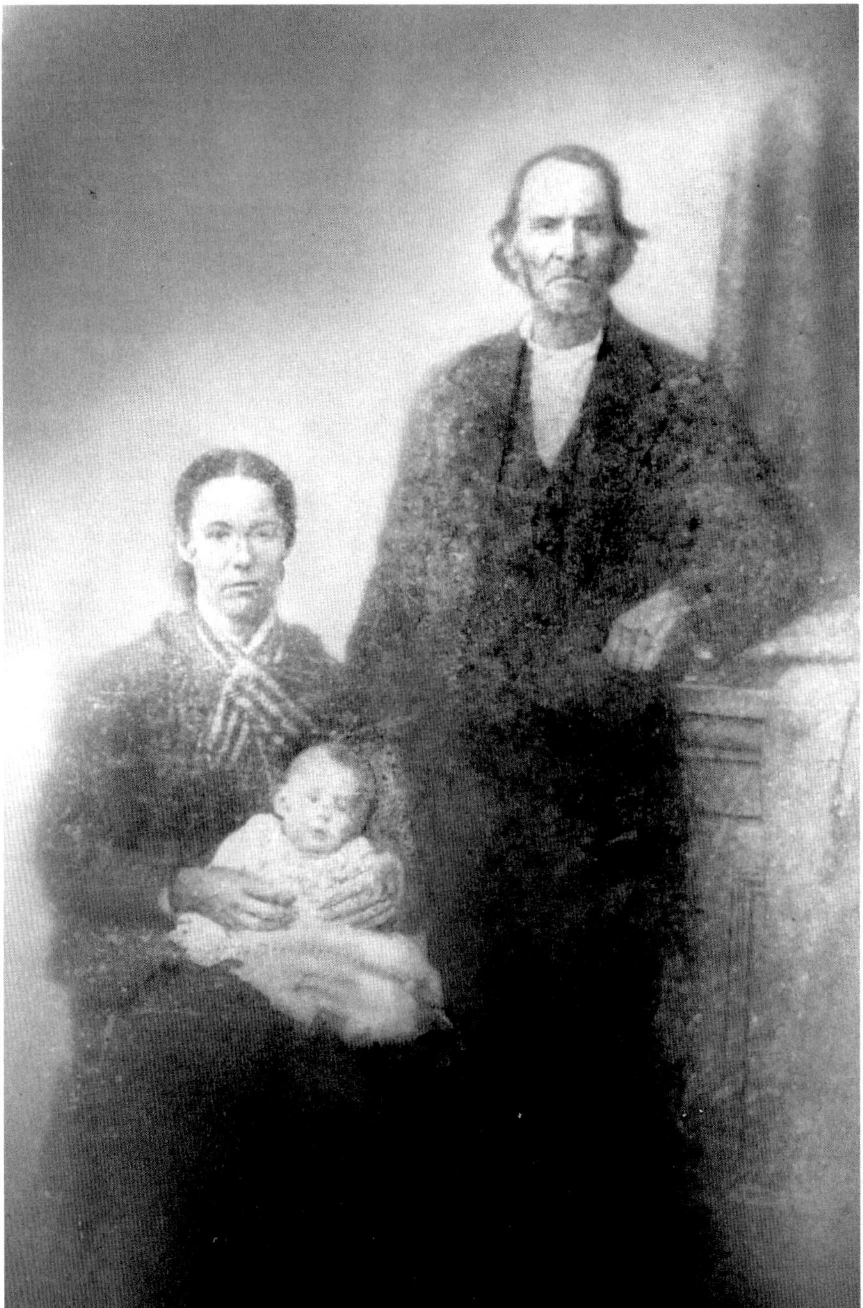

Miguel Antonio Vallejos and his second wife, Paula Martin. *Courtesy of Janice Martinez.*

for their arrival, women at the *hacienda* of Miguel Antonio Vallejos baked bread in outdoor *hornos* (beehive-shaped *adobe* ovens) "from morning til night." This bread, called *pan de comanche*, was a favorite trade item.[61] Vallejos and Juan Benito Valdez were some of the Cuchareños who spoke Ute and understood their culture and customs. When Vallejos hosted Ute chiefs and their warriors at his hacienda, the topics of discussion focused on the United States, its mistreatment of Indians and Hispanos and its disregard for their lands. Ute chief Shavano and his band attended some of these "*fiesta grandes.*" Shavano was said to be friendly with new Anglo settlers. He often asked the young men in his band to help settlers round up their livestock. In return, the settlers gave him a calf or a sack of flour.[62]

Indian discontent continued over loss of land and growing scarcity of wild game. The U.S. government responded to Anglo complaints by establishing military forts and moving and confining the Utes and Navajos to reservations. U.S. treaties continued to confine the Utes to smaller areas in eastern Utah and southwestern Colorado. In 1863, Colorado's southern Utes reluctantly surrendered their main hunting areas. In exchange, the U.S. government annually distributed blankets, food and livestock from its agency at Fort Garland. Like many Indian agencies in the territories, Fort Garland did not have enough goods to distribute, and its food was rancid. When the United States failed to provide promised goods, Mouache Ute chief Kaniache[63] and his warriors traveled to the adobe residence of John M. Francisco in the Upper Cuchara Valley and aggravated several Anglo men.[64] When Francisco traded some cattle for their safety, Kaniache left the area. The Indians "weren't mean, they just wanted to eat."[65]

By 1866, the southern Ute Indians were reassigned to the Indian Agency in Cimarron, New Mexico Territory, more than 125 miles away. The conditions there were such that the Utes went hungry and were near-naked because the agency was undersupplied. Because Indians were forbidden to hunt, they could not obtain animal hides for clothing and wild game for food. In addition, chief Kaniache's son was killed by a Hispano sheepherder near Fort Union in New Mexico Territory.[66] Frustrated, Kaniache and his band traveled north into Colorado and conducted raids on settlements. During a raid near Trinidad, Kaniache explained to the Anglo settler that cattle he had not taken would reproduce and the settler's herd would be replenished;[67] nature would provide. About two years later, Kaniache and his band camped near La Veta to meet with Colonel Dudley and officers from Fort Garland. Colonel Dudley was the superintendent of Indian Affairs for the Territories of Arizona,

Colorado and New Mexico. Fred Walsen, who was returning to la Plaza de los Leones from Ojo Caliente, New Mexico, stopped at the James G. Hamilton Ranch and apparently invited himself to this council. During council, Kaniache presumably agreed to leave the area and remain west of the mountains. Three days later, the chief returned and another council convened near Hamilton's ranch at North Abeyta. In preparation for this council, Hamilton transported goods and provisions from la Plaza de los Leones to La Veta. During council, Colonel Dudley told Kaniache that the U.S. president, "the Great Father in Washington," wanted the chief to accept and sign the treaty and remain west of the mountains. To persuade Kaniache to leave, the colonel offered butchered meat, food and provisions for his band. Kaniache corrected Colonel Dudley, saying, "The only Great Father is in Heaven." Kaniache misinterpreted Colonel Dudley's reference to the Great Father in Washington as the Great Spirit. The Utes believe the Great Spirit or Creator is everywhere and in all things and that the Creator's energy is associated with the sun. When a Ute dies, his or her spirit is reborn through reincarnation.[68] After Kaniache's reply to Colonel Dudley, Fred Walsen asked the chief where his Great Father was. Kaniache answered, "In Heaven above." Kaniache was familiar with the concept of heaven and hell from Spanish Catholic influence at pueblos and missions. Walsen then provoked him by asking, "What will then become of us White people?" Growing tired of explaining that the Utes "fought, bled, and died" for the land, Kaniache replied, "You will all go to Hell!"[69]

Kaniache spoke Spanish but limited English. He wore a blue army coat with brass buttons and had a tall hat with eagle feathers. He enjoyed making speeches, had strong convictions and was a man who "lived up to his ethics." Kaniache, who had two wives and several children, was a "popular man" at la Plaza de los Leones. His young children enjoyed watching every movement of Anglo and Hispanic housewives. Settlers at Cucharas, la Plaza de los Leones, Bear Creek and Santa Clara reported friendly relations with the Indians. Kaniache served as chief of the Mouache band until 1881. Louis B. Sporleder, who arrived at Walsenburg in 1874, said, "It was an interesting and illuminating experience, even if only for a few short years, to have lived in close contact with the Indians."[70]

During the Indian Wars, white settlers' animosities over loss of lives and livestock were pitted against Indian resistance to their loss of land and hunting areas. In 1868, Ute leaders signed another treaty that further reduced their land. In 1879 at the White River Indian Agency, agent

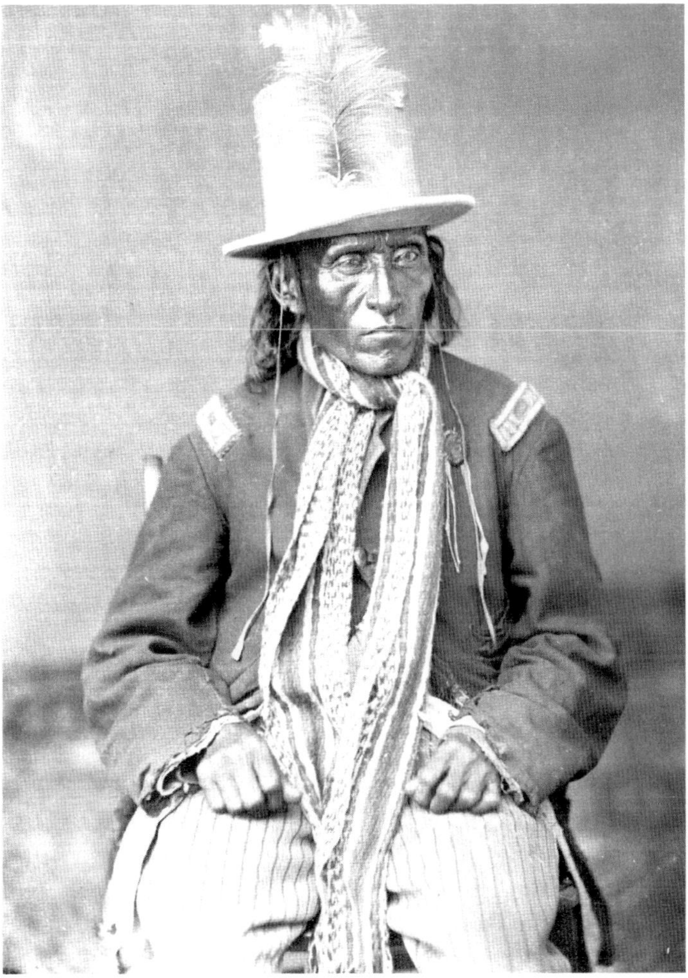

Twin brother of Ute chief Kaniache, Cu-ra-can-to, Mouache Ute war chief. *Courtesy of Denver Public Library Western History Collection, Rosenstock, X-30463.*

Nathan Meeker and the Utes clashed in what Anglos called the Meeker Massacre. In response, the government moved several Ute bands to Utah. In May 1881, five D&RG trains passed through Cucharas, Walsenburg and La Veta as it transported U.S. soldiers ordered to escort Utes off a reservation in southern Colorado to one in Utah.[71] The government permitted those of mixed breed with families to remain.[72] During this time, the Navajos in New Mexico Territory were being forcibly relocated to Bosque Redondo. By 1882, the Utes were the last tribe confined to reservations. The loss of hunting and gathering grounds, and the lack of and quality of food and provisions provided by the U.S. government, reduced many Utes and Navajos to starvation and disease.

CAPTIVITY

Documented instances of captivity in southern Colorado record an interesting and essential account of coexistence. Indian and Hispano trade in captives was a part of Southwest culture and norm. Hispanos and Indians acquired captives through trade or during raids to retrieve stolen sheep, horses and family members. Children, infants and women under age forty-five were acquired as the spoils of war through kidnapping, in trade or exchange or through abandonment or birth.[73] Captivity played a crucial role in both societies. It helped each culture learn about the other in language and custom, which resulted in both cultures living in relative peace. Captives toiled as household cooks and caregivers, sheepherders and shearers, weavers, acequia laborers, crop tenders and camp laborers who tanned hides and prepared and dried meat. Traders sold children for fifty to one hundred dollars.[74] Girls and women performed household duties and prepared and wove wool, while young boys herded sheep.[75]

Weaving was an important activity that provided fabric or material for clothing, bedding, carpeting, sacks, window and door covers and saddle blankets. According to folklore, Spider Man instructed the Navajo women how to build the first vertical weaving loom, and Spider Woman taught the Navajos how to weave. Women and girls who knew how to weave trained other captives. Because the Navajos wove on vertical looms, weaving could be done outdoors between two trees or indoors between two wooden supports.

When an Indian captive was brought into a Hispano household, he or she was assimilated through the act of a Catholic baptism, during which the captive was given a new name and adopted into a family. These captives subsequently learned Spanish, followed Catholic doctrine and assimilated into Hispanic culture. Because some female captives bore children of their owners, her children became the property of her owner, who in some cases was her child's baptismal godparent.[76] Such children became additional household help.

Members of the U.S. Congress had been discussing captivity in light of the Civil War, Negro slavery and the Emancipation Proclamation. In 1865, Colorado Territorial governor John Evans asked all Indian agents within the territory to report instances of Indians held captive as slaves. Ute Indian agent Lafayette Head[77] interviewed owners in Conejos and Costilla Counties and 149 of their Indian captives. His detailed reports provided information about captive owners and the captives they owned. His reports listed the owners' names and places of residence as well as information about each captive (e.g., age, gender, tribe, year captive was purchased, group who sold the captive, area where captive was purchased and whether the captive wished to return to his or her tribe). Some owners, from the Taos and San Luis Valleys, crossed Colorado and New Mexico Territory lines. Lafayette Head also listed Anglo owners of Indian captives but failed to include himself and his wife on the list. By doing so, he damaged his relationship with his Hispano neighbors.[78]

In 1866, Congress enacted the Civil Rights Act, and holding slaves became a violation of U.S. law. Charles Autobees, who settled along the Huerfano River, had a Cheyenne Indian captive named Mike. Mike was saved during the Sand Creek Massacre by Mariano Autobees. At the time, Autobees served as second lieutenant in Company H of the Third Colorado Cavalry. He gave Mike to his father, Charles Autobees, who "raised him as a son."[79] Others ignored the law as Indian servants were still being recorded in various records. While ministering at Taos, New Mexico, in 1870, Father Gabriel Ussel had a male Indian captive named Agustine.[80] Indian servants were also recorded on Huerfano County census records, even as late as 1880. Joseph Bourcy, from la Plaza de los Leones, had a female Indian servant named Guadalupe.[81] Cuchareños Maria Rosa Gomez and her husband, Manuel Gonzales, brought five Indian captives with them when they moved from Rio Colorado, New Mexico.[82] In 1880, Gomez, then a fifty-year-old widow, had two additional captives in her household.[83] With the assistance of hired laborers and Indian captives, she raised crops and 1,500 sheep.[84] By 1900, she lived with her adopted son and servant, Jose Florentino Gonzales.[85]

Jose Benito Maes brought two Navajo captives with him when his family migrated from the San Luis Valley to Huerfano County in 1868.[86] Maes purchased Antonio, a twenty-four-year-old Navajo, in 1864 from (New) Mexicans trading in Colorado Territory. Although Lafayette Head's report indicated Antonio was purchased from Mexicans, Head likely meant Hispanos from southern Colorado or New Mexico as some engaged in this type of raid commerce. Antonio had a child and therefore did not wish to return to his tribe.[87] If a Navajo captive was married and had children, he or she did not have to return to their tribe and be forcibly relocated by military escort to the Bosque Redondo reservation in New Mexico. Although Head wrote that Navajo captives in Colorado Territory should be returned to their tribe and transferred to Bosque Redondo, captives residing in southern Colorado were spared from this relocation. The second captive held by Jose Benito Maes was named Antonia, a twenty-three-year-old Navajo.[88] After the death of his first wife, Maria Paula Sanchez, Maes married Antonia at Walsenburg.[89]

Teodoro Maes and his wife, Maria Josefa Suazo, brought several captives with them when they migrated from Conejos to the Upper Cuchara Valley.[90] Maes, considered the greatest buffalo hunter in Huerfano County, had several horses trained specifically for hunting buffalo. Every fall, when he traveled east from Cucharas beyond Rattle Snake Buttes to hunt buffalo and antelope, he returned with "three or four wagon loads of meat that he sold to neighbors or dried for future use."[91] His captives accompanied him on the hunts to prepare and dry the meat and tan the hides.

Juan Benito Valdez, from Taos County, served in the New Mexico Territorial House of Representatives.[92] He later became an interpreter for the U.S. Army and was often seen in the company of soldiers. During military expeditions, his family and captives accompanied him. Small children traveled in large baskets hung on pack mules.[93] When Congress enacted the Civil Rights Act in 1866, holding slaves became in violation of U.S. law. Members of the New Mexico Territorial District Court accused 170 Taos County residents of holding Indian captives. A grand jury ruled that indictments would be issued only if their captives swore their owners forcibly restrained or treated them poorly. Those accused, who later had ties to southern Colorado, included Juan Benito Valdez; Pablo Beaubien, son of Charles Beaubien; Jose "Rafael" Sotero Chacon; Jose Julian Espinosa; and Maria Luisa Branch, mistress of Ceran St. Vrain. Because the social and economic exchange of captives played such a crucial role in Hispano and Indian societies, the court dismissed many of these cases.[94] As a result of the New Mexico Territorial District Court's ruling, 10 captives owned by Juan Benito Valdez were freed. Whether any of his freed captives migrated with him to Cucharas is presently unknown; however, when Valdez settled in Cucharas, he had "50 young Indians."[95] Valdez established dual residencies in Huerfano and Taos Counties. Census records show he had 9 captives between 1860 and 1870. His biological son and daughter, Jose Leonides and Maria Caterina, grew up among his Indian captives and were accustomed to the practice of having *criados* (servants). (Although most Hispanos are familiar with the term *criado* [Indian caregiver or servant], current historians use the term captive.) Jose Leonides became a prominent Cucharas sheepman, farmer and grocer.[96] Maria Caterina Valdez and her husband, Juan Bautista Martinez, had two Indian captives. The captive named Lupita washed, cleaned, cooked and took care of other household duties; she also helped with the harvest.[97]

The Vallejos brothers, Miguel Antonio, Jose Maria and Antonio Jose, each had Indian captives in their households. Antonio Jose Vallejos was one of the eight men who wintered in the Lower Cuchara Valley in 1862.[98] He and his wife, Maria Soledad Romero, brought two captives with them when they permanently settled at Cucharas. Maria Dolores, a sixteen-year-old Navajo, was baptized at Arroyo Hondo, New Mexico, on April 7, 1865; her owners served as godparents.[99] Between 1867 and 1885, Antonio Jose fathered six children by Maria Dolores.[100] After the death of his wife and seventeen days after the birth of his last child with Maria Dolores, Antonio Jose married Maria Dolores on August 29, 1885. Before parish priest Father Gabriel Ussel, the groom declared that the previous three children by Maria Dolores Vallejos were his and that "he legitimized them through this marriage."[101] The following day, Father Ussel christened their infant daughter named Maria Soledad.[102]

When Antonio Jose Vallejos died in 1892 at age eighty-five, he left his estate to Maria Dolores and his children.[103] Among his named children was Jose Hilario, a Navajo captive, who had been with the Vallejos family since 1860 at the age of two.[104] Because Jose Hilario was acquired at an early age, Maria Dolores not only became his surrogate mother, but she also was a link to his Navajo heritage.

Louis B. Sporleder thought captives in the area were kindly treated and raised the same as the owner's children. He considered Indian captivity a mild form of slavery. Sporleder commented that these captives often married into their owner's family and became established in the family business.[105] He did not take into account that captives, who witnessed the slaughter of their family members during raiding expeditions, were forced to live and work among total strangers. As captives assimilated into another's culture, many lost their native identities and heritage.

Few histories have been recorded about Hispano and Anglo men taken captive by Indians. Jose Salome Jaquez and Sisto Martinez were two Hispano captives who had ties to Huerfano County. Jaquez was raised in captivity of Ute Indians until his family paid his ransom.[106] He later became one of the original settlers of San Luis,[107] and in 1862, he was one of the men who drove sheep into the Lower Cuchara Valley and wintered there for the first time.[108] His son, Jose Gregorio Jaquez, married the daughter of Francisco Antonio Manzanares, a Ute Indian. As a boy, Manzanares was captured by (New) Mexican traders and raised in the Lower Chama Valley of New Mexico Territory in the household of Jose Antonio Manzanares and Maria Ascencion Martin. He and his owner often traveled and hunted with Jose Salome Jaquez. All spoke Ute and Spanish and were well acquainted with Wiminuche Ute chief Ignacio. By

1860, Francisco Antonio Manzanares was in Costilla, New Mexico, and by 1870, he was in Huerfano County living at Crestones.[109]

Sisto Martinez, born at Abiquiu, New Mexico, in 1834, was seven years old when he and twenty other Hispano children were captured by Indians. In 1842, he was sold to Navajos, with whom he remained for twelve years. After his freedom, he became an interpreter for the U.S. Army and was a guide in the government's Navajo relocation effort. He helped gather the Navajos for the three-hundred-mile Long Walk to Fort Sumner at Bosque Redondo, New Mexico, in which many Navajos lost their lives. Then after the Treaty of 1868, he assisted in the return of the Navajos to their land,[110] which the United States vastly reduced in size. About 1877, Sisto Martinez and his wife, Josefa Trujillo, migrated to Huerfano County and settled at Talpa. Later they lived along the Santa Clara River south of Cucharas.[111]

Robert D. Rice became a member of chief White Antelope's Cheyenne Nation as a young man. Rice had adopted the Cheyenne mode of dress and language. When Indian trader Joseph B. Doyle first met Rice east of Rattle Snake Buttes, Rice was dressed as a Cheyenne and spoke their language. Years later, Doyle persuaded Rice to "return to his own" (white) people. Rice lived in the Doyle household and became a freighter.[112]

RECREATIONAL ACTIVITIES

Native Americans, Hispanos and Anglos gathered for foot and horse races, monte card games and dances. In preparation for one important foot race, men leveled a road using dirt scrapers and logs. Jose Jacobo Vallejos, son of Miguel Antonio Vallejos, was the favored athlete, but when some Anglos secretly fixed the race, Vallejos lost the race by "the last jump."[113] One horse race was known as the *corrido del gallo* (rooster pull), in which a rooster (or sometimes a chicken) was buried with its head and neck protruding from the ground. In turn, each horseman displayed his skill as he galloped toward the gallo at top speed. Leaning over the side of his horse, he tried to pull the gallo from the ground. The winner swung the bird in the air, shouted his triumph and taunted his rivals who raced to overtake him and the gallo. Corrido del gallo contests, held during the feast days of *Santiago y Santa Ana* (Saint James and Saint Ann), were traditionally held at Gardner, northeast of Walsenburg.

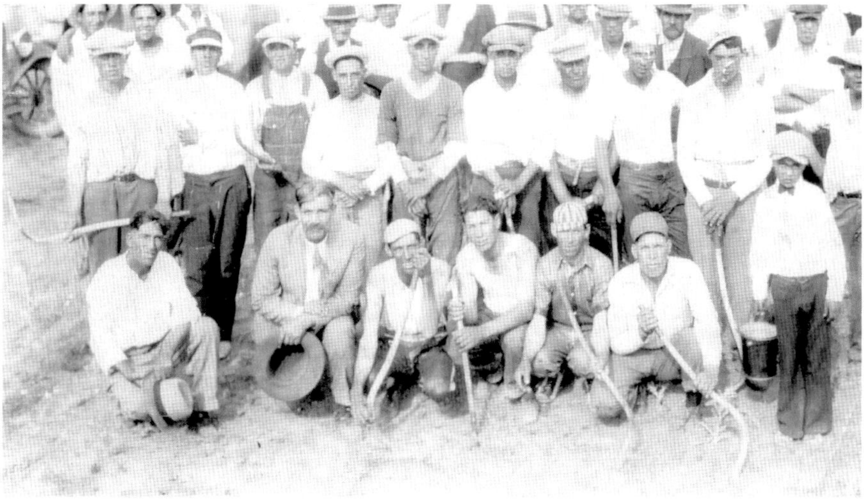

Chueco team in Vollmar, Colorado, July 4, 1930. *Courtesy of Teresa Herrera.*

The games played by Indians and Hispanos were quite similar. They both enjoyed horse racing, wrestling and gambling. Two games played by the Indians and Cuchareños were *el Chueco* and *el Cañute*. Chueco, played in the Cucharas area around 1870, was a team sport similar to ice hockey, only played on the ground. The Ute Indians had a similar game called Shinney; however, it was primarily played by women. In the Ute language, the stick was called *beher* and the puck or ball *pokunump*.[114] In Spanish, the stick was called a chueco and the ball *pelota*. The ball, about the size of a baseball, was a wad of rags covered in leather and tied with sinew (animal tendon). (Later, the wad was covered in gunny and tied with strong twine.) According to Ute women's rules, players could kick and grab other players' sticks.[115] A team won when it reached its plaza or home base. The winning team kept the ball as a trophy until the next game. Each player made his or her own hockey stick from available wood. Hispano players selected a good-sized piece of wood, soaked it in water and then shaped the stick. In contrast, Utes whittled their sticks. Teams played from one plaza or home to another as there was no set playing field. Several communities enjoyed pitting their teams against each other. For example, the Chueco team from Malachite played against the team from Gardner.[116]

The other team sport, *el Cañuto* (pipe), also known as el Cañute, originated from the Tewa Pueblo Indians. It was a guessing game played by two or more adults or children using a pin and four cylindrical, hollow sticks made from

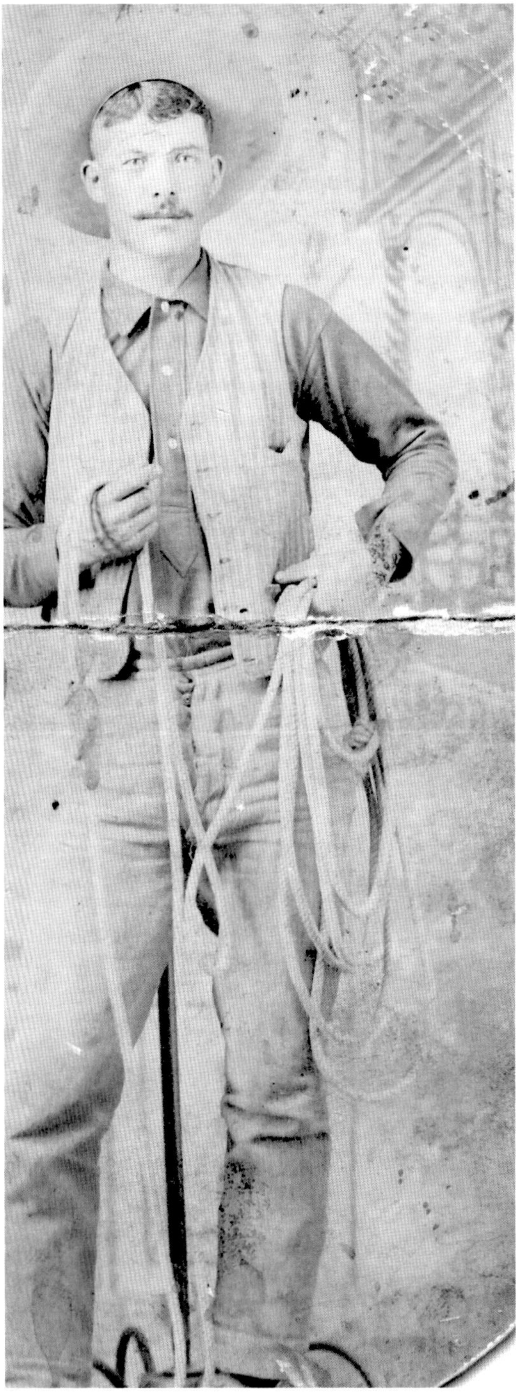

Jose Mucio Vallejos, son of Miguel Antonio Vallejos. *Courtesy of Janice Martinez.*

green cottonwood or pine branches. Players (*cañuteros*) were separated into teams. Each team used beans, kernels of corn or pebbles to keep score. When played indoors, the sticks generally were four inches long and a quarter inch in diameter. When played outdoors, the sticks were up to a foot long with a two-inch diameter and were placed in two piles of loose dirt, one pile for each team. Each stick had decorative markings or stripes burned onto it. Each stick had a name—*el uno, el dos, el hinchado* (or *el cinchado*) and *la mula* (or *el mulato*). A player placed a pin or nail made of wood, bone or iron inside a stick. Players often arranged the sticks in a star, house, triangle or some other shape or position with ends touching or with open space. The object of the game was to correctly guess which stick contained the pin. The cañutero had up to four chances to guess which stick had the pin. Depending on the stick selected, a certain number of points was subtracted for each wrong answer. The team with the highest score won the game.[117] The

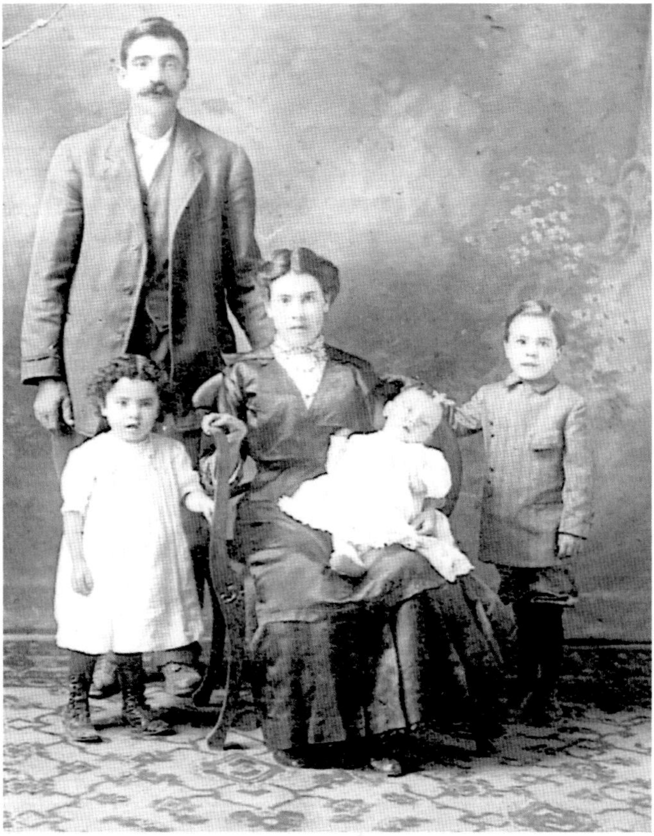

Antonio Abad Vallejos, son of Miguel Antonio Vallejos. *Courtesy of Janice Martinez.*

defending team often sang verses of a song to provide clues or simply taunt an opposing team.[118]

Allá viene el cañutero	*There comes the cañuto player*
El no halla el palito	*He will not find the pin*
El perdió el juego	*He lost the game*
Há-lla-lo, há-lla-lo, hálla-le, cañuto.	*Find it, find it, find it for him, cañuto.*

For the most part, gatherings were peaceful; however, a shooting occurred on October 8, 1898, during a dance held in a Cucharas schoolhouse. A gunshot fired at Jose Maria "Mucio" Vallejos ricocheted off the pocket watch he wore on his vest. Vallejos, son of Miguel Antonio Vallejos, took a shot that also ricocheted. After another shot was fired, Vallejos lay dead.[119] Cuchareños Antonio Domingo Valdez, Miguel de Jesus Maes and Juan Geronimo Bustos were arrested for the murder of Vallejos. Valdez was the son of Juan Benito Valdez; Maes was the son of Huerfano County sheriff Jose Vicente Maes; and Bustos was a prominent rancher in Cucharas whose father operated the first Cucharas stage relay station. Bustos was also married to a daughter of Cucharas sheriff Jesus Maria Manzanares. Each posted a $2,000 bail, and four lawyers were hired to defend them. In the end, a jury found them not guilty.[120] The fact that each man was financially able to post his bail and pay lawyers' fees attests to the financial success of some Cuchareños. Vallejos had been married for a year and a half and had a fourteen-month-old son.

SUMMARY

Like in other places in the Southwest, the Cuchareños incorporated many of their Native American neighbors' customs, including captivity. Their contact with various nations, with whom they fought and traded, had a significant influence on them. For many years before U.S. military intervention, Hispanos and Indians lived in relative harmony. The Cuchareños learned to accept visits from their Native neighbors. In contrast, Anglo settlers in the United States demanded military protection and wanted them removed. The documented instances of captivity in southern Colorado only tell the stories of harmony, friendships and familial bonds. Yet to be told are the stories of loss, heartache, language and cultural differences and punishment.

Into the Beautiful Circular Valley

"Fat" Jack, was 5' 4" tall and 4' 2" around the middle.[121]
—John H. Beadle

In Denver at 7:30 a.m. on May 7, 1872, eastern newspaper correspondent John H. Beadle boarded a D&RG train.[122] Santa Fe was his final destination. The first D&RG narrow-gauge train had two baggage, two smoking and two passenger cars. Although some D&RG locomotives were imported from abroad, most were made in the United States by Baldwin Locomotive Works.[123] The passenger car was "unique" yet comfortable. "It look[ed] like a dry goods box fitted by ingenious hand[s] into what is called a car." At the time, D&RG passenger cars measured seven feet by thirty-five feet. Each was divided into two compartments with double seats on one side of the aisle and single seats on the other. To balance the car, seats in the other compartment were arranged in the opposite manner.

Later that day, Beadle's train arrived at Pueblo, an end-of-the-line station. After dinner, Beadle boarded a Barlow and Sanderson stagecoach to continue his trip south.[124] The stage driver handled teams of two to six horses (or mules), depending on the number of passengers and weight of any freight being transported. During their night ride, "Fat" Jack stopped the stage at three stations for a quick change of horses. Before reaching Cucharas, the stage would have stopped at the Miller Station near Muddy Creek, the Greenhorn Station on Alexander Zan Hicklin's ranch and the Butte Valley Station.[125]

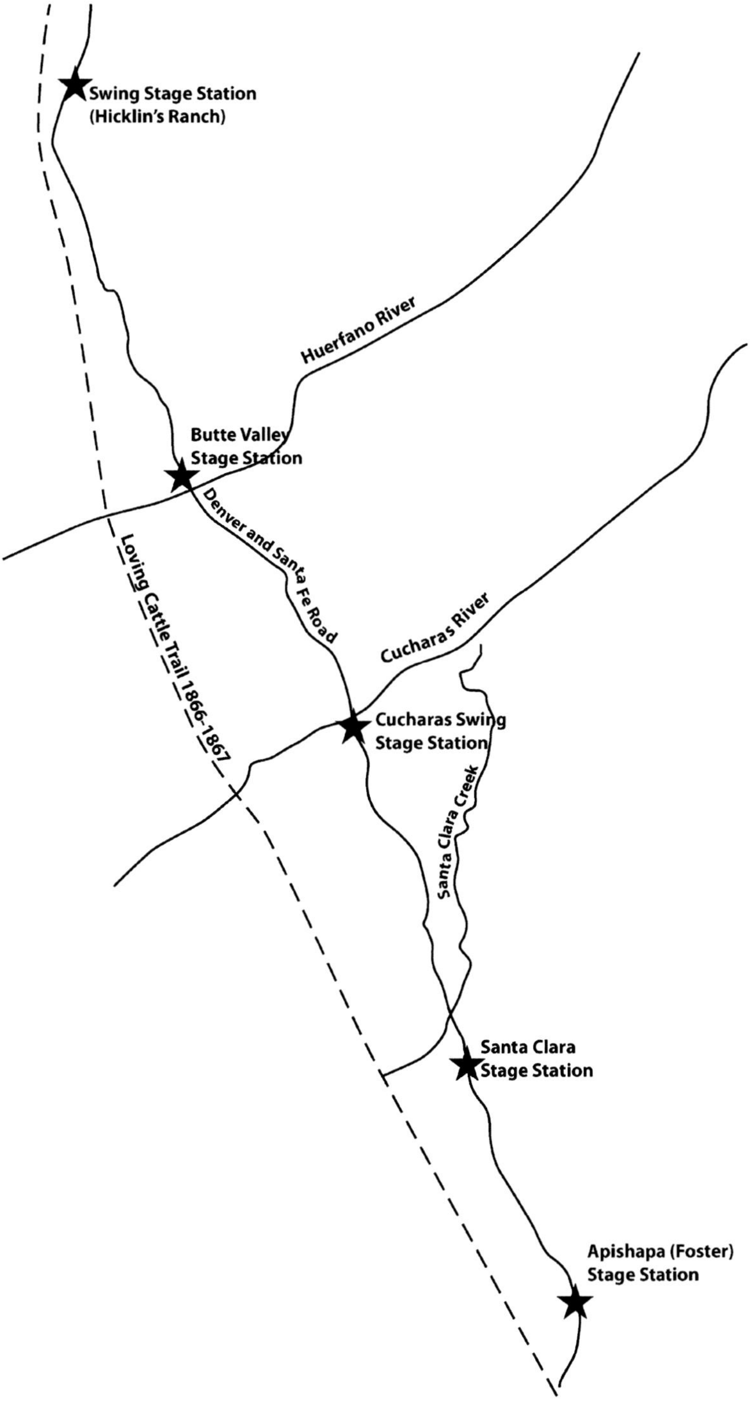

Huerfano County north–south stagecoach stations.

The following morning, Fat Jack drove the team toward an "old-style Mexican *hacienda*" in the "beautiful circular valley" of Cucharas.[126] The Cucharas Station was located on the Bustos property where the Denver–Santa Fe Road crossed the Cucharas River. A bridge was constructed to protect an irrigation ditch from damage caused by horses and coaches traveling on the Denver–Santa Fe Road. The station was located south of the Cucharas River in an area known as *la Posta*, Spanish for stage stop.[127] Once Fat Jack brought the horse team to a full, dusty stop, he set the wheel break and climbed down out of the driver's box. Beadle climbed out of the coach as Fat Jack went to exchange U.S. mail with the Cucharas postmaster.[128] Jose Alejo Bustos and his brothers, Jose de Gracia Bustos and Jose Maria Bustos, were there waiting to meet the stage. They were the stocktenders responsible for the care of the Barlow and Sanderson horses and mules. One of the brothers released the pin that fastened the team to the coach. As he led the hot and tired team toward the barn, the other brother moved a fresh team in place and fastened the harnesses, collars and bridles. As stocktenders, the Bustos brothers cared for about forty head of horses and mules. After a team was brought into the stable, stocktenders blanketed each tired horse and removed its harness, collar and bridle. Then they rubbed and brushed each horse. Later, they fed and reblanketed each horse and led it into a stall. Stocktenders also performed minor coach repair and blacksmithing.[129]

Inside the Cucharas Station a "plump and pretty *señorita*" had prepared coffee, wheat *tortillas*, *huevos* (eggs) and mutton stew. As Beadle ate breakfast, she combined "a pleasing variety of smiles and graceful gestures" to teach him the Spanish words she wrote in his journal.[130] When Fat Jack announced he was ready to leave, he and Beadle climbed back onto the stage. Once the stocktender reinserted the coach fastening pin, the 2,500-pound stagecoach was on its way to the next stop. Beadle did not mention other passengers traveling with him. When Beadle reached Trinidad, he still had a three-and-a-half-day stage ride to Santa Fe.[131]

Before 1863, there was no organized mode of transportation south from Denver to Santa Fe.[132] People traveled via small-time independent carriers, rode on horseback or rode in covered wagons. To transport goods, farmers and merchants hired independent freighters or hauled their goods by horse and wagon or pack animal. Between 1863 and 1870, several stagecoach companies operated between the two territories. At first, rather than traveling directly south from Denver to Trinidad, their coaches took the long, indirect route southeast to La Junta and then southwest along the Mountain Branch of the Santa Fe Trail to Trinidad. Once they reached Trinidad, passengers

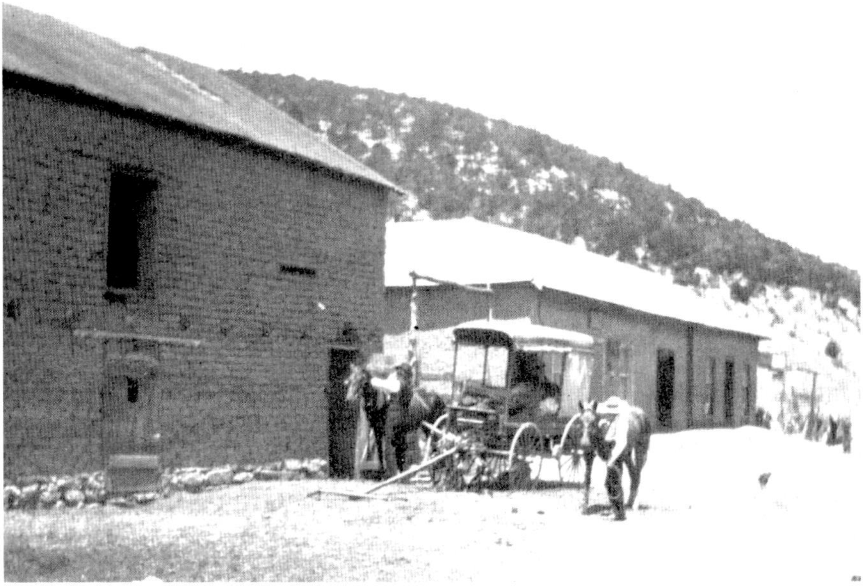

Stage station at Badito, Huerfano County, August 1904. *Courtesy of Colorado Springs Pioneers Museum–Starsmore Center for Local History, Francis W. Cragin Collection.*

continuing south boarded Barlow, Sanderson & Company stagecoaches. On April 3, 1867, Barlow and Sanderson offered direct stagecoach service between Denver and Trinidad along the Denver and Fort Union Road.[133] The road was extended and called the Denver and Santa Fe Road. Barlow and Sanderson coaches were on hand to transport passengers to areas not yet available by rail.

Stage companies did not stay in one location for too long. To reach a share in the transportation market, stage companies stayed one step ahead of the coming railroad. Barlow and Sanderson wanted the Cucharas stage station moved closer to the D&RG. On September 10, 1874, the *Pueblo Daily Chieftain* advertised that George H.F. Work hoped to rent the station "to the right man." As a result, he hired Samuel Todd, a former resident of Trinidad, to manage the station. On November 7, 1874, the *Trinidad Enterprise* reported that the station was one of the better stops en route to Pueblo where "meals could be purchased at a reasonable price."

With an increasing demand for passenger and freight service west into the San Juan Mountain mining region, Barlow and Sanderson began its first major west-bound line to Del Norte. On March 23, 1876, the *Pueblo Daily Chieftain* reported that D&RG rail cars delivered ten red Barlow and

Sanderson stagecoaches and horses to Cucharas City. From Cucharas, the stage line traveled northwest to Badito along the Huerfano River and then over the Sangre de Cristo Pass into the San Luis Valley.[134] Daily, twenty to thirty miners arrived and obtained provisions for the 110-mile stage ride into the mountains. The Bustos family continued to work for Barlow and Sanderson as stocktenders until May 3, 1876, when the last south-bound stage departed to Trinidad.[135] They continued to work for independent transportation companies or as *fleteros* (freighters) for area merchants. Jose Abundo and his brother, Juan Geronimo Bustos, assisted as stocktenders when they became of age. They were sons of Jose Alejo Bustos.[136] Independent and small stage companies continued to operate in remote areas of Colorado until the early twentieth century.

Fleteros

Although many Hispanos supplemented their farm income by taking on freighting jobs, little has been written about southern Colorado's fleteros. For fifty years, from 1821 to 1872, fleteros also played a big part in the transportation of goods along the Mountain Branch of the Santa Fe Trail. In 1870, fleteros hauled track near Denver for the Kansas Pacific Railroad. That May, nearly five thousand ox teams and one hundred mule teams were driven by fleteros. Newspaper reporters were in awe of the way "vast quantities of ties [were] hauled a 100 miles with teams subsisting on grass alone."[137]

Freighting was hard and dangerous work; many lost their lives due to injury and illnesses. On overnight trips, small independent freighters slept under their wagons or tarps. For protection and assistance on longer trips, they often traveled as family groups in caravans using various types of wagons. They shared meals and doubled their teams to assist each other when climbing steep mountainous terrain and in managing the animals and load during difficult descents. Fleteros were responsible for the contents they transported and the care of their wagons and animals.

By 1872, most freighting was still being handled by "picturesque Mexican hands in wagons drawn by ox teams."[138] In many cases, they pooled what money they had to purchase a team and wagon. The following year, fifty "Mexican freighting teams," hauled by two to five yoke, were seen near Trinidad. If needed, two or more wagons were coupled and pulled by

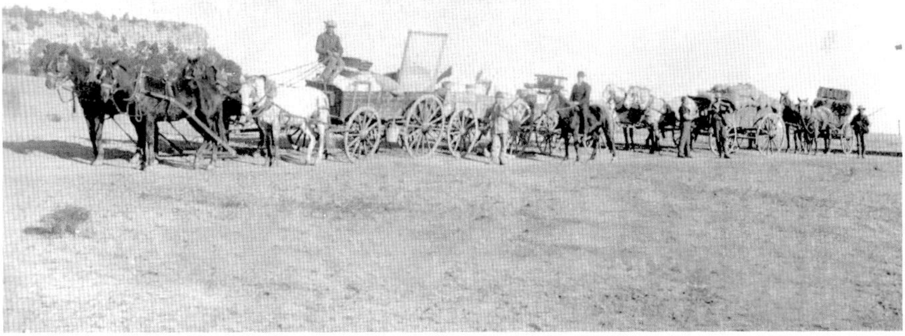

Unfug Brothers supply train to Rouse, Colorado. *Courtesy of Denver Public Library Western History Collection, Sporleder Collection, WH916, Ph Bx 3.*

multiple yokes. Oxen were used to haul the heavier goods; mules were used for lighter goods such as supplies, hardware and dry goods.[139] Four-horse and six-horse teams were also used. Horses were easier to maneuver when backing wagons to loading areas.

Many freight wagons, large and small, traveled along the Denver–Santa Fe Road and through the Bustos property. During the construction of the railroad, fleteros hauled rails, ties, foodstuffs, tents and tools to construction crews along the Front Range. Because merchants, commission houses, mines, lumber mills and the D&RG preferred Anglo commercial users over "small-scale" fleteros, few Hispano-owned freighting firms existed.[140] During early 1873, rail freight rates were so high that merchants employed fleteros with mule or ox at lower wages than their Anglo counterparts.[141] Hispanos tended to bid low to assure they would be given the job and, thus, obtain money for their families' needs.[142] They obtained work through an Anglo contractor, an Anglo freight company, a Hispano freight company or freighted as independents.[143] Three known Anglo-owned freight companies were Field and Hill, F.S. Struby and Company and the Unfug Brothers.[144] Between 1886 and 1893, Louis B. Sporleder drove a wagon and delivered goods throughout Colorado for August T. Unfug and Charles O. Unfug.[145]

Mining was big business in southern Colorado. Many Cuchareños supplemented their farm income as miners and as fleteros. Fleteros were on hand to transport coal, silver, gold and needed goods.[146] In 1876, fleteros hauled coal from mines around Walsenburg to coal chutes located in the northern section of the D&RG railyard near Cucharas City. There, laborers used scooped shovels to manually unload coal onto rail cars for shipment north to Pueblo or, later, south to the Trinidad area. During the 1880s, fleteros continued to haul crops, wool and goods to and from railway points and warehouses. As additional freight was moved by rail—and much later by motorized vehicles—the need for fleteros diminished.

The Cucharas Post Office

To be granted a post office, a town had to have a road an authorized transportation company could use. In addition, a petition requesting a post office had to be circulated among the townsfolk. Generally, the person circulating the petition became the town's first postmaster.[147] In 1870, attorney John Foster Read completed and submitted the form for a post office at Cucharas. Due to his unfortunate spelling error, the post office was first established as the Cacharas post office. Post office department forms required information about the nearest post office "on-stage and off-stage" routes. In 1870, the nearest post office north of Cucharas on the stagecoach route was located at Butte Valley. The nearest post office south of Cucharas on the same stage route was at Trinidad. By December 8, 1870, the Cucharas post office was in operation where the Denver–Santa Fe Road crossed the Cucharas River on the property of Jose Alejo Bustos. Joseph Adams was appointed postmaster. For some reason he did not serve out his term, so Read served in his place. Although the post office at la Plaza de los Leones was already in operation by this time, it was not on the Barlow and Sanderson stage route.[148] By government contract, a stagecoach driver

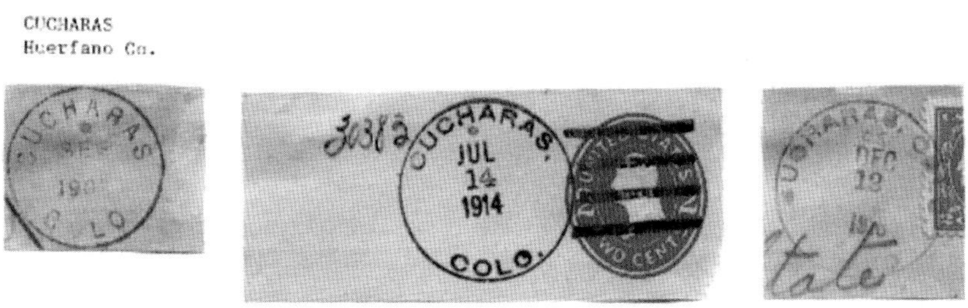

Cucharas postmarks. *Courtesy of Margie Pfund Memorial Post Mark Museum and Research Library.*

was not authorized to carry mail to towns not on his route. When a post office was off route, the postmaster of the nearest on-route post office was authorized to transport mail to that post office.[149] If an authorized stage driver dropped off mail at the Cucharas post office destined for la Plaza de los Leones, the Cucharas postmaster was responsible for delivering it to la Plaza de los Leones. Subsequently, this changed when la Plaza de los Leones became Walsenburg and stage and rail transportation services became available there.

Once rail track reached the railroad town of Cucharas City on February 26, 1876, mail that arrived from Trinidad by coach was delivered to the Cucharas postmaster. He sorted the mail and then took any mail going north to the D&RG for delivery by rail. The Cucharas post office closed on July 12, 1877, because it no longer had "traffic in stamps." All Cucharas mail was then delivered to Walsenburg.[150] Interestingly, two weeks later, the sale of U.S. postal stamps improved, and the government reinstated the Cucharas post office.[151] Although it continued to use its former name, the post office was relocated to the D&RG town of Cucharas City.

Cucharas Postmasters

DATE ASSIGNED	NAME
December 8, 1870	Joseph Adams[152]/John Foster Read
February 23, 1871	Peter S. Albert
June 14, 1871	Benjamin F. Logier
January 4, 1872	John Foster Read
September 20, 1872	Nasario Chavez
1873	John G. Self
December 8, 1874	George H.F. Work
March 12, 1875	Robert B. Stanley

DATE ASSIGNED	NAME
July 3, 1876	Mrs. Sarah O. Adams
July 26, 1877–1879	John Grady[153]
September 6, 1880	Walter V. Stevens
March 22, 1886	Fred O. Roof
June 21, 1888	William F. Korte
January 16, 1889	Walter V. Stevens
December 31, 1889	Robert Ames
May 4, 1891	Juan M. Valdez
October 18, 1892	Walter V. Stevens
August 23, 1894	Servellyn A. Parkhurst
November 22, 1894	Richard M. Limm
April 11, 1895	William Upton
August 24, 1898	Nettie Tanguary
September 21, 1899	Walter V. Stevens
April 7, 1904	Mary Aiken
August 12, 1904	Mary Aiken
December 15, 1904	Ray Josephine Jones
July 24, 1908	Katherine Cooney
January 16, 1909	Forest A. Chalk

DATE ASSIGNED	NAME
February 4, 1910	James Benjamin Stevens[154]
October 22, 1912	Harry W. Compton
March 4, 1914	John N. Miller
March 30, 1916	Nestor Guerrero
1920	Nestor Guerrero

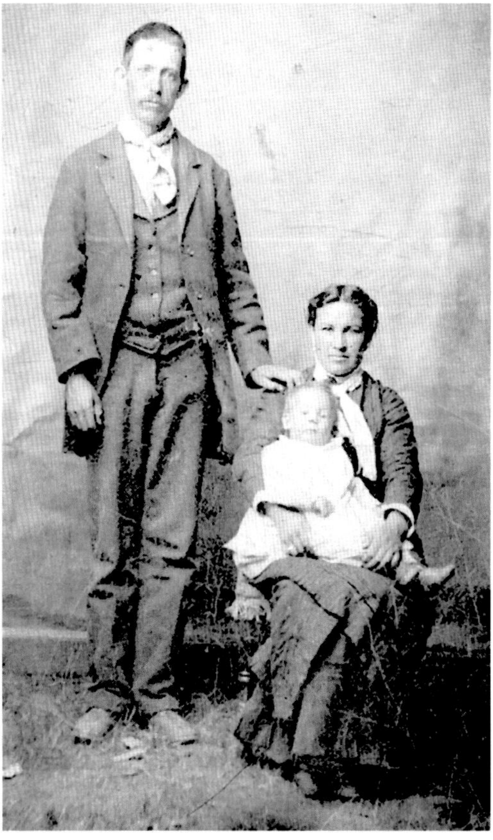

Cucharas postmaster Nestor Guerrero with his wife, Maria Andrea Bustos, and child. *Courtesy of JoAnn Beadeaux.*

Although the population of the area continued to be predominantly Hispano, between 1870 and 1920, only three out of twenty-seven appointments were made to Hispanos; four appointments were made to Anglo females.[155] Postmaster Nasario Chavez served in 1872. He also ran a store at Cucharas.

Postmaster Nestor Guerrero was appointed in 1916. Occasionally, he had his stepdaughter take the mail bag to the D&RG depot. Eighteen-year-old Gertrude Vallejos rode about a mile on horseback to the depot.[156] In 1884, he operated an independent passenger and freight service.[157] Guerrero served as a justice of the peace in 1896 and again in 1902. He owned a store and continued

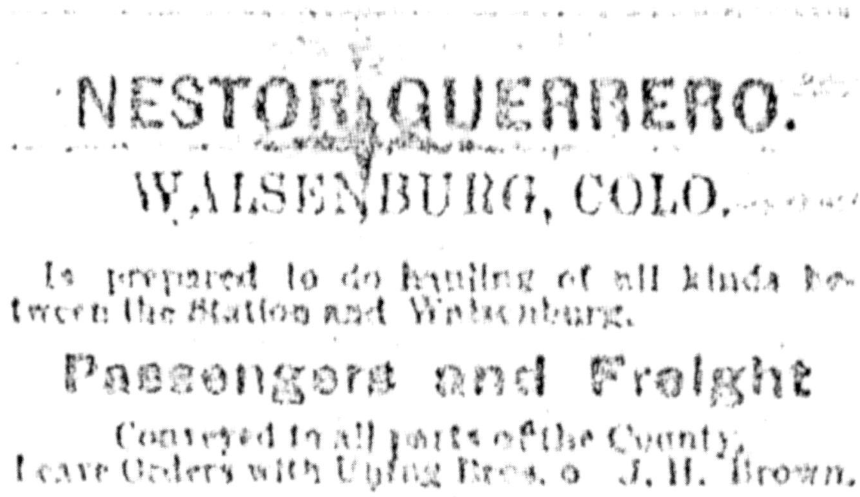

Guerrero Passenger and Freight Service advertisement, May 10, 1884. *Courtesy of* Walsenburg World.

to serve as postmaster until his death in 1920.[158] He was the last appointed postmaster of Cucharas. The Cucharas post office officially closed on January 15, 1921.

Lumber Mills

There was a tremendous need for timber. D&RG needed logs for ties and bridge works. Depending on the grade, every mile of railroad track required between 2,500 and 3,500 wooden ties.[159] Coal mines needed logs for support props, and Anglo newcomers preferred lumber, rather than earth-friendly adobe, for their homes and businesses. Timber for coal mines came from the Trinchera Estate in the San Luis Valley, of which General Palmer was also associated. Fred Walsen and his partner, future brother-in-law Alexander Levy, provided props, poles and ties for the D&RG.[160] In turn, General Palmer's D&RG transported logs, ties and timber props to coal mines near Walsenburg, including the Walsen Mine owned by Fred Walsen.[161]

Loggers felled trees using axes and double hand saws. Freighters hauled the timber to mills, where logs were cut into props, board lumber and ties. In 1873, there was a sawmill in *Cañon de Agua* (literally water canyon). The mill

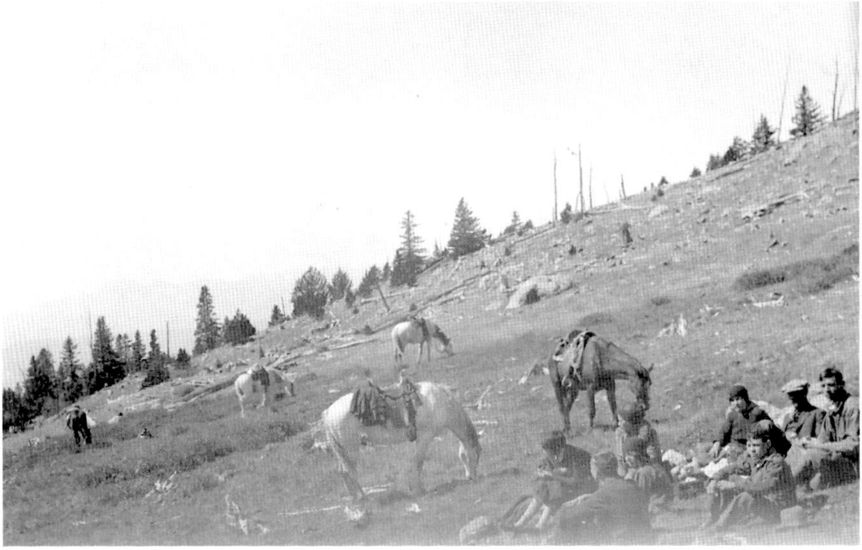

Horse riders picnic in area stripped by logging. *Courtesy of Helen Cisneros Vigil Family.*

was located about thirty-five miles from Cucharas and had an abundance of pine timber.[162] Jose Simon Abelino "Lino" Maes and his younger brother, Jose Vicente Maes, were two of the Cuchareños who worked in a ties camp.[163] Freighters hauled this cut timber to Cucharas City for rail transport to mines and other locations. P. Craig and B.K. Simpson operated a lumber mill there in 1875. Their partner was Cucharas City town trustee Thomas Wilkins. As the D&RG moved west from Cucharas, a D&RG subsidiary advertised the need for 260,000 feet of lumber hauled to points along the line.[164] Sporleder commented that before 1875, the forest—"the soil's protectors" on both sides of the Cuchara River—was never disturbed.[165]

> *The great trees and the bushes and vines suffered destruction. These "newcomers," with the characteristic greed of their own kind of civilization, cleared the land and plowed to the very edge of the river's channel. Spring freshets and summer floods* [washed] *away hundreds of acres of the richest soil.* [These] *"disastrous results"* [caused the area to look as it does] *now, a dreary, dead-looking waste of gravel and sand, with here and there thickets of scrubby willows and a few crooked, dwarfish trees.*

Summary

Cucharas as a stagecoach stop on the Denver–Santa Fe Road is an important historical find. Cucharas, located ten miles from the Butte Valley Stage Station and ten miles from the Santa Clara Station, was an excellent stopping place for a change of horses and mules. This piece of history corrects Colorado stage maps and introduces the Bustos family who worked as stocktenders. What a sight it must have been to see the stage come to a dusty stop and the stocktenders quickly unhitching and replacing the tired teams.

Helen Hunt Jackson saw thirty "white-topped" freight wagons pulled by ten to twenty mules.[166] The information presented about Hispanos in fletero occupations communicates that they were in demand and that many Hispanos did this type of work. Fleteros worked long and hard, and it was a difficult and dangerous occupation that must be recognized.

The establishment of the post office at Cucharas was an important milestone. Because Cucharas was on the Denver–Santa Fe Road, stages transporting mail stopped there and not at la Plaza de los Leones, the parent village of the surrounding Hispano villages. John Foster Read served as the first Cucharas postmaster for about nine months. He became a Huerfano County surveyor in 1880 and a county clerk in 1884. In 1885, Read and his second wife, Maria Cleofes Quintana, and their two sons moved to Denver where sons Henry and Antonio attended school.[167]

The post office, newspaper office and later the telegraph office were popular places where important information circulated. Postmasters, newspaper editors and telegraphers dealt with important news on a daily basis—information that was not readily accessible to the townsfolk. Cucharas postmasters John Foster Read, John G. Self and Frederick Osborne Roof were associates of Fred Walsen. Fred Walsen was said to be instrumental in helping Read change the name from la Plaza de los Leones to Walsenburgh (later Walsenburg).[168] In 1873, when Postmaster Self learned the D&RG was going to lay track west from Cucharas to Walsenburg, he purchased prime real estate north of the Cucharas River. The following year, he deeded a right of way to the D&RG.[169] Postmaster Roof became Huerfano County clerk in 1891. By 1900, he lived in Walsenburg and worked as a cashier for the Walsen Banking Company owned by Fred Walsen.[170] This company was later known as the Fred Walsen Bank. Roof managed the bank until Fred Walsen Jr. completed his education.[171] Fred Walsen Sr. thought highly of Roof and named him as executor of his will, for which Roof received $300 a year.[172]

La Plaza de los Leones did not officially become Walsenburg until 1873; however, Colorado territorial maps dated before this time incorrectly used the name Walsenburg or shortened la Plaza de los Leones to Placita, or incorrectly as Placito. (*Placita* in Spanish means little *plaza* or town.) In addition, some published references incorrectly cite La Veta as the site of the Cucharas post office in 1871 and Cuchara Junction as the site of the Cucharas post office in 1872.[173] (La Veta was an off-stage route during 1871, and rails at the junction were not in place until 1876.)

When the stage station and the post office were moved to Cucharas City, people flocked to the new surroundings. Mail, passengers and all types of freight then arrived by rail.

FAITH, SACRIFICE AND SERVICE

Bendito San Jórge.	*Blessed be St. George.*
Bendito Su altar.	*Blessed be His altar.*
Bendito los campos donde	*Blessed be the field on which*
Hemos de andar.	*We must walk.*

Like all pioneering families, the Cuchareños lived difficult lives. Women died in childbirth and sometimes as a result of accidental cooking fires. Men lost their lives on the farm and range, and children died of disease, drowning and snakebites. They prayed for comfort, aid and protection and to give thanks for the blessings bestowed upon them. Some families knelt as they daily prayed the rosary before candlelit home altars. Because there were many rattlesnakes in Cucharas, many carried long sticks when they walked to the corral, "even at night." Before leaving her house, Gertrude Vallejos, granddaughter of Miguel Antonio Vallejos, prayed to *San Jórge* (Saint George) for his protection.[174]

Between 1861 and 1869, the Catholic Archdiocese of Santa Fe served as far north as the Arkansas River in Colorado Territory. Because there were not enough priests to serve the growing county, priests could only make occasional monthly visits to the area. During the three-year period between 1866 and 1869, Mass was celebrated at Cucharas in the homes of Justice of the Peace Albino Cordova and Lorenzo Romero.[175] In 1869, Archbishop of Santa Fe Jean Baptiste Lamy sent Father Louis Merle to establish a parish church at la Plaza de los Leones. Unfortunately, attempts to have a parish church met with disaster. Fires destroyed the first rustic church in 1873 and the second

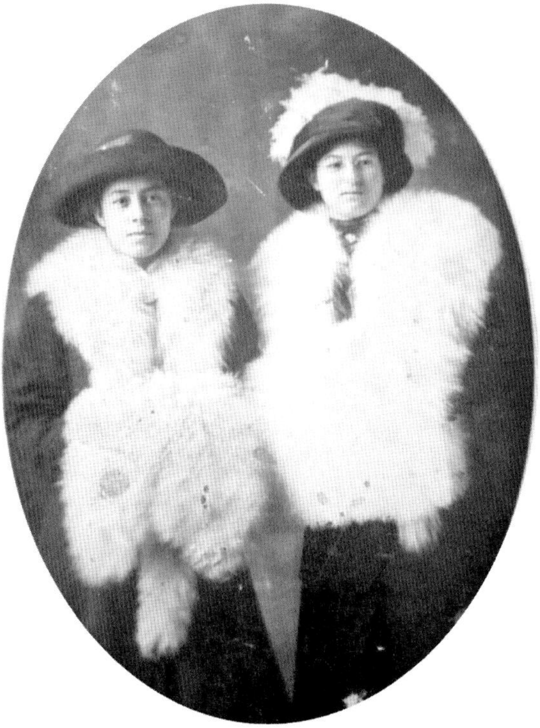

Maria Paula Vallejos Atencio and her sister, Gertrude Vallejos Farr. *Courtesy of Janice Martinez.*

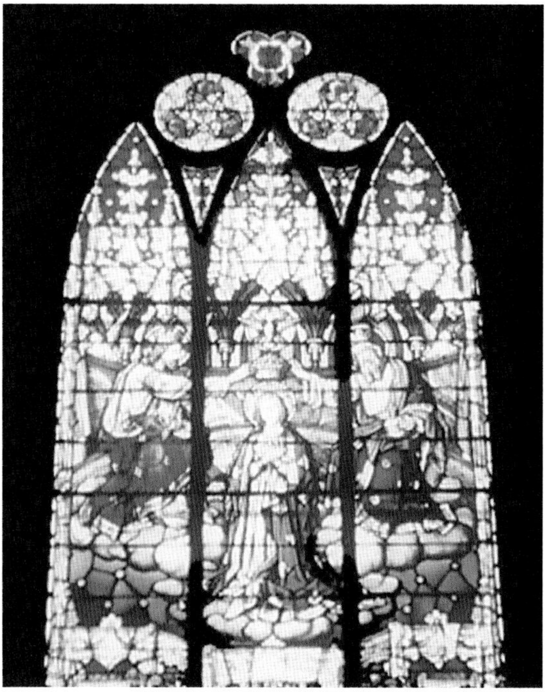

Stained-glass window donated by Jose Leonides Valdez, Saint Mary Parish Church, Walsenburg, Colorado. *Courtesy of the author.*

built in 1876. On October 15, 1876, Bishop Joseph P. Machebeuf of Denver installed Father Gabriel Ussel as parish priest of *Nuestra Señora de los Siete Dolores* (Our Lady of the Seven Sorrows), present-day Saint Mary Church. Prior to arriving at Walsenburg, Father Ussel ministered at Taos, New Mexico Territory.[176] After another flood destroyed a third church in 1878, Father Ussel was instrumental in building a new church. Jose Leonides Valdez loaned Father Ussel $3,000 for the new church in 1892. Two years later, he donated the entire loaned amount. He and Judge Jose Anastacio de Jesus Valdez (J.A.J. Valdez) each donated a stained-glass window for the new church.[177]

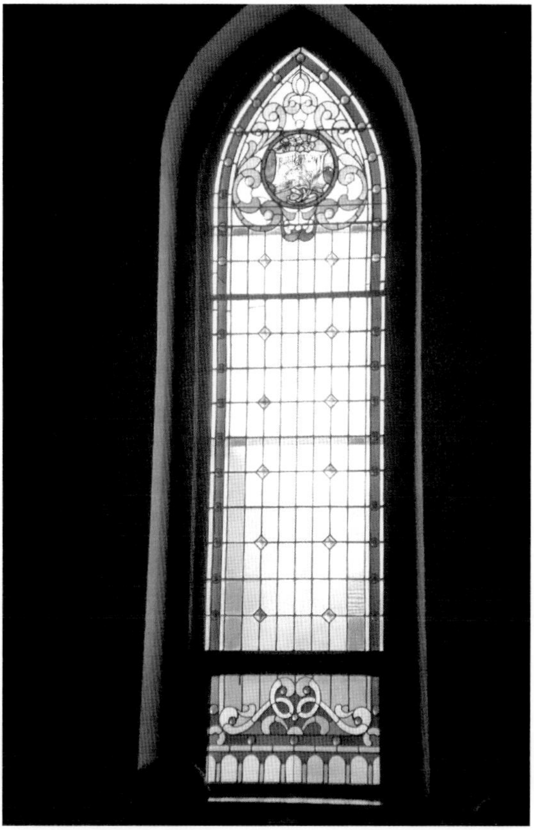

Stained-glass window donated by Jose Anastacio de Jesus Valdez, Saint Mary Parish Church, Walsenburg, Colorado. The brass plate inscription reads: "In Memory of JAJ Valdes." *Courtesy of the author.*

Feast Day Celebrations

People from nearby communities celebrated saints' feast day events at Walsenburg and Gardner. In celebration of the *Corpus Christi* (Latin for Body of Christ) feast day celebrated at Walsenburg, members of the *Sociedad de la Unión Católica* (Sacred Heart Society) constructed one of four outdoor altars and decorated each with flowers.[178] This feast day, which centered on the sanctity of the Eucharist and the presence of Jesus Christ, was a very popular event. Before entering church to celebrate Mass, the parish priest carried a

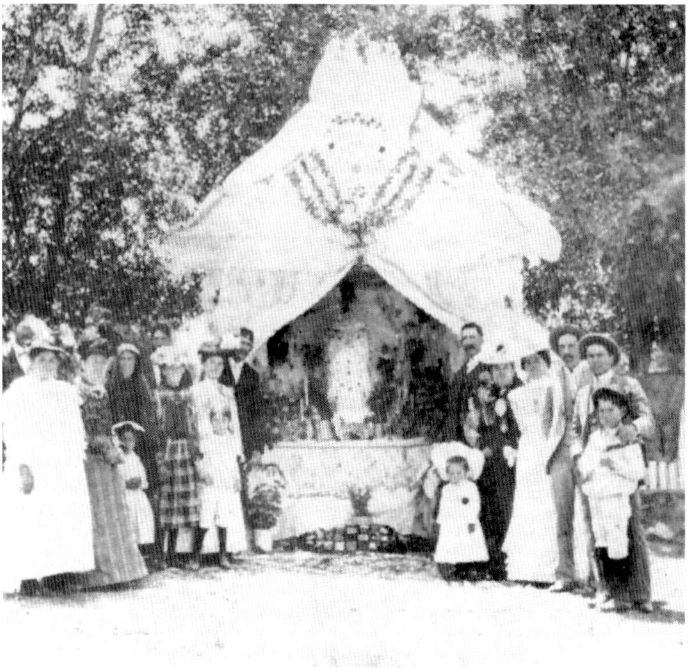

Outdoor altar erected by the Sociedad de la Unión Católica. *Courtesy of Howard L. Delaney.*

monstrance displaying the consecrated host and led the congregation in procession, pausing at each outdoor altar to pray.[179] J.A.J. Valdez founded the Sociedad de la Unión Católica in 1894 and served as its *mayordomo* (organizer). He successfully organized this feast day's celebrations for many years.[180]

Another important celebration was the feast of *San Isidro Labrador* (Saint Isador the Laborer, the patron saint of farmers). On this feast day, the priest, or a mayordomo, carried a statue of San Isidro; with the congregation following behind, he walked through crop fields asking for blessings and plentiful harvests.[181] After a feast day Mass, the congregation gathered and shared a meal. The day's activities also included various types of entertainment, such as horse races, foot races and a variety of games. Booths provided treats, such as watermelon, candy, sodas and homemade ice cream.[182] The day usually concluded with a dance where local musicians performed in a dance hall or schoolhouse.[183] To the music of two violins and one guitar,[184] couples enjoyed dancing *las cuadrilles* (square dances), *valses* (waltzes),[185] polkas and *el chotís* (the schottische).[186] Musicians of the time included Agapito Montoya,[187] Jose Leon Medina,[188] Jose Daniel Martinez[189] and Seferino Sandoval.[190] Martinez was the grandson of Juan Benito Valdez.

The San Antonio Church

The Cuchareños hoped one day to have their own church built on the Cucharas plaza. In late 1894, Jose Leonides Valdez sold two lots on the plaza to the Right Reverend Nicholas Matz, bishop of the Catholic Archdiocese of Denver. The price of the sale was one dollar.[191]

By the following year, the Cuchareños named their church *San Antonio* for Saint Anthony. They placed a bell in the wooden bell tower above the adobe church. The adobe church measured about eighteen by thirty feet and had six windows.[192] Carved *santos* (holy images), statues and crucifixes housed in the church were made by parishioners or purchased from commissioned *santeros*.[193] Once a month, a priest arrived in Cucharas to celebrate Mass.[194] Father Gabriel Ussel, *Padre Gabriel* as the Hispanos called him,[195] arrived on horseback or in a two-seat, horse-drawn carriage.[196] After Mass, the visiting priest was given a meal hosted at a parishioner's home.[197] Later, St. Anthony Church was dedicated a chapel.[198]

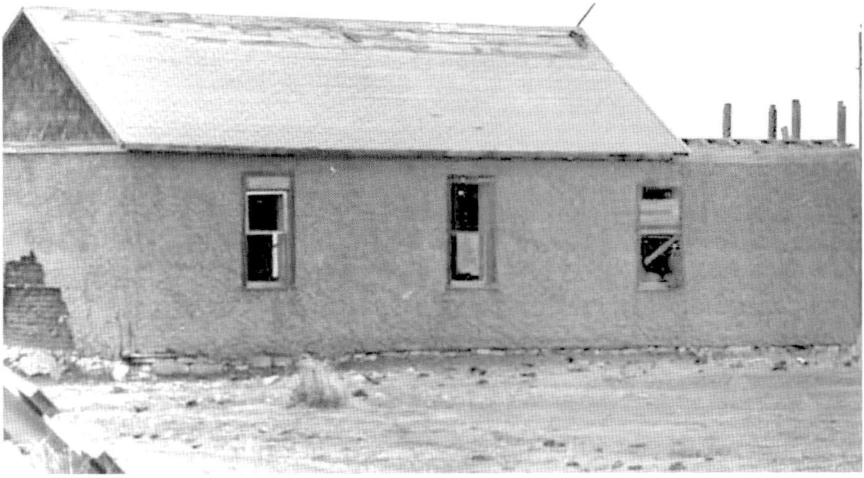

West wall of the San Antonio Chapel, Cucharas. Photo by Sara Murphy, 1981. *Courtesy of Colorado Historical Society Office of Archaeology and Historic Preservation.*

BAPTISM

Parents of an infant or young child and their selected *padrinos* (godparents) traveled to Walsenburg to have the child baptized in the parish church. Padrinos served as role models and sponsors for the child. Padrinos could be a married couple, a grandmother and her son, a grandfather and his daughter, an older brother and sister or a prominent married couple of the community. Generally, grandparents served as padrinos for a first-born grandchild. For the baptism ceremony, the *madrina* (godmother) dressed the baby in a handmade long, white baptismal gown.[199] The padrinos then presented the child before the parish priest. *María* was often part of a girl's baptized name in honor of Saint Mary. The names *Jesús*, *Cruz*, *José*, *Juan* or *María* were part of a boy's baptized name in honor of Jesus, the holy cross or saints Joseph, John and Mary. With the arrival of Anglos from the east, baptized names were either dropped or shortened. Jose Anastacio de Jesus Valdez became J.A.J. Valdez, Juan de la Cruz Esquibel became J.C. Esquibel and Jesus Maria Manzanarez became J.M. Manzanares.

DEATH AND BURIAL

The solemn ringing of the church bell announced the death of a member of their community. Family and friends arrived at the home of the mourners to offer comfort and support. The body was bathed, dressed and placed on the cloth-draped board for the *velorio* (wake) held in the deceased's home. Later, with the availability of milled lumber, wooden coffins became available. Relatives and neighbors gathered in the candlelit room to pray. At midnight, those in attendance ate a meal and then prayed until dawn. When a person became tired, he or she took a nap. "In shifts, some prayed while others slept."[200] They prayed to free the deceased from the burden of sin and to prepare his or her place in heaven. The burial took place the following day.

Prior to 1869, when the parish church and cemetery were built, burials took place out on the prairie. The body was wrapped in a shroud, if available, and placed in a grave. If the ground was frozen, they covered the body with rocks. The grave and rocks helped to prevent animals from destroying the deceased's remains. In 1982, workers digging a carbon dioxide pipeline through Cucharas exposed human remains from an unrecorded burial site. Nine unidentified bodies of Hispanic and/or Native American descent were buried there between 1860 and about 1868. Each was wrapped in a *mortaja* (shroud); their ages ranged from under thirty days to forty years.[201]

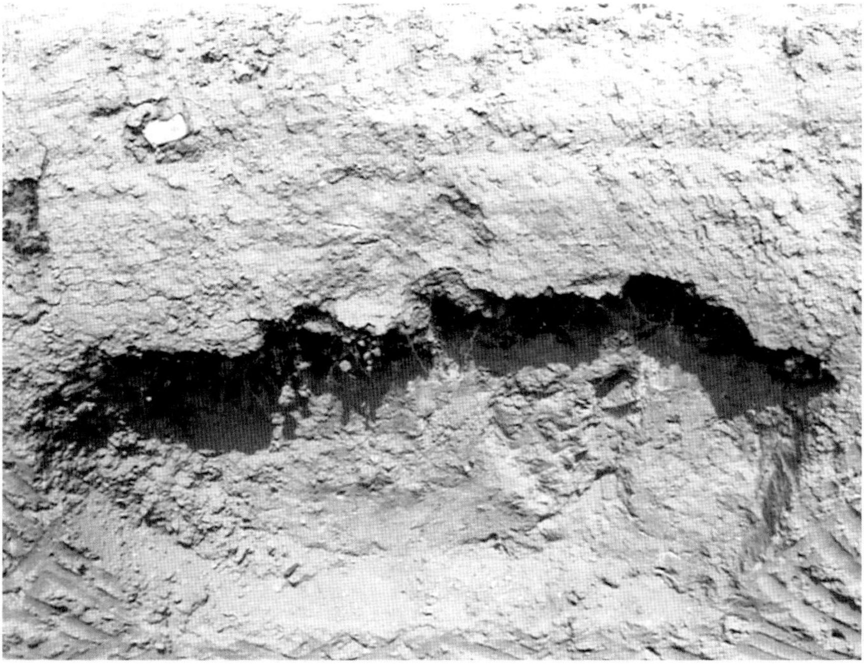

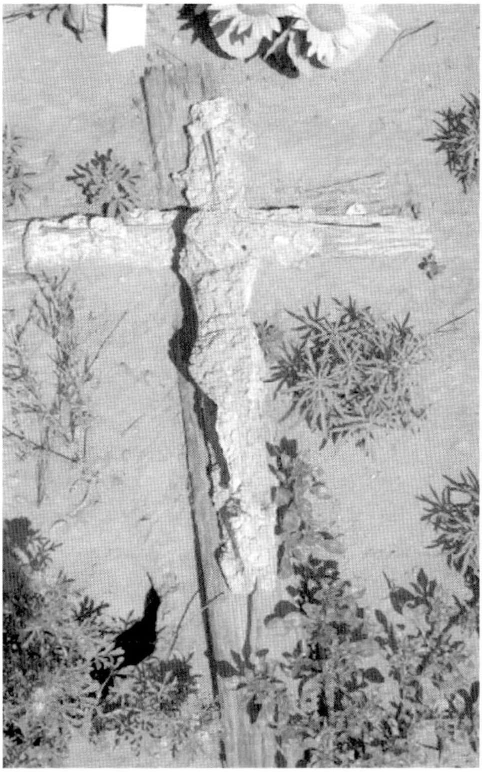

Above: Burial cavity, Cucharas, 1982. *Courtesy of Office of Contract Archeology, University of New Mexico.*

Right: Weathered hand-carved crucifix on an unmarked grave in the Bustos Cemetery, Cucharas. *Courtesy of the author.*

The Cucharas community had at least three cemeteries in place after 1870. The Vigil Cemetery was located about three miles northwest of Cucharas. It was a family cemetery and is no longer in use. The Valdez Cemetery, first known as the Cucharas Cemetery, was in use by 1869. It is still in use today but is known as the Valdez-Cordova Cemetery. The Bustos Cemetery, which is still in use today, was established in 1890. Cucharas City businessman Walter V. Stevens sold land for this cemetery to Bishop Nicholas Matz for one dollar.[202]

Families dressed in black and mourned their loss for at least one year. After this period of time, it was quite common for a widow, or a widower, to remarry. A widowed mother often needed help with her farm and livestock, and a widower needed help with his young children and someone who could manage household duties.

HOLY WEEK AND THE BROTHERHOOD OF *PENITENTES*

In preparation for the Lenten Holy Week, a week of prayer and fasting in remembrance of the Jesus's death on the cross, the Cuchareños doubled up on their chores. They performed no heavy work, including the chopping of wood. By tradition, families fasted at breakfast and only ate a light meal at dinner; they played no music or games.[203] Cucharas had a *penitente* group known as *La Fraternidad Piadosa de Nuestro Padre Jesús Nazareno* (the Pious Fraternity of the Brothers of Our Father Jesus the Nazarene). Penitentes were not ordained priests, and they could not administer the holy sacraments (e.g., baptism, marriage, communion and penance). Because few priests were available to minister to the people, the Brotherhood led prayers, visited the sick and helped bury the dead. They also provided aid to widows and the poor.

During the late 1880s, the penitentes of Cucharas constructed a *morada*, a building where they met and practiced rituals of penance, song and prayer. They constructed their morada of upright ties plastered with adobe.[204] This type of building was called a *jacal.* The Brotherhood named their morada *el Corazón de Jesús* (the Heart of Jesus) and prayed before several santos.[205] Later, the Brotherhood constructed a two-room adobe morada. The larger room served as an *oratorio* (chapel). It measured about twelve feet by twenty feet. Nonmembers were allowed to visit the chapel and pray before the santos kept there.[206] The smaller room served as a meeting room

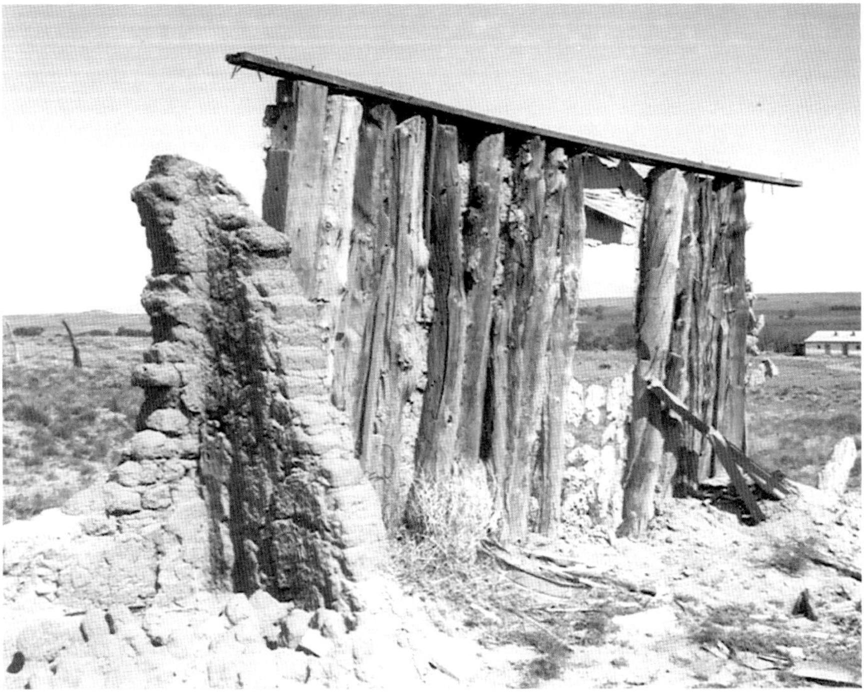

Remains of adobe and jacal morada in Cucharas. *Courtesy of Office of Contract Archeology, University of New Mexico.*

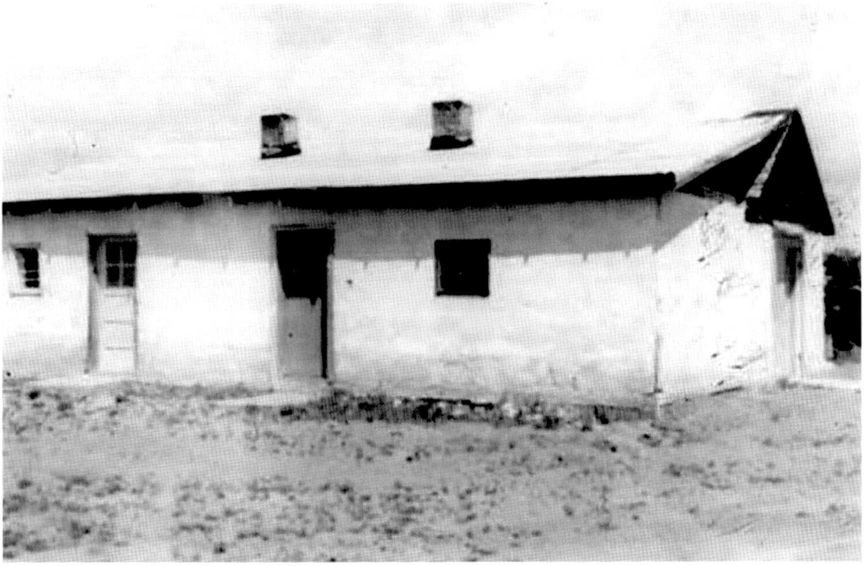

El Corazón de Jesús Morada in Cucharas. Photo by Sara Murphy, 1981. *Courtesy of Colorado Historical Society Office of Archaeology and Historic Preservation.*

where the Brothers met and ate. It had a table and handcrafted chairs and benches. It measured about ten feet by twelve feet.[207] Father Ussel was known to have visited the many moradas that once dotted the Huerfano County landscape.[208]

Penitentes followed traditional practices passed down from their northern New Mexican ancestors. On Good Friday during the *Procesión de Madera* (Procession of the Cross or Way of the Cross), one penitente carried a large cross. He was followed by additional cross bearers and then by other Brothers and the wives or female relatives who served as auxiliaries. Penitentes not carrying crosses flagellated themselves with *azotes* (whips). Some made their way toward *Calvario* (Calvary) on their knees. Calvario, located a few miles from the morada, was an area that symbolized where Jesus was crucified. As they prayed along their way to Calvario, a *pitero* (flute player) played ascending and descending melodies to symbolize sadness. The procession periodically stopped to sing a special hymn or relieve cross bearers. The procession concluded at Calvario with the reenactment of the Crucifixion of Jesus. Penitentes

Log cross near a Cucharas morada. Photo by Sara Murphy, 1981. *Courtesy of Colorado Historical Society Office of Archaeology and Historic Preservation.*

performed these practices to atone not only for their sins but also for the sins of all men and women. They offered their suffering up to God to heal the world of sin. According to an 1878 account, eleven wooden crosses were seen at Calvario in Cucharas. Some were nine to ten feet long. After the re-creation of the Passion of Christ, two crosses stood upright on the prairie and nine lay overlapped on the ground.[209]

During the evening of Good Friday, those in the procession returned to the morada for a service in the chapel commemorating the hours of darkness when Jesus died. An *hermano mayor*, an elder Brother, lit thirteen candles on a candleholder with several arms or branches (candelabrum). Two penitentes chanted the *Miserere* (Latin psalm for have mercy). Other penitentes answered the chant with a hymn about the Passion. At the end of a verse, a penitente extinguished a lit candle on an end of the candelabrum. Each extinguished candle symbolized the apostles' abandonment of Jesus. At the conclusion of the *Tenebrae* (Latin for shadows), the hermano mayor led prayers for the living and the souls in purgatory and extinguished the last remaining candle. Now in total darkness, the sound of the handmade wooden cog clacker (*matraca)*, the twirl of a ratchet and the shaking of chains symbolized the anguish of Jesus's death.

Many Anglos criticized penitente rituals and exaggerated about them in newspapers and books. In 1876, a Colorado Springs newspaper inaccurately wrote, "The mode of punishment and its severity was in proportion to the sins a penitente committed during the past year." The article also incorrectly stated that being a penitente for three years automatically assured his place in heaven, and that after this period, "this lowest type of humanity [was free to] raise hell on earth." Without regard to religious rights, the article concluded, "In the heart of free America… civil power [should] suppress the heathenish practice."[210] Because published criticism drew many onlookers, the Brotherhood became more secretive in their Lenten rituals and practices.

By 1923, the Ku Klux Klan had quite a following in Colorado. Hispanos, African Americans and immigrants dealt with warnings of "clinging to old ways" or speaking with accents.[211] Vandals shot at the Cucharas morada and stole several santos.[212] When two Anglo men tried to burn a cross on the Cucharas prairie, armed penitentes prepared to confront the presumed Klan members. After more attempts to burn the last wooden cross that stood upright at Calvario, a Brother moved it for safekeeping.[213] As traditions, practices and forms of worship changed through the years, more and more moradas permanently closed as fewer younger Hispanos became penitentes. Between 1980 and 1986, Huerfano County had only three active moradas.[214]

Non-Catholic Ministries

Methodist and Protestant missionaries also served in Huerfano County. In 1873, the Reverend A.H. Quillan started the Methodist Church at Gardner. He served the Methodist Church until 1897.[215] The following year, the Reverend C.H. Kirkbride, a Methodist local elder from Pueblo, ministered at Cucharas City.[216] He was replaced in September by thirty-five-year-old Reverend Oscar P. McMains.[217] About 1895, the Reverend Refugio Jaramillo, a Presbyterian, ministered to the Spanish speakers near Walsenburg. Later he opened a Spanish school for adults and children where thirty-one students were enrolled. By 1904, Walsenburg had a Mexican Presbyterian Church.[218] Reverend Jaramillo still held Protestant services in the area in 1910.[219]

In 1895, Presbyterian reverends T.F. Kirkwood from Colorado Springs and F.M. Gilchrist from Del Norte ministered in the San Luis Valley and started the Presbyterian College of the Southwest at Del Norte. Many Hispanos were ordained and received into the Presbyterian faith and attended this school. Former Catholic Antonio Jose Rodriguez became a Presbyterian minister and ministered to the Southern Ute Reservation at Ignacio, baptizing about eighty Ute Indians. The first Ute Presbyterian, Julian N. Buckskin, helped translate English hymns and scriptures. Ute chief Severo Capote and many in his band were received into the Presbyterian Church in 1897. Reverends Rodriguez and Manuel de Jesus Sanchez also organized Presbyterian missions and churches at Saguache, Trinidad and Walsenburg.[220]

Protestant missionaries discouraged centuries-old Catholic practices such as home chapels, devotion to the saints, praying the rosary, penitente rituals and other practices engrained in Hispano religious custom. The Theatine Order of Catholic Priests felt Protestant missionaries were too eager to convert and "rob" Hispanos of their Catholic education, faith and heritage.[221] Although there were some conversions, the majority stayed devoted to their Catholic faith, custom and tradition.

Summary

The foundation of the Cuchareños was grounded in faith, sacrifice and service to others. Prayer, sacrifice and celebration brought them together as they prayed for good crops and blessings and supported their neighbors in times of need. But their religion was in conflict with their Anglo neighbors. Helen Hunt Jackson described Hispano santos, *retablos* and home chapels as "gaudy Roman Catholic prints and effigies and shrines."[222] She and others also criticized the penitentes and their practices.

Parish priests continued to offer regular monthly Mass in the San Antonio Church at Cucharas until the 1950s.[223] In time, fewer Cuchareños were left to maintain the church and morada. By 1982, the small bell and tower on the San Antonio Church were gone. Upon the land where the last morada lay sits a doublewide trailer home. And, by 2004, the last remaining symbol of their Catholic heritage was a melting adobe wall and the dismantled roof of the San Antonio Church.

Linked by Water, Linked by Blood

"Newcomers," with the characteristic greed of their own kind of civilization, cleared the land and plowed to the very edge of the river's channel.[224]
—*Louis B. Sporleder*

After establishing permanent settlement in Cucharas, the community dug an *acequia* (irrigation ditch) to move water to their farmlands. Acequia construction was a developed skill that was passed down from generation to generation. Its construction required a careful review of the lay of the land and analysis of the soil. Using the flow of gravity and following the curve of the land, an acequia moves water in a snakelike pattern.[225] Early acequia construction required the use of simple wooden tools to cut through and move dirt. Dirt and rocks were placed on large pieces of rawhide that was moved from the worksite by mule or oxen.

Miguel Antonio Vallejos was the *patrón* (leader) of the Cuchareños. As patron, he "supervised the [division] of land and directed the building of acequias."[226] Through "centuries of experience" in the Southwest, his ancestors found long lots more compatible with the lay of the land and available water than the square-grid layout used in the eastern part of the United States. Long lots were perpendicular to the acequia to maximize the number of *parciantes* (a group of farmers) who had access to water.[227] As an *acequero*, a person knowledgeable and experienced in the construction of acequias, Vallejos directed the parciantes in the physical work needed to dig, test and use an acequia. Acequeros had no written instructions; they

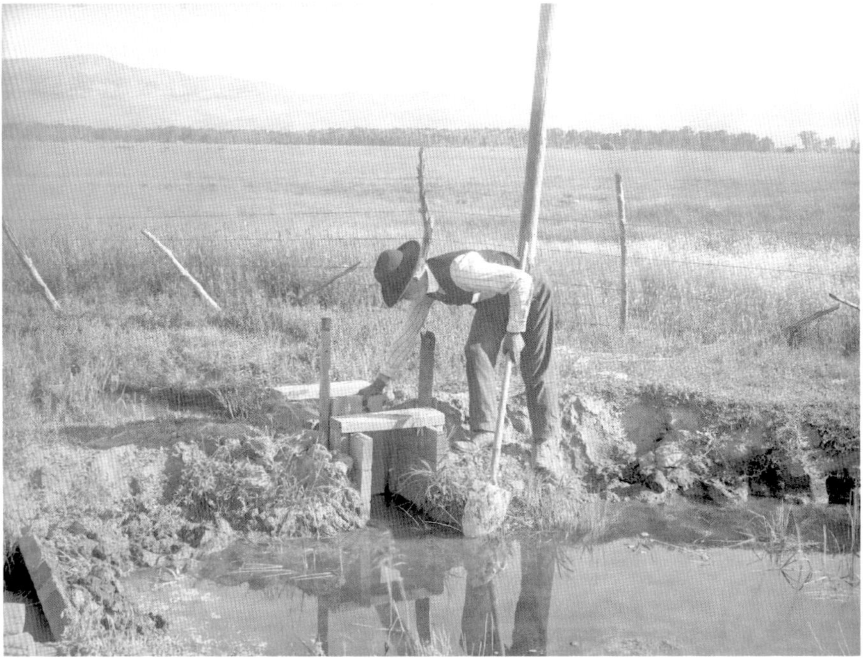

Controlling the flow of water through a wooden head gate. *Courtesy of Denver Public Library Western History Collection, L.C. McClure, MCC 1349.*

relied on practices from long-standing rules and custom established by their ancestors who settled in New Mexico.

Water for each acequia in Cucharas came from selected points along the Cucharas River. Where water would enter the acequia, they constructed a *presa* (dam) using piled logs, rock and branches. The presa held back water from the river, thus keeping the acequia dry during construction. It also kept water from spilling into the main gate at the inlet.[228] A *compuerta* (wooden headgate or floodgate) at the inlet controlled the flow of water into the acequia. It also helped keep out debris and could be locked to shut the flow of water flow.[229] An insufficient flow of water could create sinkholes, causing water loss. Too much water flow could destroy the dam, the acequia and the embankments.

Once the acequia was in operation, parciantes could irrigate their fields. Water was distributed on a rotation basis beginning with the parciante closest to the main headgate. After water was given to the first parciante for an established amount of time, it went to the second parciante and so forth until every parciante of an acequia had a chance to irrigate.[230] When it was a parciante's turn to irrigate, he slid the plank (headgate) in a wooden track to direct the water onto his field. A wooden box held the plank in place and kept the water from washing out the earthen bank.[231] When one furrow of his field was sufficiently irrigated, the parciante made a mud dam to allow water to flow into the next furrow. When his turn to irrigate was over, he closed his headgate to allow water to flow to the next parciante's land. Parciantes followed traditional Hispano water distribution values: distribute first to those in greatest need, take water only when it is your turn and take no more than the amount you need. By custom, each parciante cultivated and weeded his field so as not to waste water on a deserted or lost crop. These values were especially important when water was scarce. The prevailing principle was "to safeguard crops for food and subsistence."

Managing an Acequia

According to Hispano custom, a mayordomo was elected annually by parciantes of an acequia association to enforce their agreements and manage their ditch.[232] The mayordomo was elected based on his knowledge and experience of irrigation techniques and propriety and justice in handling parciante water disputes.[233] An experienced mayordomo could tell how much water ran in the ditch. He also knew how much each farm's share of water was and how long each farmer's headgate should remain open. Each parciante was entitled to a *surco* (unit) of water sufficient to irrigate a section of land as determined by the mayordomo. By tradition, a surco was equal to the amount of water that flowed through the hub of a cart wheel.[234] The water measurement used in Colorado Territory was the miner's inch, which measured water flow from a one-inch-square opening through a two-inch piece of wood. This measurement originated in California after the 1849 gold rush and evolved into the cubic foot per second unit used today.[235] Ideally, each parciante was careful not to take more than his allocated amount; and when a parciante violated this custom, he was assessed a fine. Each knew if he interfered with the acequia in any manner, took water without permission of the mayordomo, irrigated when it was not his turn or had unpaid fines, the mayordomo could lock his headgate.

Irrigating out of turn, making an unauthorized cut in the ditch or irrigating for too long a period of time were considered water theft by acequia norms and punishable by Colorado Territorial water law. In 1885, the Madrid Ditch No. 2 association set the fine for taking water without the mayordomo's permission; the minimum fine was one dollar and a maximum was three dollars, as determined by the mayordomo.[236]

The mayordomo was responsible for collecting payment of fines and could refuse a parciante's use of the water based on the incurred fines. Fine payments went into the acequia fund. A good mayordomo maintained cohesion among the parciantes and encouraged reciprocity and mutual aid.[237] His on-the-job training, experiences as a parciante and his knowledge and understanding of acequia culture and governance provided him with the skills he needed to act as mediator, leader, ditch manager, conciliator and negotiator. The mayordomo was accountable to the parciantes of his ditch. He interpreted and enforced acequia standards according to local custom and practice or documented rules and procedures. Because responsibilities of the mayordomo were passed down from mayordomo to mayordomo, his responsibilities were well understood.

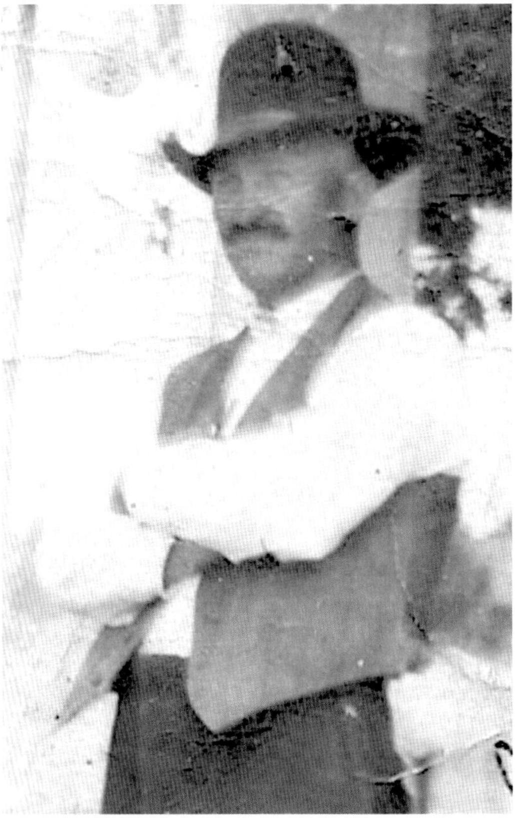

Madrid Ditch mayordomo Teofilo Bustos, husband of Maria Virginia Lucero. *Courtesy of Richard Bustos.*

Antonio Tircio Bustos served as mayordomo of the Madrid Ditch No. 2 (hereafter Madrid Ditch) in 1907 and 1908. He was associated with the Madrid Ditch until at least 1915.[238] In 1885, he served as one of four sheriffs safeguarding Cucharas City.[239] He was elected county assessor in 1889.[240] His younger brother, Teofilo Bustos, served more terms as mayordomo than any other parciante. Expertise as a skilled and equitable leader likely contributed to his repeated elections. He was associated with the ditch for at least twenty-five years.[241] Their mother, Maria Manuela Maes, and brothers Juan Basilio and Jose Agustin were also parciantes.

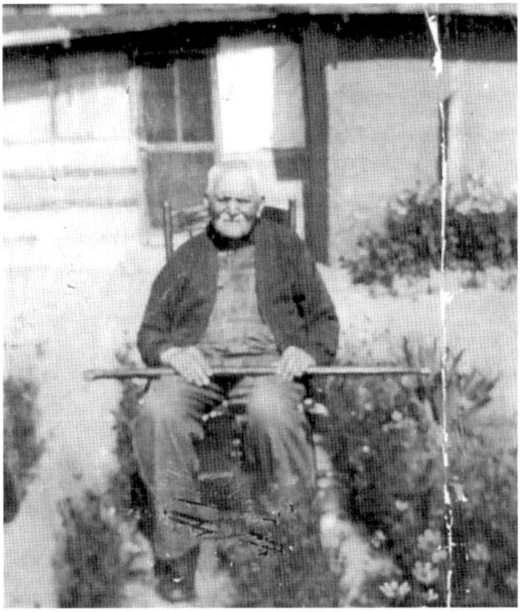

Right: Madrid Ditch mayordomo Juan de Jose Florentino Chavez. *Courtesy of Donald Romero.*

Below: Madrid Ditch mayordomo Jose Concepcion Cisneros and his mother, Juana Maria Coppee (Copas). *Courtesy of Helen Cisneros Vigil Family.*

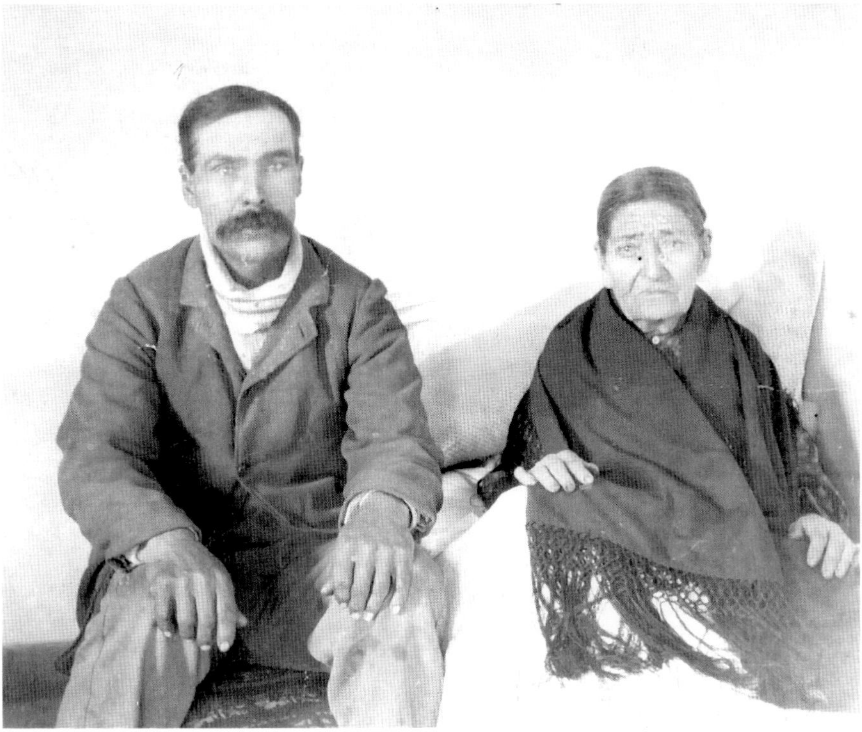

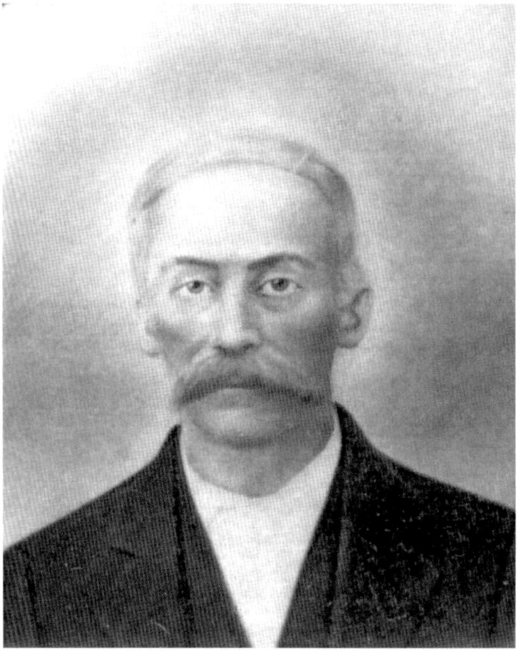

Madrid Ditch mayordomo Manuel Antonio Lucero. *Courtesy of Donald Romero.*

Juan de Jose Florentino Chavez served at least one known term as mayordomo in 1916. He was associated with the ditch from at least 1888 to 1923. During the 1930s, he grew beets on his farmland.[242] His son, Jose Federico, was twenty-eight years old when he served as mayordomo in 1902. He was associated with the ditch from 1891 to 1903. In 1900, Jose Federico supplemented his farm income by working as a D&RG section hand.

Jose Concepcion Cisneros served as mayordomo in 1895. The following year he provided the association with a tangible monetary asset, which greatly helped its treasury. He purchased a colt for $5.80. A parciante gave it to the association as payment of her accumulated dues and fines.[243]

Jose Eluterio "Chatito" Lucero served as mayordomo in 1917. He was associated with the ditch from 1896 to 1923. He periodically supplemented his income by herding and shearing sheep in Wyoming and working as a D&RG section hand.[244]

Manuel Antonio Lucero, no relation to Jose Eluterio Lucero, served three intermittent terms as mayordomo between 1905 and 1923. He was associated with the acequia from 1884 to at least 1923.[245] He and the Bustos mayordomos were brothers-in-law.

Jose Eulogio Martinez (born about 1840) was a parciante of the ditch from 1884 to at least 1923; he served as its mayordomo in 1912. Beginning about 1888, he supplemented his farm income by plowing and cultivating John Foster Read's land. During the fourth year he worked for Read, Martinez planted and cultivated ash and maple seeds. In all, Martinez planted about ten thousand trees![246]

La Limpia: The (Spring) Cleaning

One of the most important events was the annual spring cleaning of the acequia. For this important cleaning, the mayordomo planned and organized the work needed on the acequia. Because only those parciantes who invested labor in their fields were allocated water for their crops, acequia associations imposed fines when parciantes did not attend the first spring cleaning. Mayordomos recorded the names of parciantes who defaulted on any work assignments and the amounts of work each parciante worked and owed. All proceeds collected went toward the maintenance of and improvements to the acequia. Parciantes who were delinquent in the payment of their assessment and/or failed to perform the required work could lose their right to the water.

Acequia associations imposed fines when parciantes were absent from the first spring *limpia* or *saca* (cleaning or clearing). Absence due to illness was not considered a valid excuse. If a parciante could not answer the mayordomo's call for work, he (or she) was obligated to send in his place a *peón* (laborer) to perform work equal to that of the other parciantes or laborers. A parciante could not send a boy to do a man's job. The spring cleaning and periodic emergency ditch repairs were (and continue to be) family and communal affairs engaging the participation of multiple generations and perhaps served as a child's rite of passage into the community.[247] Older parciantes and former mayordomos shared their knowledge of irrigation techniques and water-flow control.[248] It was a time when local rules, practices and standards were passed down from mayordomo to mayordomo, from parciante to parciante and from generation to generation.

Water Scarcity and Drought

During times of water shortage and drought, each mayordomo examined fields irrigated by his acequia to determine the greatest need. Rules for water sharing during such times were based on delivering the most benefit to the parciante community. By custom, available water was measured in units of time, not by priority number or quantity, as established by Colorado Territorial law.[249] In an equitable and fair manner, each mayordomo partitioned or apportioned the available water among his parciantes by limiting the amount of time each could irrigate, first serving those in greatest need. Although not every parciante received all the water desired, each received a portion of it. Parciantes shared the water in times of scarcity, and when they did not need the water, they passed it on to those who did. A mayordomo could be removed from his duties and/or fined if he failed to distribute water equitably among his parciantes.[250] And under no circumstance could he favor his relatives or "mistreat anyone in word or deed" when water was scarce.[251] This system worked to avoid loss of any water or any parciante's right to the water.

Los Americanos (The Americans)

With the arrival of the D&RG came a continued influx of Anglo settlers, land speculators, miners and cattlemen and economic pressure to sell the land and, thus, the water. During times of economic stress, some parciantes resorted to selling off parts of their land and water rights. Major issues surfaced when Anglos became members of the acequia association. In addition to not knowing how to speak Spanish, they were unfamiliar with acequia terms, irrigation custom and rules. Between 1870 and 1923, William B. Wayt and George Mitrovich were the only two Anglo parciantes of the Madrid Ditch. Mitrovich acquired water rights after purchasing land from Felix Lucero in 1897.[252] Wayt, who was in Colorado by the 1880s,[253] was a parciante in 1901, 1902 and 1908. In 1901, Wayt was fined five dollars for disobeying a directive and irrigating without the mayordomo's permission (*por disobedencia, tomo agua*).[254] Because mayordomos possibly did not know how to spell or pronounce the names Wayt and Mitrovich, various ledger entries recorded them simply as "*americano*" or "*el americano*" (American or easterner). Mayordomos may have referred to them critically as americano because they distrusted the easterners who took the water and the finest land or because the two outsiders disregarded acequia norms and traditions and represented economic, social and political change. According to the ledger entries, no americano was a parciante of the Madrid Ditch between 1909 and 1923, and none was elected to serve as mayordomo.

Female Parciantes

Women assumed the role of parciantes by several means: their purchase of land irrigated by an acequia, marriage to a parciante, the death of a spouse or father or relationship to mothers or brothers who were parciantes. The names of six women appeared in the Madrid Ditch ledgers between 1884 and 1908. The ledger entries associated with these women included receipt of monetary donations, work entries, fines and miscellaneous donations to the acequia. They were only a few of the independent parciantes who, in their husbands' absence, became heads of households and managed all domestic affairs from the house to the fields.

Viviana Cisneros married widower Quirino Maes at Conejos in 1868; she was his third wife.[255] At the time, Maes held four Indian captives.[256] By 1870, Viviana was no longer in his household.[257] By 1885, Viviana, now divorced from Maes, was living in Cucharas where she worked as a cook.[258] Because the Indian captives were the property of her husband, she presumably took none with her when she moved to Cucharas. She purchased land in Cucharas from her brother and became a parciante in 1895.[259] By

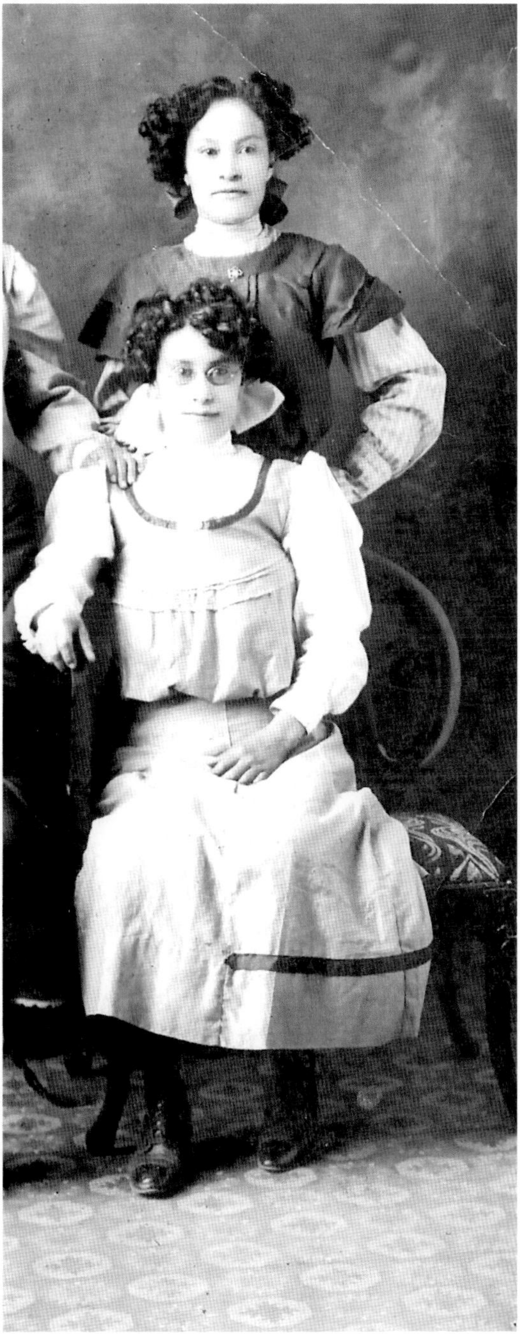

Maria Damiana Cisneros and Virginia Catalina Cisneros, daughters of Jesus Maria Cisneros and nieces of Viviana Cisneros. *Courtesy of Helen Cisneros Vigil Family.*

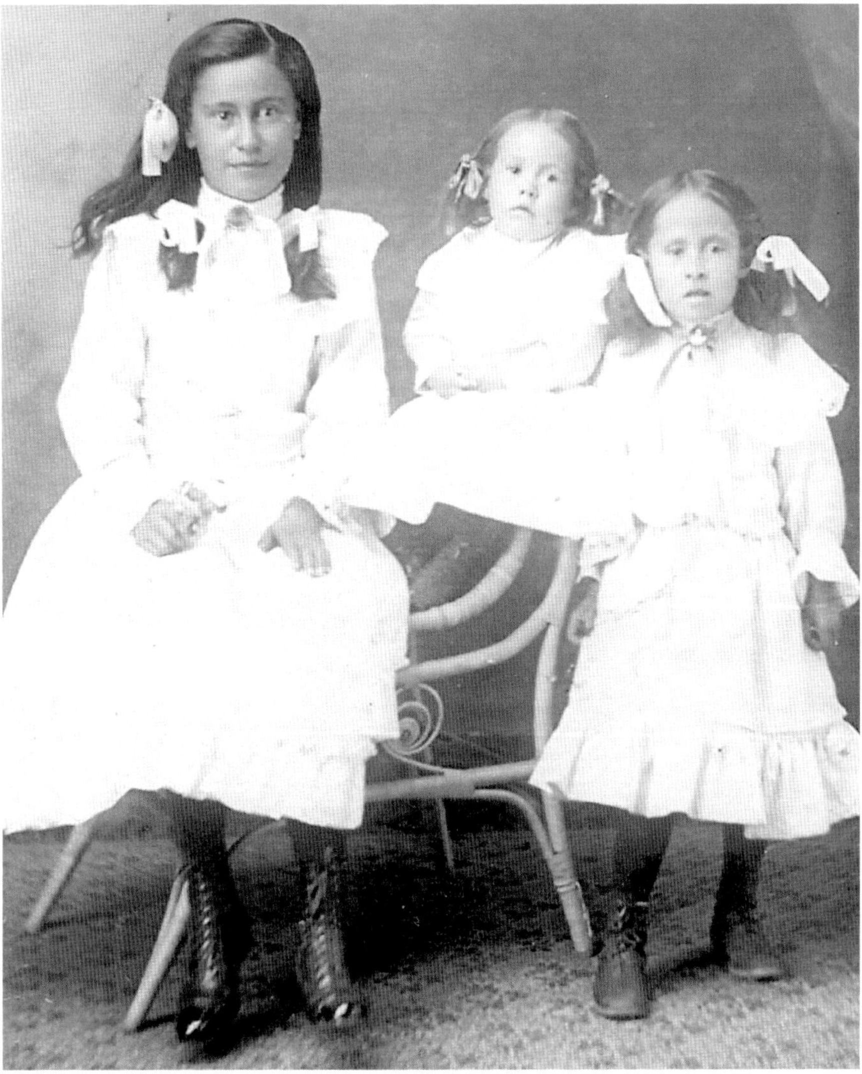

Virginia Catalina, Elena "Helen" and Lucila "Lucille" Cisneros, daughters of Jesus Maria Cisneros and nieces of Viviana Cisneros. *Courtesy of Helen Cisneros Vigil Family.*

1900, Viviana, now about age fifty-one, was living with her mother, Juana Copas, and a twenty-two-year-old woman named Onofre.[260] She was a parciante until 1902. Her brothers Jose Antonio, Jose Concepcion and Jesus Maria Cisneros were also parciantes of the Madrid Ditch and likely helped Viviana maintain her crops.

Maria Rosa Gomez was the fifty-year-old widow of Manuel Gonzales by 1880.[261] By 1885, she raised crops and 1,500 sheep with the assistance of hired laborers and Indian captives.[262] She was a parciante from at least 1884 to 1888 when she received a patent on her land.[263]

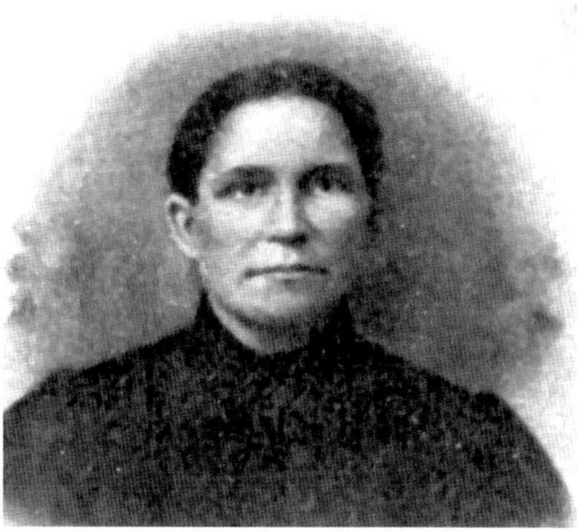

Maria Virginia Ramona Bustos, daughter of Jose Maria Bustos and Maria Manuela Maes and spouse of Manuel Antonio Lucero. *Courtesy of Donald Romero.*

Maria Manuela Maes was the wife of Jose Maria Bustos. He was one of the stocktenders at the Cucharas stagecoach stop. Maria Manuela was about forty-two years old when her husband died in 1881.[264] She became a parciante nine years later, when she purchased land irrigated by the Madrid Ditch from her son, Juan Basilio Bustos.[265] In 1896, she was fined seventy-five cents for a day's work that was supposed to be done by her son-in-law's father, parciante Jose Crispin Lucero. For some unrecorded reason, Lucero refused or declined to work on her behalf. According to a ledger entry, she was only able to pay fifty cents of this fine.[266] Her sons were parciantes of the Madrid Ditch and helped maintain her crops. Maria Manuela Maes was a parciante from 1892 to 1896.

Maria Marcelina Martinez was the second wife of Gabriel Madrid,[267] for whom the Madrid Ditch was named.[268] She was a fifty-three-year-old widow when she became a parciante in 1902. The following year, she was fined three dollars for not appearing at a designated workday called by mayordomo Antonio Tircio Bustos. Her brother, former mayordomo Jose Eulogio Martinez, paid her fine. Maria Marcelina was a parciante from 1902 to 1908.

Elfida Roybal was the daughter of Jose Andres Roybal, one of the men who wintered his sheep in Cucharas in 1862. She married Juan Basilio Bustos in 1886. By 1902 at age forty-three, she was a widow and a parciante. She likely raised her two young children and maintained her crops through the help of her brother and brothers-in-law. She was a parciante for seven years. By 1920, she was living with her father at Walsenburg. Of the six women named in the ditch ledgers, she was the only one who left a will. Elfida Roybal Bustos left her estate to her sister Alcaria Roybal Espinoza of Walsenburg.[269]

Maria Dolores Vallejos was a sixteen-year-old Navajo when baptized at Arroyo Hondo, New Mexico, in 1865. Her owners, Antonio Jose Vallejos and his wife, Maria Soledad Romero, served as godparents.[270] Between 1867 and 1885, Maria Dolores bore six children to Antonio Jose. They officially married in 1885.[271] When Antonio Jose Vallejos died seven years later at age eighty-five,[272] he left his estate to Maria Dolores, six biological children and Jose Hilario Vallejos.[273] Maria Dolores received "all household furniture, books, fuel, and provisions" that had been collected and stored.[274] Maria Dolores was about thirty-seven when she became a parciante in 1884. Because ditch associations had no real source of income to offset expenses, its parciantes paid annual dues and gave occasional contributions. Sometimes they paid dues in trade, as little cash flowed through the Cucharas community in the late nineteenth century. In 1896, Maria Dolores gave the acequia association a two-year-old female colt—*portranca*—in payment of her accumulated dues and fines.[275] She maintained her crops through the help of Jose Hilario Vallejos, a Navajo captive in Antonio Jose's household. By 1900, Maria Dolores took in boarders while living with Jose Hilario and his family. She was a parciante of the Madrid Ditch from 1884 to 1902.

Historically, acequia associations assessed a tax in lieu of a woman's actual physical work during the spring cleaning.[276] Ledger entries of the Madrid Ditch do not indicate that its association assessed such a tax. Although some women were financially able to hire peones to work the spring cleaning on their behalf, they likely paid them in livestock or barter rather than in cash. They were active members of the acequia association; with help from their Indian captives, peones and family members, they worked on the ditch and maintained their crops and fields. Ledger entries do not indicate whether they actually performed physical labor on the acequia, but it is important to remember that these women belonged to pioneering families. Women and their older children knew how to ride a horse; how to bridle and harness a team of draft animals; how to hitch the team to a wagon, plow or other farm equipment; and how to maneuver the team to haul rocks and branches to and from acequia work sites when needed. They knew irrigation techniques and acequia custom and rules.

They took care of their family gardens and, in the absence of their menfolk working far from home, irrigated, tended and harvested crops. And when their husbands, fathers or brothers periodically or permanently left Cucharas to work as laborers for the railroad or in steelworks at Pueblo, in area coal mines or as sheep shearers and crop workers, these women irrigated their crops and, during times of water shortage, took their turns to irrigate at night. According to the Madrid Ditch entries, no woman was elected to a position of acequia leadership.

Acequias in Cucharas

The Cucharas community had as many as eight acequias and one reservoir. These acequias were the Ballejos Ditch, Duran Ditch, Lucero Ditch, Madrid Ditch No. 2, Old Time Ditch,[277] McCaskill Ditch, Mexican Ditch, Sanchez Ditch[278] and the Stevens Reservoir. Because Colorado Territorial law initiated the decree system about 1870, these acequias were said to have been constructed in 1870. The Ballejos Ditch was named for Antonio Jose Vallejos. In 1892, Jose Hilario Vallejos became a landowner and a parciante of the ditch. Antonio Jose's son-in-law, Jose Antonio Martinez, and grandson, Jose Eusebio Martinez, were also parciantes. Water from the Ballejos Ditch irrigated a total of two hundred acres. Water appropriated for the ditch was transferred upstream near La Veta in 1931.[279]

The Duran Ditch was named for Jose Reyes Duran and his brother, Manuel Duran. It irrigated a total of 25 acres of land owned by Manuel Duran, Walter V. Stevens and Jose Leonides Valdez. By 1874, water was also used by the D&RG and residents of Cucharas City.[280] Like other railroads of the period, state, county and municipal governments granted the D&RG special privileges to access and harvest natural resources. During this time, many privately owned reservoirs were built specifically "for the purpose of selling the water stored in them."[281] Stevens Reservoir, constructed east of the D&RG's land in 1872, encompassed an area of nearly 180 acres and was fed by water from the Cucharas River through the Duran Ditch.[282] When the Huerfano County District Court amended the Duran Ditch decree twenty years later, it authorized the ditch to irrigate only 25 acres, while it allowed the Stevens Reservoir to stand at "full capacity." Upset by this inequity, Jose Hilario Vallejos filed suit, but the court found in favor of the reservoir's owner, Walter V. Stevens.[283] Unfortunately, the court failed to acknowledge that water from Stevens Reservoir was diverted to fill D&RG wells and water tanks.[284] By 1903, the D&RG required more than the water appropriated for the Duran Ditch, so the Lucero Ditch was transferred into the Duran Ditch. Today, the Duran Ditch continues to feed water from the Cucharas River into the Stevens Reservoir.

The McCaskill Ditch was named for Dr. John McCaskill. It irrigated one hundred acres, and its water was claimed by the Cleveland and Colorado Cattle Company and Jose Leonides Valdez. In 1930, its water was transferred upstream above La Veta.[285]

The Madrid Ditch No. 2 ran through an area of Cucharas called *el Palomar* for the wide variety of birds that nested there. Not to be confused with Madrid Ditch No. 1, which obtained water from the Huerfano River, the Madrid Ditch No. 2 obtained water from the Cucharas River, a tributary of the Huerfano. In 1870, it had eighteen parciantes.[286] The Madrid Ditch was named for Gabriel Madrid, who may have been its first mayordomo or acequero. By 1896, it was the largest acequia in Cucharas, irrigating five hundred acres.[287]

The Mexican Ditch was the second-largest acequia in Cucharas. It ran 8,643 feet somewhat horizontally along the south side of the Cucharas River.[288] Jose Andres Roybal was a parciante of this ditch.[289] He was one of the eight men who wintered his sheep in the Lower Cuchara Valley in 1862. The Denver–Santa Fe Road ran through this area of Cucharas on the property of Jose Alejo Bustos. By 1930, the Mexican Ditch irrigated 245 acres of land, and at least four descendants of its original fourteen parciantes irrigated with its water. It is still in use today; because the old Denver–Santa Fe Road runs through its path, water from the Mexican Ditch flows underground through a culvert. How the Mexican Ditch got its name can only be assumed.

The Sanchez Ditch was claimed by Pablo Sanchez and his mother, Maria Magdalena (Martin de) Sanchez. She was the widow of Manuel de Jesus Sanchez. (He is not the Reverend Manuel de Jesus Sanchez discussed in the previous chapter.) The Sanchez Ditch irrigated two hundred acres.[290] By 1880, her farm was valued at $1,200.[291]

Summary

The water divided among the eight acequias in Cucharas was now being further divided for upstream and downstream use. Upstream, Walsenburg needed additional water to satisfy its growing population, and numerous coal mines in the area required more water for their industrial operations. By 1884, Walsenburg town officials were considering ways to afford a waterworks project to pipe water into the city from nearby lakes and reservoirs. By 1890, its population reached 1,033.[292] Downstream, the D&RG likewise required water to operate its steam-driven trains, which transported coal, minerals, lumber and passengers.[293]

Many changes throughout the years tested the parciantes' ties to the community and ties to the water. Their strong commitment to their cultural principles and traditions of acequia management were tested by the increasing loss of water. In turn, the increasing loss of water threatened their acequia system as fewer dues-paying parciantes were left to work the spring cleaning. In light of the profound changes Anglos brought to southern Colorado, these parciantes continued to practice Hispano acequia custom and water-sharing rules. As evidenced by Madrid Ditch acequia ledgers, they retained their language, customs, culture and traditions.

Hispano irrigation norms and practices are a vital piece of Colorado's water history. As early as 1861, the Colorado legislature officially incorporated acequia governance and custom into its water laws. These laws established duties of the mayordomos and regulations for their elections, regulated the use of water by acequias over mills or other industry and gave mayordomos power to regulate compulsory labor from parciantes who use the water. In 1864, the Colorado Territorial legislature recognized the Doctrine of Appropriation—first in time, first in right—which basically stated that during periods of limited water supply, the priority number of a water right determined when water could be diverted and delivered relative to other water rights. By law, the earliest water user had access to all the water needed before the next user in line. Entries in the Madrid Ditch ledgers show that its parciantes continued to use acequia rules when water was scarce. The entries also show that male and female parciantes depended on one another and came together for the common cause—to keep the water flowing and to keep the crops growing. Although several Cucharas acequias no longer carry water and blown dirt has filled their trenches, the remains of these acequias and their snakelike paths are reminders of their function and significance to Colorado's Hispanic culture and history.

From a Dusty Road to a Railroad

The lands in the lower bottoms are all under ditch and cultivated...mostly [by] *Mexicans, who are willing to sell out at from $250 to $300...American families...are very anxious to have more...whites for their neighbors.*
—Pueblo Daily Chieftain, *May 20, 1872*

In 1872, many changes were taking place as the D&RG was making its way south from Pueblo. General William Jackson Palmer and his associates purchased land along projected rights of way.[294] Through subsidiary companies, they purchased 2,640 acres for the railyard, 1,000 acres for the railroad town site and additional mineral land in the area.[295] They planned to build a new town three miles northeast of the old Cucharas plaza and relocate the stage station and post office. In 1873, newcomers arrived and settled east of the railroad's new land. Their settlement was known as the Kansas Colony as sixteen of its nineteen inhabitants were from Johnson and Miama Counties, Kansas.[296] Several colony men later ran successful businesses at the new railroad town of Cucharas City.[297]

On February 14, 1876, nineteen men met to plan a celebration for the arrival of the D&RG to Cucharas City. The celebration committee chairman presided over the meeting and named a chief parade marshal. In addition, the committee discussed whether Mr. Ruibal and two other men should visit with commanders of Fort Garland, Fort Lyon and Territorial New Mexico's Fort Union to borrow one cannon for the celebration. The meeting ended after the committee agreed liquor would be sold during the celebration.

Although the track was still three and one-half miles away from Cucharas City, the "grand celebration" continued as planned ten days later. The parade began in front of the town hall with the parade marshal leading the procession. Participants in the parade included United States, territorial and county officials; members of the fire department; citizens on horseback and "on foot"; Civil War veterans; D&RG officers; a guest speaker; and the local clergy.[298] The parade continued through the main streets of Cucharas City until arriving at the depot grounds.[299] The front door of the depot faced west toward Cucharas City overlooking First Street.[300] Several activities were on the agenda. At Union Depot, Judge Jim Ford spoke about the rise and progress of American railways. At the conclusion of Judge Ford's speech, Masonic lodge officers of the Ancient Order of the Children of Montezuma performed the symbolic laying of the cornerstone.[301] Then Fred Walsen and Mr. Bigney, former editor of the *Walsenburg World Independent* newspaper,[302] drove the golden spike as a cornet brass band performed.[303] With the assistance of the train engineer, young ladies dressed in white draped

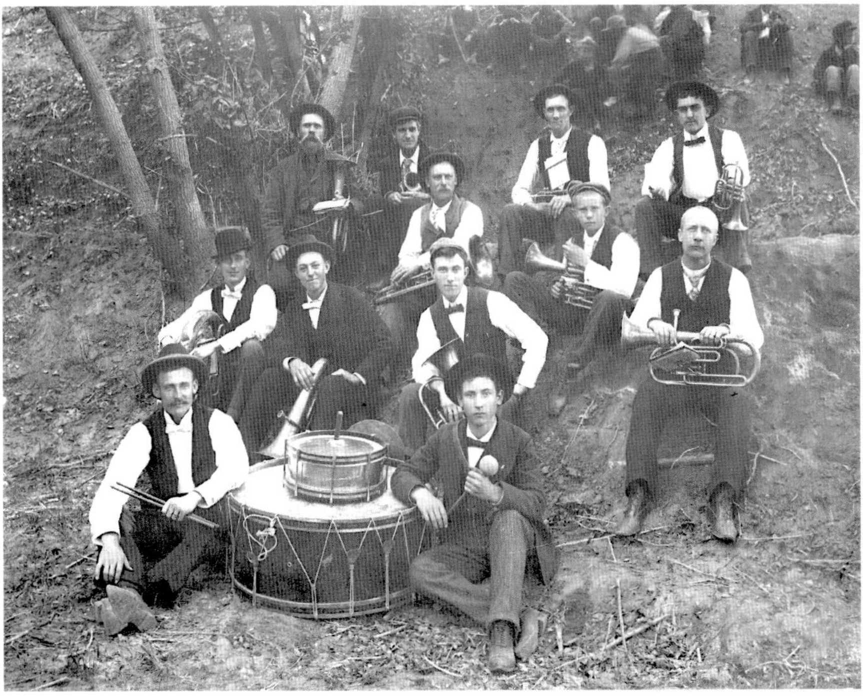

Walsenburg Band, circa 1893. Louis B. Sporleder, director, is in the second row on the far right, and W.B. Wayt is in the fourth row on the far left. *Courtesy of Denver Public Library Western Collection, Sporleder Collection, WH916, Ph Bx 2.*

Locomotive No. 103 with garlands of flowers. Representatives of the D&RG then presented the train conductor with two gold-flecked ticket punchers. Charles R. Youle led a group in singing "All Hail the Iron Horse," and then E. Thompson, from Rio Grande County, gave a speech in Spanish.[304] As civil engineer J.D. St. Lawrence "unfurled the stars and stripes," the Saint Michael's Cathedral choir performed a piece by Beethoven. Following this, Honorable D. Mitchell read an essay called "The Influence of Our Railway System on Popular Education." After the celebration, a grand ball and banquets were held at the homes of D&RG civil engineer James R. De Remer, Thomas Wilkins and B.K. Simpson.[305]

Cucharas City was platted on August 1, 1874, but not incorporated until February 24, 1876. It was destined to become an important town with a long, prosperous life. English-language newspapers from Denver, Colorado Springs, Pueblo, Walsenburg and Trinidad worked with the D&RG to promote their town to investors as an "established" town complete with Anglo town trustees, businesses and landowners.[306] Its promoters, including Read and Hayt, worked "a great deal" to publicize the town and hoped Cucharas City would overtake Walsenburg in size and importance. Many

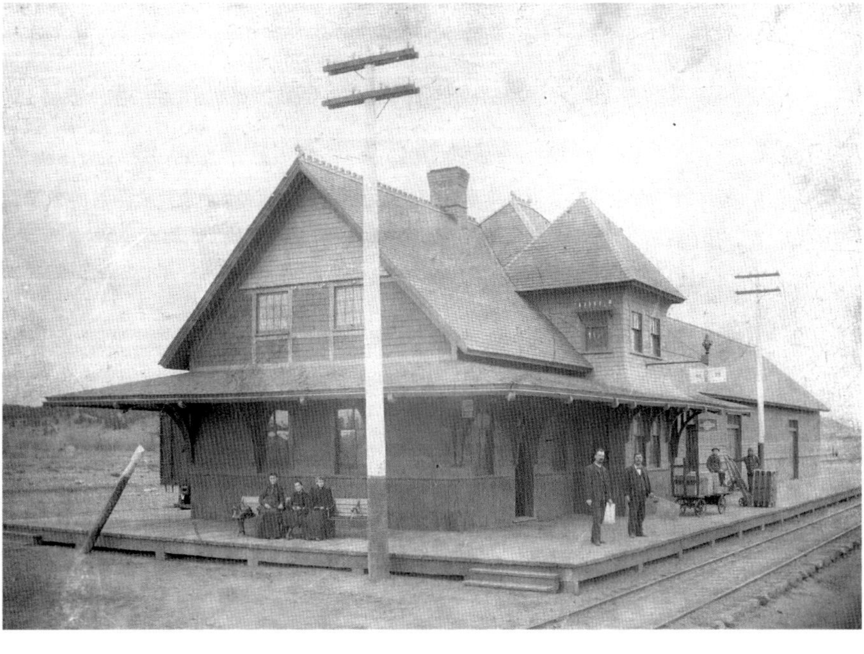

D&RG depot at Walsenburg, Colorado. *Courtesy of Denver Public Library Western History Collection, Sporleder Collection, WH916, Ph Bx 2.*

submitted articles to local newspapers.[307] Newspapers and state directories listed Cucharas City with overstated populations. New businesses were drawn to the new railroad town, which ultimately changed the economics and political structure of the established Cucharas community.

Cucharas City was laid out in blocks, streets, alleys and lots. A subsidiary company of the D&RG offered town lots and company land for sale.[308] Judge John Foster Read and his partner, Charles D. Hayt, of the real estate and legal firm Read and Hayt, specialized in surveying and filing land claims and procuring titles under the homestead, preemption and mining laws.[309] They had offices at Cucharas City and Walsenburg. On August 20, 1874, their firm purchased 160 acres for $555 ($3.46 an acre) from Cuchareño Juan Jose de Aguero.[310] De Aguero's application for a land patent was still in process at the time;[311] little did he realize that his valuable tract of land was near the proposed D&RG train depot and along the right of way. The following day, Read and Hayt sold 120 acres of this land to Fred Walsen.[312] Walsen then leased the land along the right of way to the D&RG.[313] Hayt, Read and businessman Walter V. Stevens also purchased land along the rights of way.[314]

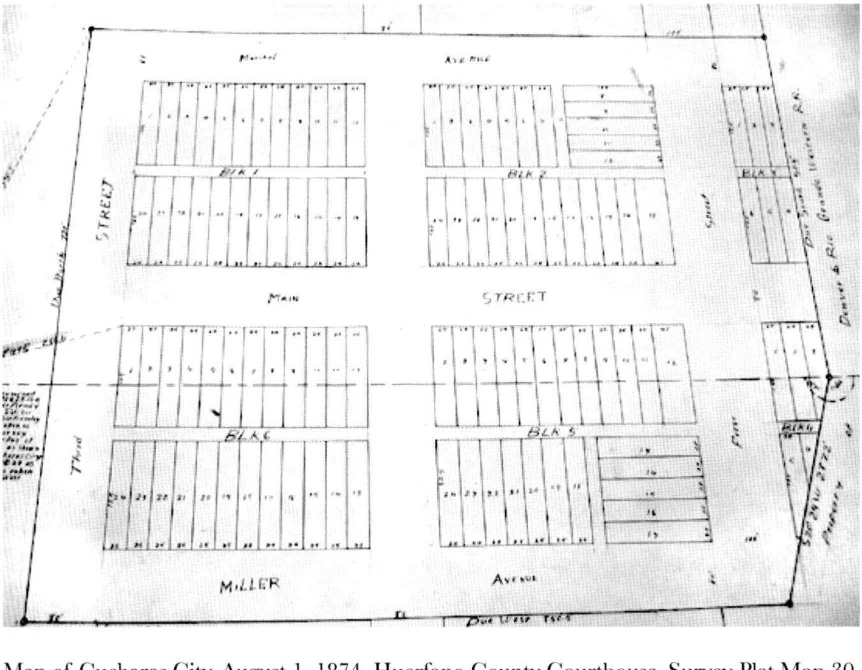

Map of Cucharas City, August 1, 1874, Huerfano County Courthouse, Survey Plat Map 30, 1922. *Courtesy of the author.*

By 1875, Cucharas City had two or three stores and twenty wooden houses.[315] By November, there were a dozen "good" houses and more under construction. It continued to grow to a town of considerable size and became the center of activity where people, including "many Walsenburg people… liked to shop."[316] By May 1876, Cucharas City had every type of business, except shoemaker. Hispanos Ruibal and Martinez purchased a lot "near the business center [for] a large store room to accommodate their rapidly increasing business."[317] J.M. Murphy and Company opened a large store that sold dry goods, clothing and cookware.[318] Charles D. Hayt ran the livery stable where travelers arriving by stage and rail could rent horses, carriages and wagons. Cuchareño Jesus Maria Manzanares served as constable (sheriff or police) of Cucharas City from 1875 to 1885. His office was located in the town hall. Manzanares, a community leader, lived to the age of 103.[319]

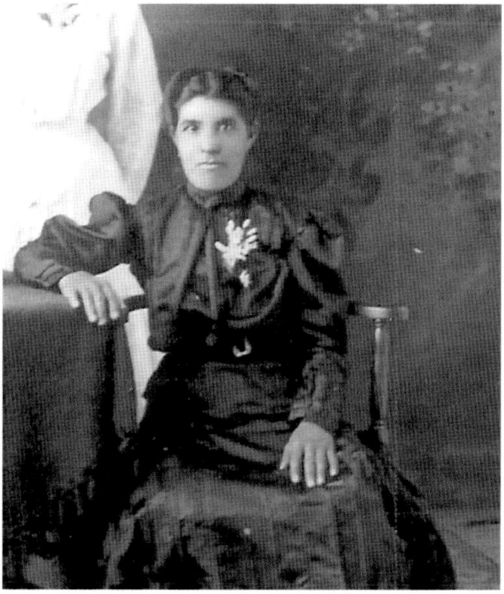

Maria del Carmen Manzanares, daughter of Jesus Maria Manzanares. *Courtesy of Donald Romero.*

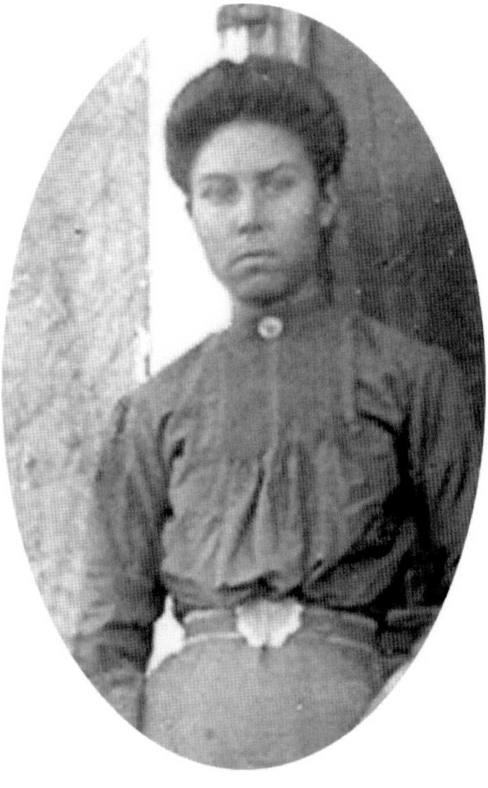

Maria Isabel Manzanares, daughter of Jesus Maria Manzanares. *Courtesy of Stella Hernandez.*

Cucharas Businesses

Business	Businessmen
Attorney	E.W. Baker
Band leader	Prior B. Mayo
Cucharas House Hotel	John Stockman
D&RG civil engineer	George Hurlburt
Drugstore	E.P. Snydam and Samuel S. Adams
Groceries and provisions	George Walter Morton
Hardware	Thomas Wilkins
Judge	William A. Offenbacker
Livery	Charles D. Hayt
Lumber	P. Craig, B.K. Simpson and Thomas Wilkins
Meat market	Henry Lewis
Minister	C.H. Kirkbride
Notary	Charles D. Hayt
Physicians	Dr. S.S. Adams and Dr. Say
Postmaster	George H.F. Work
Real estate	Charles D. Hayt
Schoolteacher	Miss Scott

Business	**Businessmen**
Southern Colorado Improvement Company	Thomas Wilkins, president; J.V. Offenbacher, secretary
Stage agent	Charles D. Hayt
Town trustees	Thomas Wilkins, Thomas Miller, T.A. Sloan, J.V. Offenbacher and William A. Offenbacker

By late 1874, the D&RG had a passenger depot and railyard in place on its land east of Cucharas City. For the convenience of rail passengers, a hotel was built close to the depot. In 1874, John Stockman ran the Cucharas House Hotel. By 1876, its name changed to the National House, operated by thirty-three-year-old Samuel Todd. It was an "exceptional hotel [with] excellent accommodations." In 1889, it was replaced by a new large brick hotel called the Fitzgerald.[320] Mrs. T. (Etta) Fitzgerald and her twenty-four-year-old daughter, Maggie, managed the hotel and its restaurant. Edith Wilford, age twenty-five, and eighteen-year-old Jeaney Seroody were hotel maids. Seroody arrived in the United States in 1880; she was from Bohemia. Cuchareño Alfonso de Jesus Valdez, age sixteen, worked as the waiter.[321] He was the grandson of Jose Leonides Valdez. The Fitzgerald Hotel was later known as the Pictureville Hotel. It was owned by James Benjamin Stevens, son of Walter V. Stevens, and later owned by William B. Wayt.[322] Maria Librada de Herrera Duran supplemented her family's income by working there as a laundress and dishwasher for fifty cents a day.[323] She was the spouse of Manuel Duran, who first settled in la Plaza de los Leones in 1868.[324]

Many men of different nationalities came to the Cucharas area in search of jobs. Jonney Miwon, age thirty-six, worked as a cook at the Fitzgerald Hotel.[325] Forty-eight-year-old Chong Wooyon, aka Wooyou Chong, was not enumerated with the other Fitzgerald Hotel employees; however, in 1900, he was employed as a cook. Wooyon may have worked as a cook in a D&RG cafeteria car. Both Miwon and Wooyon were undocumented workers from China. Additional Chinese men were enumerated in 1885 and 1900. In 1885, Ah Ying was a servant in the household of La Veta hotel keeper Samuel Todd. In 1900, Fee Wee, Kime Ola and Yee Ding worked in a laundry. Wee and Ola resided in Walsenburg; Ding at La Veta. These men may have come to Cucharas to escape the prejudice against the Chinese in places like

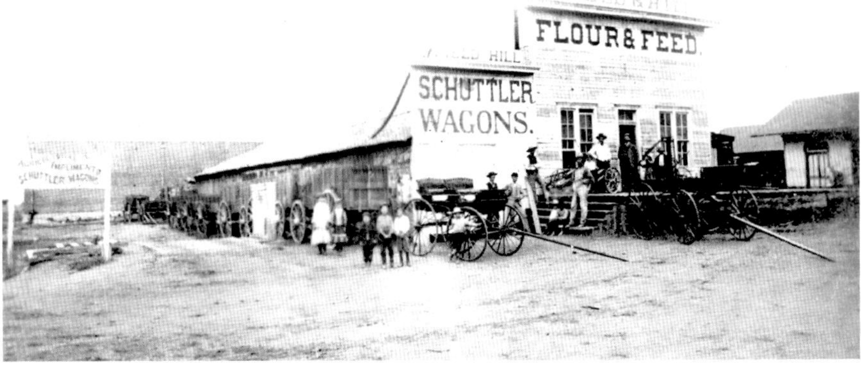

Field & Hill Schuttler Wagons and Field & Hill Flour & Seed at the southeast corner of Sixth and Hunt, Alamosa, Colorado. *Courtesy of Denver Public Library Western Collection, O.T. Davis, X-6447.*

Denver in 1880 and Rock Springs, Wyoming, in 1885. Men of different nationalities also worked for the D&RG and in coal mines near Walsenburg and Trinidad. The D&RG needed laborers at its grading camps, and miners were needed in coal mines near Walsenburg and Trinidad. By 1879, D&RG laborers were in such high demand that it hired men from around the Pueblo area and transported them to its various grading camps.[326] Those who spoke limited English were assigned to section gangs or other manual labor occupations. Younger men freighted; older men graded roads; and Irish, Chinese, Hispanos and Mexicans shoveled dirt. African American men worked as porters.[327] Unfortunately in the United States, the practice of hiring minorities only for labor positions in railroad and other industries continued for nearly eighty more years.

In an effort to capture the market of the San Juan mine trade, several warehouses were built in Cucharas City. E.P. Snydam, who also operated a billiard hall there,[328] built several forwarding and commission warehouses near the depot. Thomas M. Field and Isaac W. Hill, of the firm Field and Hill, operated a forwarding house and were hauling mining supplies to the San Juan Mountains.[329]

The D&RG officially opened for rail business on March 1, 1876. The D&RG planted forty trees along its main roads, and passengers and mail arrived daily by rail from the north and by stagecoach from the south. Walsenburg businessmen, including Fred Walsen, hoped the D&RG would make its way west through their town. To compete with Cucharas City for the San Juan mining trade, they made moderate offers to D&RG officers and convinced them to make Walsenburg a major stop on the San Juan line.[330] The rail switch was now in place for construction west through Walsenburg to La Veta. On June 30, 1877, the *Colorado Springs Gazette* reported that the Walsenburg train station was renamed Walsen Station.

Summary

When the D&RG Railroad arrived at Cucharas, Hispano farmers from Cucharas and other nearby towns hauled their wagons every Saturday to the railroad town of Cucharas City. Their wagons were loaded with squashes, string beans, potatoes and "all sorts of green stuff."[331] The rails would now transport their grown produce to other locations. At Cucharas City they sold crops and livestock and purchased or bartered for needed goods. With the arrival of milled lumber, they began incorporating wood in their homes. Pitched roofs with wooden shingles would begin to replace the traditional flat roofs and wood plank floors.

During its heyday, Cucharas City saw activity around the clock. Unfortunately its lifespan was short-lived when Walsenburg, then La Veta, replaced it as a D&RG end-of-the-line town. Many of its businessmen followed the D&RG to La Veta.[332] Helen Hunt Jackson witnessed a ploughshare cut the first rail-track furrow through the meadows of Cucharas. A year later, she traveled by train over the same area and saw the "little town" of Cucharas City "surrounded by acres of sunflowers."[333] Cucharas City became a "has-been town" with only "a handful of log-cabins and wooden shanties" along one street.[334]

On May 1913, one of two D&RG water tanks was moved to west Denver.[335] The D&RG moved and retired several cars and buildings in 1924, when its last depot was torn down. By 1937, rail service to Cucharas had stopped altogether. By 1944, all that remained of Cucharas City were the ruins of the old hotel.[336]

Education in Cucharas

To put their children on an equal footing with the children of others for the race of life.
—Colorado Superintendent of Public Instruction, 1883–6

Although there were four school districts in Huerfano County in 1869, only two of the districts had schools. Formal education in Cucharas began as early as 1871 when Jose Anastacio de Jesus "J.A.J." Valdez organized School District 4 in Cucharas and taught its first class, for which the county paid him $300.[337] Valdez and his father, Jose Mariano de Jesus Valdez, and younger brother, Juan Bautista Valdez, taught school during their lifetimes. They were strong advocates for public education. By 1871, the county's superintendent of schools reported an increase in the average number of school days from twenty-six the previous year to fifty-four; however, no new schoolhouses were constructed.[338] During this period, many in farming communities did not send their daughters to school, and sons were needed on the farm, especially during harvests. Due to the county's change in population, school districts were periodically reassigned. By 1874, Huerfano County had eight school districts located in Badito, Butte Valley, Cucharas, Gardner, La Veta, Saint Mary's, Santa Clara and Walsenburg.[339] The following year, District 4 schoolteachers at Cucharas taught lessons in a *jacal*.[340] In 1893, Cucharas was located within School District 5. Cucharas was later assigned to Districts 12 and 25.[341] Hispanos composed the majority school population. Although some Hispano parents did not read or write in English, they took an active interest in their children's education and

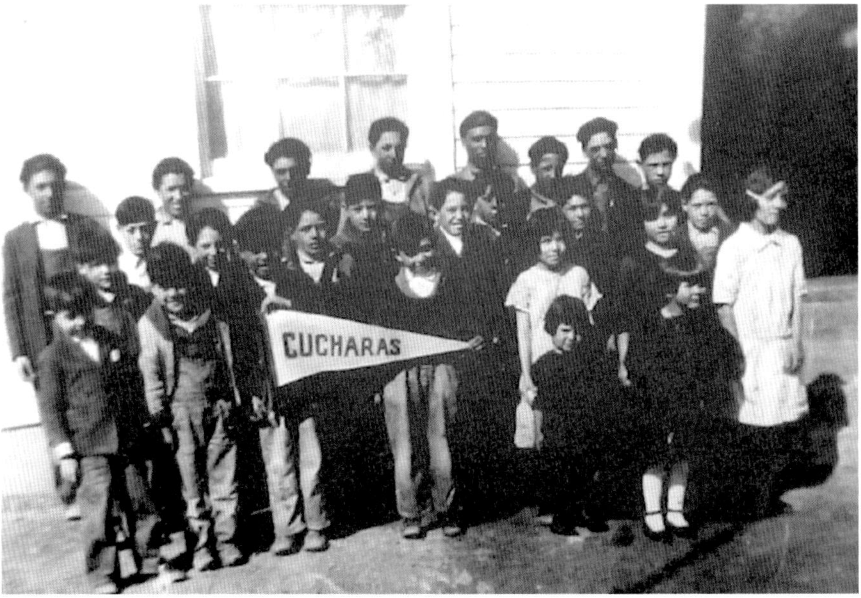

Cucharas School class photo, circa 1920. *Front row (from left):* Reinaldo Vigil, Edward Sandoval, Ben Maes, Remijio Padilla, Eloisa Lucero, Martha Hurtado (in front of Eloisa), Ernestina Vigil, Teresina Sandoval (in front of Ernestina) and Aurelia Bustos. *Middle row (from left):* Diego Sandoval, Alberto Bustos, Jacobo Vigil, Richard Sandoval, Manuel Sandoval, Manuel Vigil, Steve Golobe, Florencio Lucero and Modesto Maes. *Back row (from left):* Henry Lucero, Anselmo Padilla, Silvano Lucero, Pete Guerrero, Joe Vigil, Benjamin Guerrero, Onesimo Bustos and Baltazar Cisneros. *Courtesy of Conrad Lucero.*

served on school boards. By 1883, individuals could obtain temporary Colorado teaching certificates by petition from the state superintendent of public instruction. Unfortunately, records of the state archives do not include petitions submitted by Huerfano County residents or the names of women and men who received temporary teaching certificates. Subsequent state superintendent reports stated Hispanos were still the county's majority population whose children made up close to half of school populations. The reports also credited the county's Hispano residents for appreciating the value of education and the need to learn English.

At one time, four schools served the Cucharas community: the Cucharas City School, Fairview School, Cucharas School and New Cucharas "Bustos" School.

Cucharas City School

The first Cucharas City School was described as a log building (jacal) owned by a Mr. Sheldon. According to the February 7, 1875 edition of the *Pueblo Daily Chieftain*, the building was totally consumed by a fire that probably originated from the building's "Mexican fireplace." Between 1893 and 1898, the community constructed the Cucharas City School near the junction of the D&RG Railroad where rails turned west toward Walsenburg. The school became known as the Cuchara Junction School. By 1898, Cuchara Junction School was said to have 121 students. In 1899, Alex Guerrero, Eulalia Bustos and Pedro Manzanares were on the honor roll. Eulalia Bustos, granddaughter of Jose Alejo Bustos, later became a Cucharas teacher.[342] When a fire causing $2,500 in damage destroyed the school in 1927,[343] an adobe building served as a temporary replacement. It had a potbellied stove, a large shelf for books, school desks and a blackboard on the south wall.[344] Known teachers who taught grades one through eight included Frances Marie Nelson, Tina Martinez and Frances Reed.[345]

Fairview School

Fairview School in District 25 was located northeast from the Cucharas plaza. The school was built by Captain J.S. McHarg in 1896 on land

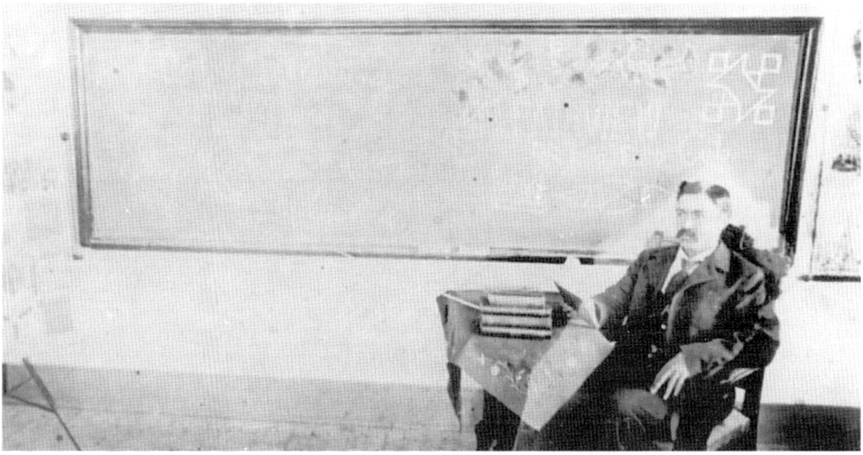

Schoolteacher Casimiro Cruz, Fairview School, District 25, Cucharas, February 11, 1907. *Courtesy of Pueblo City-County Library District.*

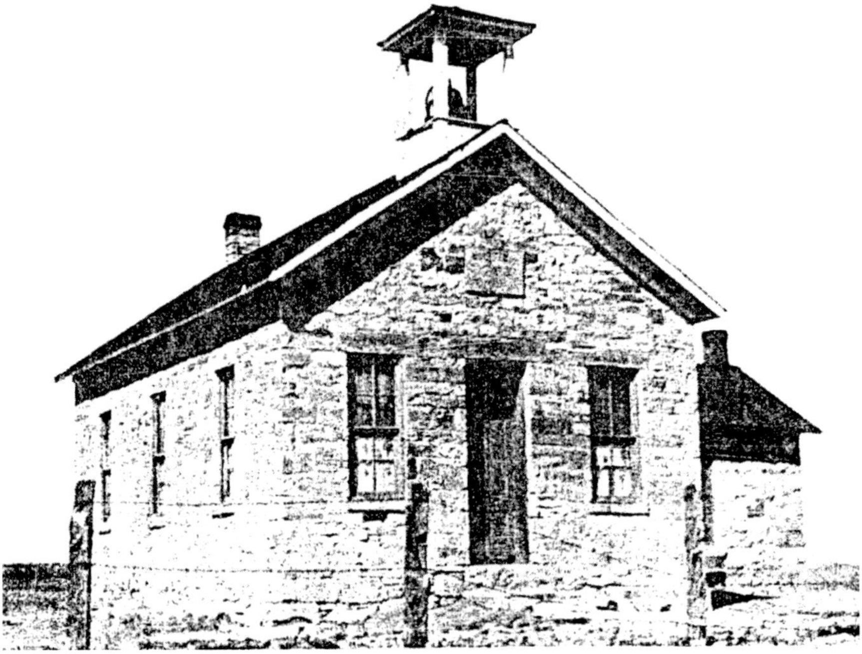

Fairview School in Cucharas. *Courtesy of* Huerfano World.

donated by Jose Leonides Valdez. Valdez served as president of the Fairview School Board, Jonathan Abercrombie served as secretary and J.B. Martinez served as treasurer. This white-limestone school sat on a bluff overlooking the Cucharas River. It measured thirty-three by twenty-one feet and had a twelve-foot ceiling. It had eight windows with solid stone sills and a bell in a square bell tower. Slate blackboards hung on the rear and side walls. A sign over the front door read "Fairview School Dist 25." By 1898, it had thirty-five students. Known teachers who taught there were Casimiro Cruz, James Fagan,[346] Dave Humphrey, Ana and Fidelia Manzanares, Jose Manuel Martinez, Mabel McKinley and Frances Marie Nelson.[347] Cruz was living in Trinidad by 1891.[348] He married Mary King at Walsenburg in 1898[349] and taught at the Fairview School in Cucharas during the 1907 school year. He returned to Trinidad by 1910 and became a newspaper printer and publisher.[350] A bulldozer demolished the Fairview School about 1950, sending its white limestone boulders into the Cucharas River.

Cucharas School

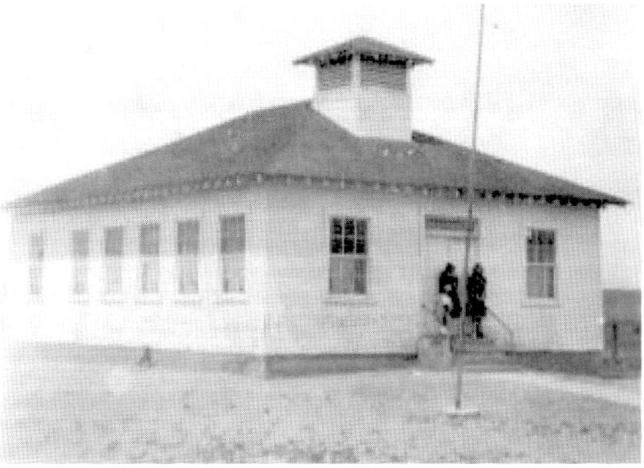

Cucharas School. *Courtesy of Helen Cisneros Vigil Family.*

Cucharas School was built east of the old Cucharas plaza. It measured thirty-five by thirty-five feet, and by 1920, it was already too small for its growing student population. The white, painted-frame schoolhouse had a shingle roof and bell tower.[351] The building still stands, but today it serves as a private residence. Travelers can see its green roof and empty bell tower from Highway 10 traveling northeast of Walsenburg. The Cucharas School was in use until about 1953.

New Cucharas "Bustos" School

The New Cucharas School in District 12 was built as a Works Progress Administration (WPA) project as part of the New Deal programs initiated between 1933 and 1938.[352] WPA projects provided employment and emphasized the use of local materials and traditional construction methods. The WPA also constructed new schools in Bear Creek, Chama, La Veta, Maes Creek and Sandy. Construction of the New Cucharas School began November 7, 1938, on property donated by Teofilo Bustos. Thirty workers constructed the adobe school at a cost of $7,182. Carmel Bustos, Richard Bustos Sr., Charlie Corsentino, Tom Rogers Sr., Alberto Romero, Teodoro Sandoval and Bennie Vallejos served as members of the New Cucharas School Board.[353] The flat roof, which had a slight pitch to allow for drainage, and the *viga* ends depicted the traditional architecture of the Southwest.[354] Vigas (wooden pole beam supports) appeared to protrude from each side of the building. Rather than supporting the roof, however, these vigas were simply meant to imitate Spanish architecture. The school was named New Cucharas School, but it was known as the Bustos School.

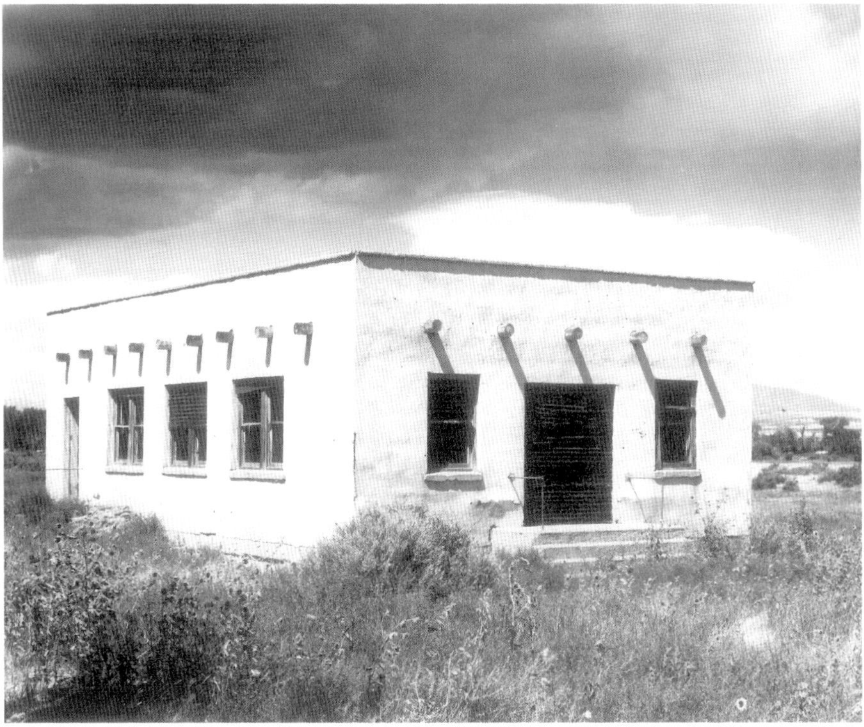

New Cucharas "Bustos" School, circa 1939. *Courtesy of Pueblo City-County Library District.*

The adobe walls of the Bustos School were eighteen inches thick, and the school measured twenty-four by forty-eight feet. The exterior was a beige color. Calcimine, an off-white finish, was applied to the interior walls. Later the interior was painted a turquoise color.[355] The school also had hardwood floors, a built-in blackboard on the west wall and modern lighting.[356] The foundation and windowsills were constructed of cement. The front east exterior had a double-hung window on each side of a doublewide front door; the south wall had three openings, each with two side-by-side double-hung windows. On the north wall were three small rectangular windows about a foot parallel to the ceiling. The front entrance had three concrete steps and a landing, and on the north and south ends of the landing were iron pipe handrails.

In 1942, a folding partition divided the large room where grades one through five met on one side and grades six to eight met on the other.[357] The Bustos School had no bell tower, flagpole or playground equipment.

During recess, parents Ruben Barela and Bennie Vallejos Sr. made time to play baseball or football with the boys. The girls played Ring Around the Rosy and other games. Behind the school were two wooden outhouses, one for the girls and the other for the boys. Each outhouse had a "double-seater."

The school kitchen and lunchroom were located in the back part of the building. The lunchroom had two big picnic-type tables built by Ruben Barela. The kitchen had a large wood-burning stove and cabinets stretched around the room. Moises Chavez was the hot lunch cook. His aunt, Cora Vasquez, often assisted him in preparing mashed potatoes, brown gravy and canned meat, a vegetable, hot biscuits with peanut butter and honey and fresh milk with or without chocolate powder. In celebration of holidays, Chavez and Vasquez baked cookies and cakes for the children. Every year, students prepared a program for their parents in which they recited poems, performed plays and danced. The children presented really nice programs at school, especially at Christmas. "Some students tap danced and some danced *La Jesusita*." Former student Guerminia Eugenia "Jean" Barela recited a poem.[358]

A basket full of goodies
To give a lonely friend,
Will make her Christmas happy,
And joyful without end.

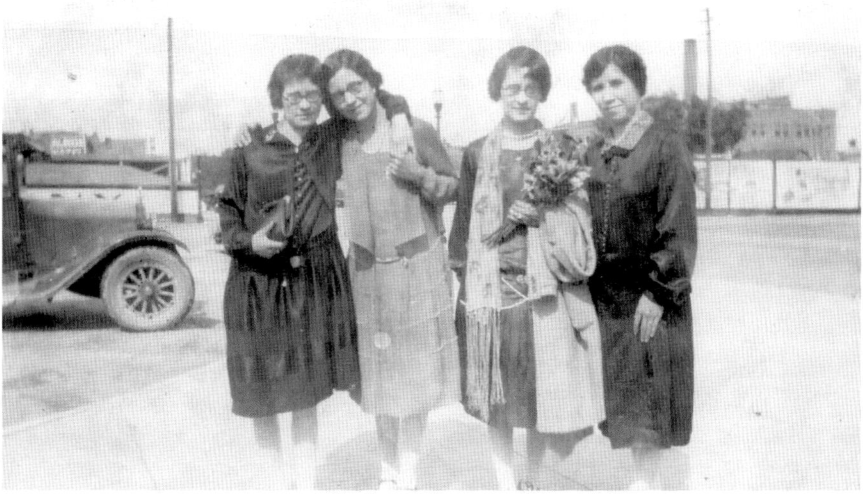

Huerfano County teachers Helen Cisneros, Ida Bustos, Lucila "Lucille" Cisneros and Eulalia Bustos Britt. *Courtesy of Helen Cisneros Vigil Family.*

Sometime after World War II, the community used concrete rather than the traditional mud and lime plaster to keep the exterior adobes from eroding. Unfortunately, moisture became trapped between the adobe and cement. Consequently, the saturated adobes could not support the weight of the heavier, drier adobe bricks, and the walls of the Bustos School collapsed. The school was nominated several times as an endangered place in Colorado,[359] but like too many of our historic adobe buildings, it was not selected because very little of the adobe walls remained. By March 2008, the east wall of the school had collapsed and plans were underway to level the remaining walls.

After graduating eighth grade, some students attended high school in Walsenburg. Pina Barela rode her white horse "Tony" as far as the Cisneros residence, and then she rode the school bus to Walsenburg. Freda and Garfield rode to Walsenburg in a Model A driven by their father, Teodoro Sandoval. During the 1941 school year, Garfield Sandoval was the only eighth-grade graduate of the Bustos School.[360]

SUMMARY

The community came together to form school districts, serve on boards and construct their schools. When not used for educational purposes, schoolhouses served as important cultural centers where community meetings, political rallies and dances were held. What remains of the schools in Cucharas are scant photographs and few documented memories. Land on which the Bustos and Fairview Schools sat is now used for grazing.

During the 1950s, the last three remaining schools in Cucharas closed. The Bustos School went into disrepair and the adobe walls began to fall. The Fairview School lay empty until a bulldozer leveled it and dumped its white limestone blocks into the Cucharas River.

The End of Cucharas

What a wonderful change would take place by the immigration of farmers from the East to take the place of Mexicans. With their customary hard work and judicious management, they would soon elevate the county to the rank it so richly deserves.
—Huerfano Cactus, *May 10, 1884*

Cucharas was a thriving, vibrant community complete with a variety of transportation services, several businesses and the all-important post office. Stages, freight wagons and later D&RG rail cars transported new and needed goods to its changing population. As the rolling plains and prairie transformed into byways for stagecoaches, freight wagons and railroads, landownership and the landscape changed. In place of plentiful sheep grazing on the prairie, the D&RG cut its way through the land. As Anglo newcomers from the east added to the county's population, they sought ways to improve the area's social and political standing.[361] They preferred the less energy-efficient buildings constructed of milled lumber, and they wanted neighbors who were more similar in language, culture and tint. Many new types of jobs came to Cucharas. Drivers, messengers and stocktenders were needed to ensure the steady operation of stagecoaches transporting mail, express freight and passengers. Laborers were in demand to build the railroad. Freighters, who were mainly acquired on contract by Anglo-owned companies, were on hand to move timber, milled lumber and goods of various sizes to merchants and their customers.

Vital information about the D&RG coming through the area passed first through a network of key Anglo friends and associates. Fred Walsen and his friends and business associates were privy to information about the D&RG's plans. Walsen was a son-in-law of August Sporleder, who owned the Sporleder Inn at Walsenburg. The Sporleders often hosted balls, dinners and celebrations. Colorado governor Alexander Cameron Hunt, Colorado Circuit judge Moses Hallett, Congressman George M. Chilcott, Congressman Jerome B. Chafee and General William Jackson Palmer of the D&RG regularly lodged at this inn. Prominent Anglo men often gathered at this entertaining place to smoke cigars, sing songs and sip beer.

Miguel Antonio Vallejos, an influential family member, sold crops and livestock to German merchants and traders in la Plaza de los Leones. He was the patrón of the Cuchareños. As patrón, he helped resolve disputes and was the political spokesman who could control local politics. Fred Walsen understood this well, when in 1874, he asked Vallejos to serve as godfather for his daughter.[362] Fred Walsen did not have many Hispano personal friends. Hispanos had a greater respect for his partner, Alexander Levy, whom they called *el Señor Levais*. Hispanos referred to Fred Walsen as "el Fred," pronounced *el Freth* in Spanish.[363] By this time, Hispano and Anglo relations were strained as events in play ultimately changed the socioeconomics of the Cuchareños. Land had already been purchased at Cucharas for the D&RG and Anglo settlers, businessmen and land speculators who were arriving at the D&RG's new town, Cucharas City. In 1872, Jose Simon Abelino "Lino" Maes was one of two Cuchareños wounded in an altercation that occurred presumably with railroad personnel.[364]

Anglos, including John Foster Read, Charles D. Hayt, Fred Walsen and Walter V. Stevens, purchased prime land from the Cuchareños. Anglo-run newspapers printed articles in English to specifically attract Anglo businessmen and farmers. To attract investors and capitalists, the county seat needed to be moved from Badito to a more popular and populous site. In 1870, U.S. congressmen George M. Chilcott, Jerome B. Chafee[365] and "a party of their friends [were on a] canvassing tour" in southern Colorado. According to the May 13, 1874 edition of the *Pueblo Daily Chieftain*, it was at this time that they approved the move of the county seat to Walsenburg.[366] Now that the county seat was in the right place, certain men worked to disassociate la Plaza de los Leones as a Mexican town and convert it to a prosperous new Anglo municipality managed by town trustees. They succeeded, and its name officially was changed in honor of Fred Walsen on June 16, 1873.[367] However, the name change had been in progress for a number of years. The fact that John Foster Read wrote "Walsenburgh" on the post office department form submitted for the Cucharas post office attests that Anglos were already using that name in 1870. The politics associated with the name change were stimulated by the discovery of coal and the arrival of the D&RG. Some may argue that la Plaza de los Leones was in a different location than Walsenburg; the fact remains that this plaza was the parent village and an important site.

Once news about the construction of the D&RG finally reached the Cuchareños, many found that to protect their holdings they had to quickly file homestead claims. Huerfano County probate judge and Cucharas postmaster John Foster Read was "very busy receiving filings of homestead claims from Mexican settlers."[368] Filing a claim was a new experience for Hispanos. To file their claims, each had to come up with cash to pay the miscellaneous required fees. In addition to the three-dollar filing fee on a 160-acre tract, there was a ten-dollar patent fee, a one-dollar recording fee and survey costs.[369] These were already difficult times for Hispanos as little cash flowed through the area.

Area newspapers continued to criticize Hispanos; on May 7, 1874, the *Pueblo Daily Chieftain* published that the Hispanos who claimed the productive valley lands were not industrious, and without much difficulty or expense, their rich grazing lands could be in the hands of "thrifty and intelligent American or Europeans." Many Cuchareños lost their homes, properties, crops, grazing land and positions of economic and political power. Meanwhile, their new Anglo neighbors were able to improve their financial conditions due to the opportunities made available only to them.

Due to their language, surnames, religious customs and ethnicity, the Cuchareños were perceived as newly arrived, non-U.S. citizens. On March 1, 1876, a grand celebration took place at Union Depot for the arrival of the D&RG to Cucharas City. Officers of a Masonic lodge performed the symbolic laying of the cornerstone. Fred Walsen and the former editor of the *Walsenburg World Independent* had the prestigious honor of pounding the golden spike. The celebration was followed by a grand ball and several banquets held in private Anglo residences at Cucharas City. Interestingly, rather than selecting an individual from Huerfano County to give a speech in Spanish, the celebration committee selected an Anglo from Rio Grande County, which was rich in silver and gold.

The year 1876 was a banner year for Fred Walsen. By the end of March, Walsen had a commission and forwarding house ready for business at

Cucharas City.[370] That year he also opened his prosperous Walsen Coal Mine. The Walsen Mine was Huerfano County's first coal mine and became the county's largest and most productive mine. (In 1869, land that later became the site of the Walsen Mine was owned by Juan Evaristo Gonzales.[371]) Fred Walsen and his brother-in-law, Alexander Levy, provided poles, ties and cattle for General Palmer's D&RG,[372] which transported logs, ties and timber props to mines around Walsenburg.[373] Walsen and his connections with General Palmer became quite lucrative. He and his associates increased their personal wealth and disassociated their growing town with those "Mexican" customs and their way of life. Clearly, Hispanos did not have the capital to compete; they were mostly not given an opportunity to compete because they were not privy to key information affecting their community. Helen Hunt Jackson captured Anglo views and the economics experienced by the Hispanos when she wrote, "Here and there...ragged [men,] half-naked boys and girls, [and barefoot women] peering...curiously at everything."[374]

The Dust Bowl of the 1930s combined with the facts that local coal mines closed, the loss of D&RG work and the general economics of the time caused the demise of many farms in southeastern Colorado, including Cucharas. Many descendants of the first Cuchareños moved to search for work. Some worked as seasonal laborers in fields and as sheepherders. For those who

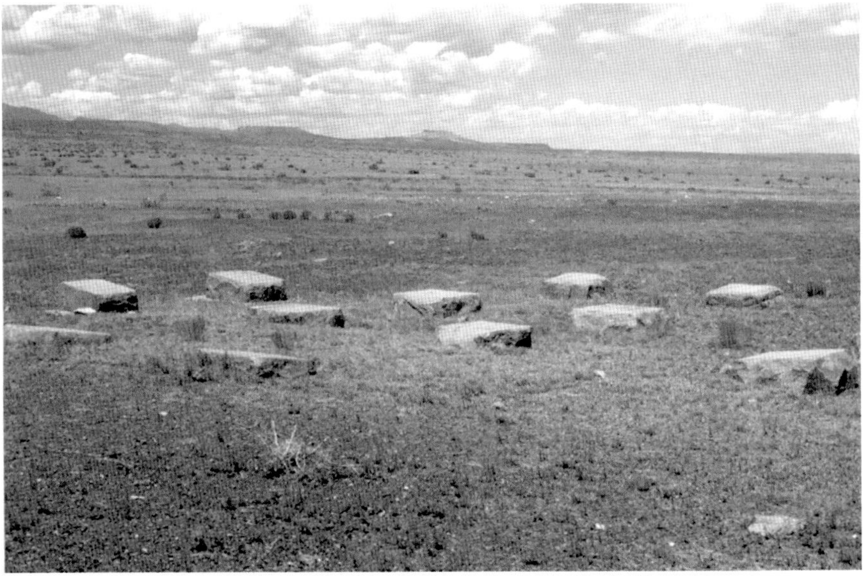

Stone pedestals for a D&RG water tank near Cucharas City. *Courtesy of Ronald L. Wadsack.*

remained, WPA jobs employed some, while others continued to survive with the available irrigation water.

The scant traces that remain of Cucharas and Cucharas City only hint at the lives of the people who once made their home there. Gone from the land are reminders of its rich transportation history from a dusty road to a railroad.

Today, only a few remnants of Cucharas lie scattered across a tiny farming and stock-raising area in Huerfano County. Unfortunately, the Cucharas stage relay station was not inventoried and surveyed nor captured by photography, and because railroad town buildings were picked up and moved as easily as they were laid down, nothing remains of Cucharas City.

This Cucharas is not the same Cucharas on today's Interstate 25 sign near Walsenburg. It is not the Cucharas Camp (est. 1906) located southeast of La Veta. This Cucharas no longer exists. Today you can drive on Highway 10, eight miles northeast of Walsenburg, and not know that nearly 150 years ago, a vigorous community thrived there. Mounds of melted adobe appear where homes of the Cuchareños once stood. Like the withered handmade cross on an unmarked Cucharas grave, time, weather and change took a toll on the Cuchareños. The surnames Walsen, St. Vrain, Bent, Boggs, Carson and Francisco live on in southern Colorado history. Fred Walsen became known as the father of Walsenburg and an important pioneer who helped develop the area's coal mines. His work on behalf of the Republican Party changed the politics of southern Colorado. At the time of his death, his estate was valued at $500,000.[375] In vast contrast to the Cuchareños buried in cemeteries on the Cucharas prairie, Fred Walsen's family stone and marble vault are in Denver's manicured Fairmont Cemetery.[376] The name Ceran St. Vrain still lives on in Colorado as a mountain range, several rivers, a school district, a state park and a fuel storage facility. The legacy of St. Vrain's friends and acquaintances, who settled along the Huerfano and Purgatory Rivers as part of the Cornelio Vigil–Ceran St. Vrain Land Grant, also lives on in historic Bent's Fort, Boggsville and Fort Francisco.

The names, stories and pertinent events that shaped the lives of the Cuchareños help document an important and forgotten part of Colorado's history. There are many other communities such as Cucharas that need to be documented and must be remembered in history. Perhaps someday soon historic markers will be placed near the sites of the Cucharas Plaza and Cucharas City to recognize and acknowledge the histories of the Native American, Hispano and Anglo cultures that once lived there.

Appendix A

Los Cuchareños—The People of Cucharas

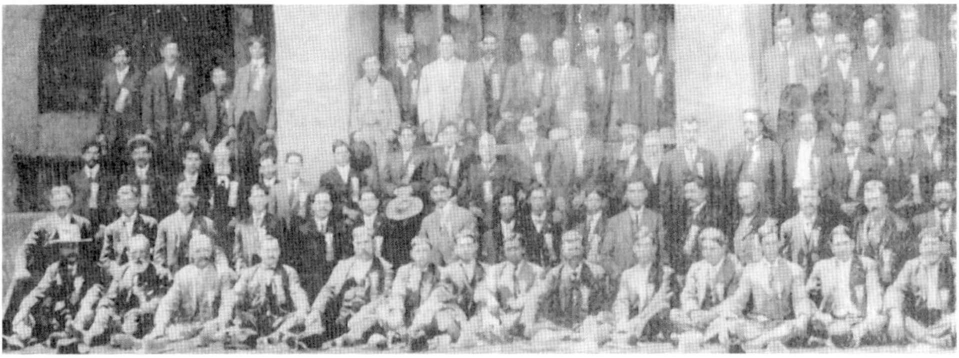

Sociedad de la Unión Católica (Sacred Heart Society), circa 1915. *Courtesy of* Walsenburg World.

APPENDIX A

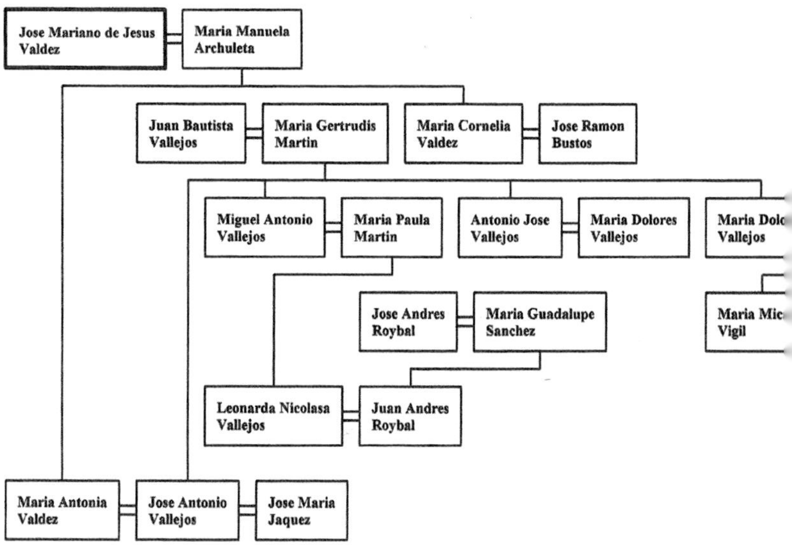
Jose Mariano de Jesus Valdez
Maria Manuela Archuleta
Juan Bautista Vallejos
Maria Gertrudis Martin
Maria Cornelia Valdez
Jose Ramon Bustos
Miguel Antonio Vallejos
Maria Paula Martin
Antonio Jose Vallejos
Maria Dolores Vallejos
Maria Dolc Vallejos
Jose Andres Roybal
Maria Guadalupe Sanchez
Maria Mic Vigil
Leonarda Nicolasa Vallejos
Juan Andres Roybal
Maria Antonia Valdez
Jose Antonio Vallejos
Jose Maria Jaquez

Family Ties
to the
Early Cuchareños

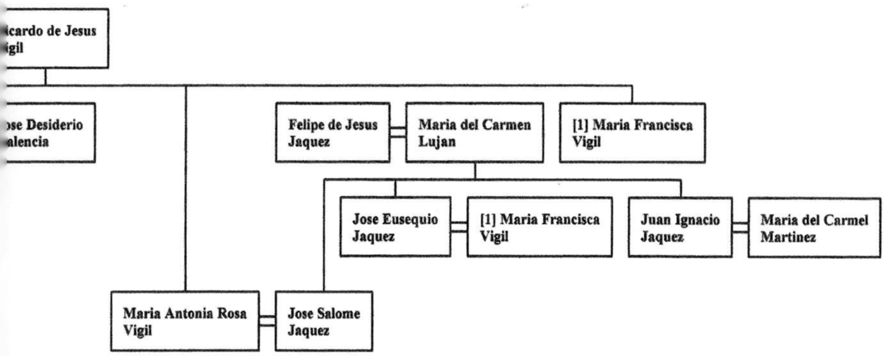

Appendix A

Direct Descendants of Jose Alejo Bustos

Jose Alejo Bustos = Martiana Maes
m: 1857

- Maria Teodosia Bustos
- Maria Teodora Bustos
- Jose Fabian Bustos
- Jose Abundo Bustos
- Jose Diego Bustos
- Maria Andrea Bustos
- Jose Eustacio Bustos
- Maria Isadora Bustos
- Dolores Bustos
- Juan Geronimo Bustos
- Jose Ramon Bustos
- Maria de la Cruz Bustos
- Juliana Bustos
- Sara de Jesus Bustos

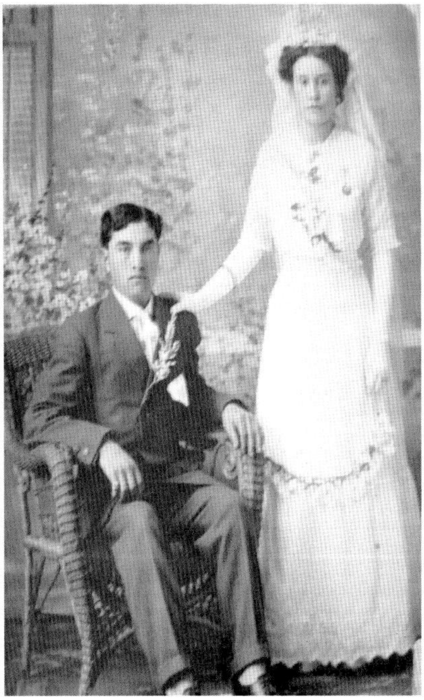

Damacio Vigil and Carmelita Torres.

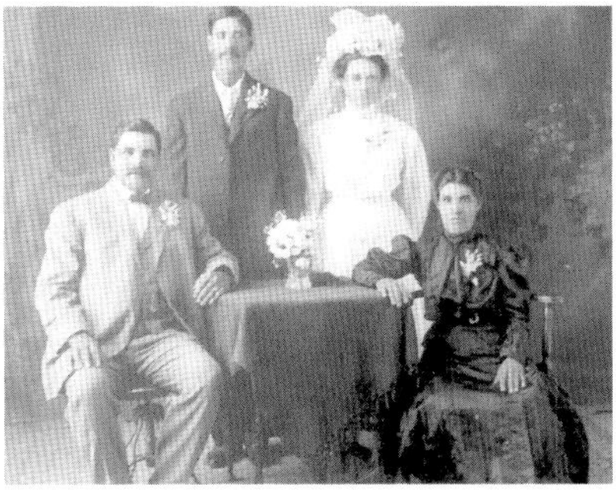

Juan Geronimo Bustos and Maria del Carmel Manzanares (both seated), with Juan Isidro Romero and Asencion Lucero.

Direct Descendants of Jose Maria Bustos

Jose Maria Bustos = Maria Manuela Maes

- Juan Basilio Bustos
- Antonio Tircio Bustos
- Maria Virginia Ramona Bustos
- Jose Gregorio Bustos
- Jose Agustin Bustos
- Maria Leonarda Bustos
- Teofilo Bustos
- Nicolasa Bustos
- Jose Teodoro Bustos
- Juan Jose Bustos

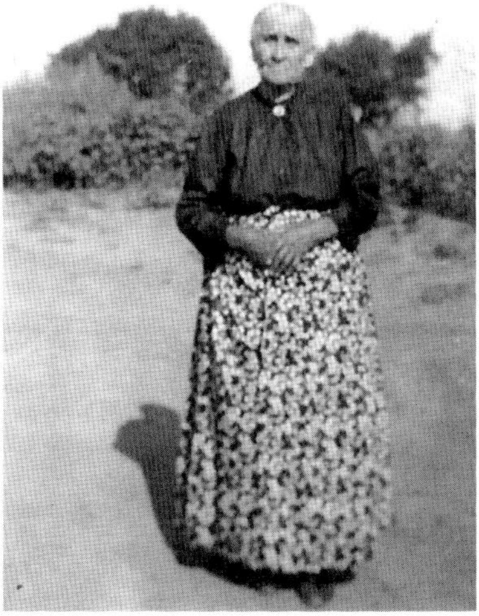

Maria Virginia Ramona Bustos.

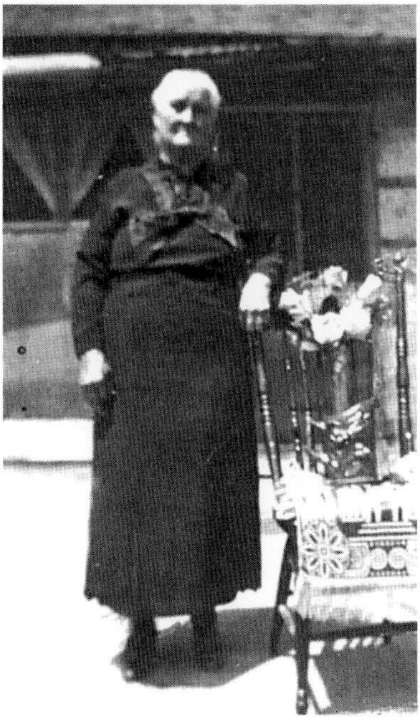

Maria Leonarda Bustos.

Appendix A

Direct Descendants of Jose Ramon Bustos

Maria Cornelia Valdez = Jose Ramon Bustos = Maria Benigna Mondragon
m: 1854 m: 1882

- Maria Francisca Bustos
  ||
  Jose Luciano Albert
- § Jose Antonio Bustos
- Maria Manuela Bustos
- Maria Emiliana Bustos
  ||
  Miguel Antonio Vigil
- Simon Lino Bustos
- Juan Bernardino Bustos
  ||
  Maria Delfina Olguin
- Francisco Bustos

- Carmel Bustos
  ||
  Rafaelita Ruybali
- Maria de la O Bustos
  ||
  Jose Espiridion Lucero
- Feliberto Bustos
- Valfidio Bustos

(§ indicates Indian captive)

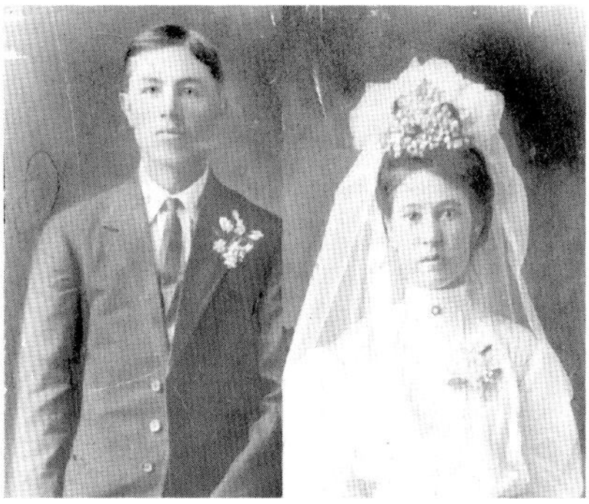

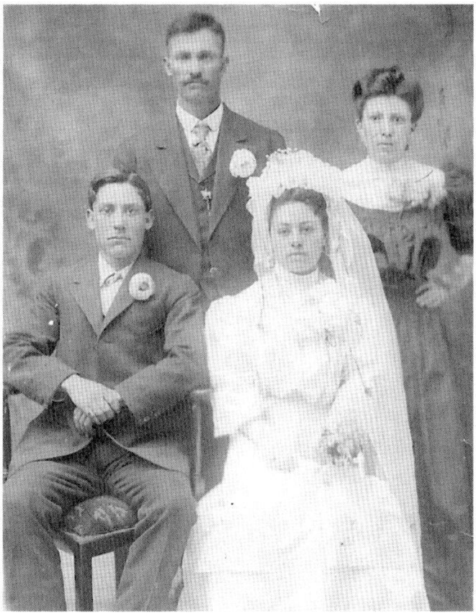

Above, left: Jose Espiridion Lucero and Maria de la O Bustos.

Above, right: Carmel Bustos (groom), Rafaelita Ruybali (bride), Teofilo Bustos and Maria Virginia Lucero.

Direct Descendants of Jesus Maria Cisneros

Jesus Maria Cisneros = Maria Romualda Martinez
m: 1884

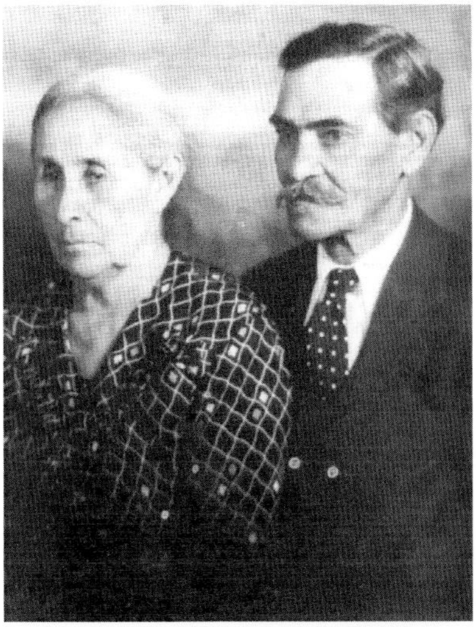

- Jose Salome Samuel Cisneros
- Ana Modesta Cisneros
- Juan de Jesus Cisneros
- Maria Damiana Cisneros
- Virginia Catalina Cisneros
- Regina Victoria Cisneros
- Lucinda Cisneros
- Lucinda Victoria Cisneros
- Maria Lucila Cisneros
- Elena "Helen" Cisneros
- Eloiza Celina Cisneros
- Cristobal Celestino Cisneros
- Victoria Ernestina Cisneros

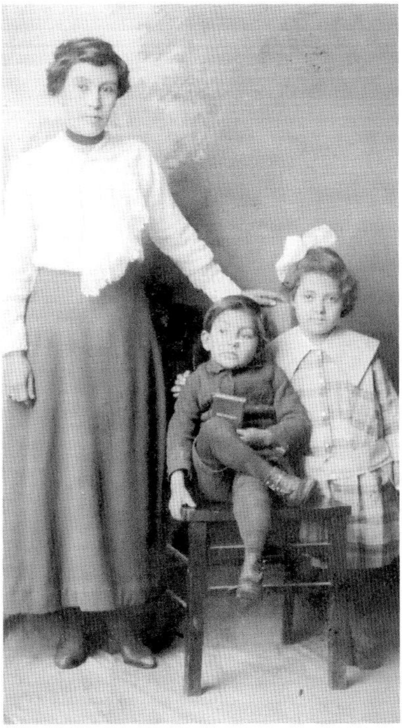

Left, top: Maria Romualda Martinez and Jesus Maria Cisneros.

Left, bottom: Ana Modesta Cisneros and children Lucretia and Pedro Maes.

Direct Descendants of Manuel Antonio Lucero

Manuel Antonio Lucero = Maria Virginia Ramona Bustos
m: 1876

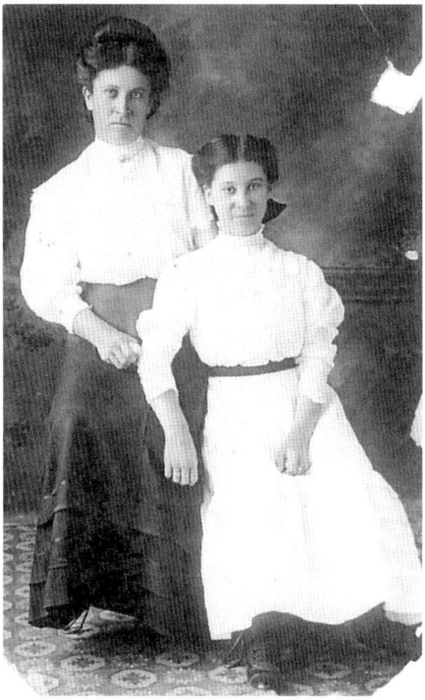

Asencion Lucero (standing) and Placida Lucero.

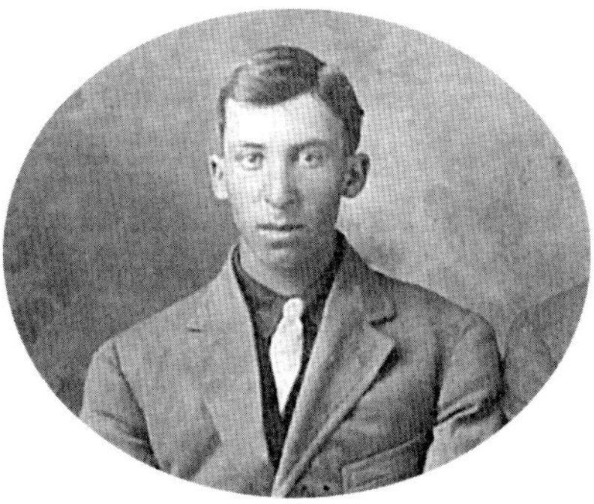

Jose Maria Lucero.

- Lucinda Lucero
- Asencion Lucero
  ||
  Juan Isidro Romero
- Jose Francisco Lucero
  ||
  Josefa Pacheco
- Elisa Lucero
  ||
  Francisco Garcia
- Jose Maria Lucero
- Placida Lucero
  ||
  Ruben Barela
- Porfirio Lucero
  ||
  Margaret Reynolds

  Josephine Reynolds
  ||
- Lucas Lucero
  ||
  Anne Quintana

Direct Descendants of Jesus Maria Manzanares

Jesus Maria Manzanares = Maria Rita Tafoya
m: 1865

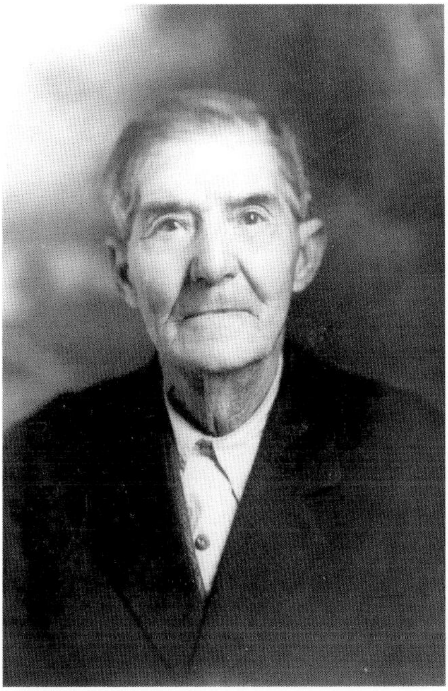

Jesus Maria Manzanares. *Courtesy of Denver Public Library, Western History Collection, Sporleder Collection, WH916, Ph Bx 1.*

- Juanita Manzanares
- Maria Adelina Manzanares
- Francisca Manzanares = Juan Francisco Chavez
- Maria Rufina Manzanares = Eustasio A. Romero
- Maria Paula Manzanares = Juan Maria Lucero
- Maria del Carmel Manzanares = Juan Geronimo Bustos
- Antonio Tercio Manzanares = Nellie Alice Deus
- Maria Isabel Manzanares = Jose Estevan Vigil

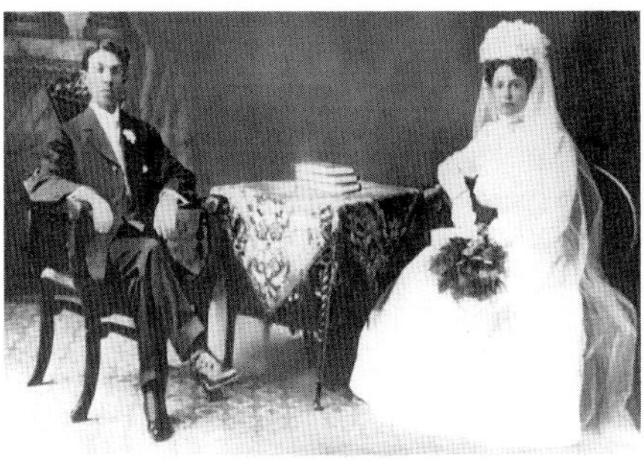

Antonio Tercio Manzanares and Nellie Alice Deus.

Direct Descendants of Diego Antonio Sandoval

Diego Antonio Sandoval = Juana Nepomucena Padilla
m: 1857

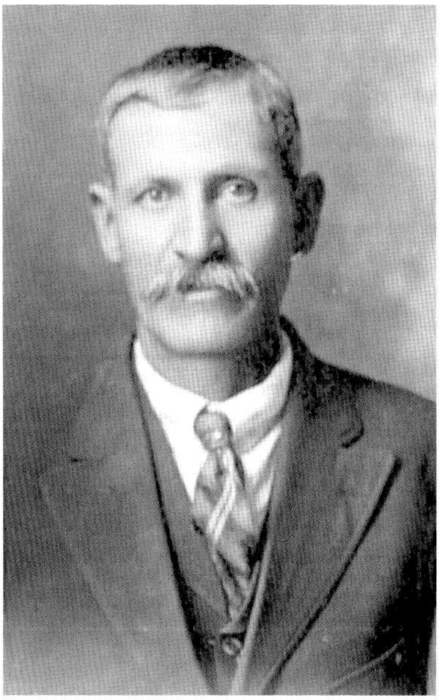

- Anastacia Sandoval
  ||
  Juan de Jesus Duran
  ||
  Margarita Martinez
- Victor Sandoval
  ||
  Sabina Atencio
- Manuel R. Sandoval
- Emiteria Sandoval
  ||
  Toribio Tolmiche
- Maria de la Cruz Bustos
  ||
  Teodoro A. Sandoval
  ||
  Elisa Maes
- Juana Maria Sandoval
  ||
  Juan Florencio Santistevan

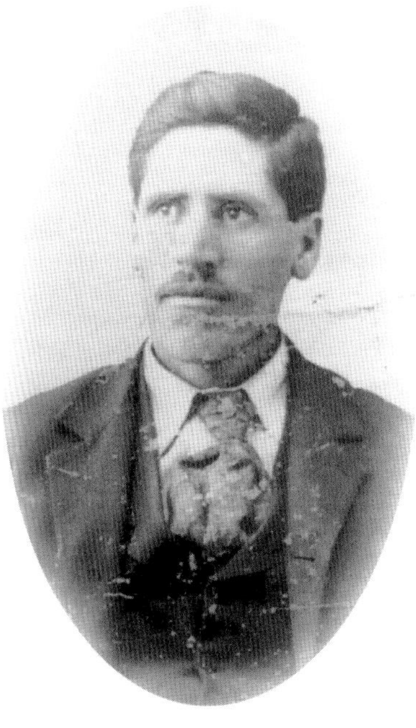

Left, top: Manuel R. Sandoval.

Left, bottom: Teodoro A. Sandoval.

Direct Descendants of Jose Leonides Valdez

Martiana Mestas = Jose Leonides Valdez = Maria Hilaria Naranjo

- Maria Dolores Valdez
  ||
  Jose Ignacio Vidal Martinez
- Juan Manuel Valdez
  ||
  Cleofes Naranjo
- Maria Ines Valdez
- Maria Eufemia Valdez
  ||
  Francisco Antonio Gonzales
- Jose Eutequio Valdez
- Maria Simona Valdez
  ||
  Juan Andres Trujillo
  ||
  Francisca Martinez
- Malaquias Valdez
  ||
  Albina Cordova
- Jose Florencio Valdez

- Teresa de Jesus Valdez
- Geronimo de Jesus Valdez
- Leonardo Martinez
  ||
  Teresa de Jesus Valdez
  ||
  Santiago Gonzales
- Antonio Leonides Valdez
  ||
  Felicitas Naranjo
- Flora Valdez
- Leofredo Valdez
  ||
  Maria Francisca Taylor
- Albina Lucero
  ||
  Abel Celestino Valdez
  ||
  Crestina Bustos
- Maria Raquel Valdez
  ||
  Jose Salomon Pino
- Ester Valdez
  ||
  Celestino Abedon Aragon

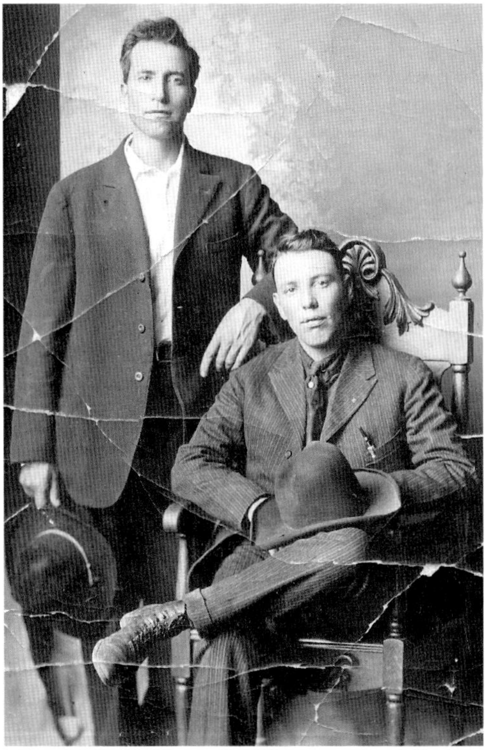

Antonio Leonides Valdez (standing) and Abel Celestino Valdez.

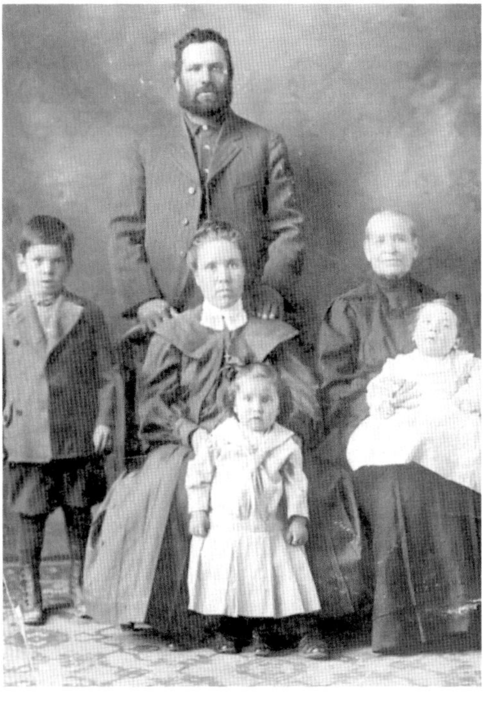

Malaquias Valdez (standing), Miguel Valdez, Albina Cordova Valdez holding Daniel Valdez and Juanita (no surname) holding Jacobo Valdez.

Direct Descendants of Miguel Antonio Vallejos

Maria Gertrudis Chavez = Miguel Antonio Vallejos = Maria Paula Martin
m: 1832 m: 1858

Children of Maria Gertrudis Chavez (m: 1832):

- Antonia Vallejos
- Maria Refugio Vallejos
- Maria Asencion Vallejos
- Antonio Jose Vallejos
- Juan de Dios Vallejos
- Maria de la Luz Vallejos
- Donaciano Vallejos
- Rafaela Vallejos
- Irinea Vallejos
- Luis Maria de Jesus Vallejos
- Lazaro de Jesus Vallejos

Children of Maria Paula Martin (m: 1858):

- Dolores Vallejos
- Josefa Vallejos
- Maria Rosalia Vallejos
- Juan Felipe Vallejos
- Juan de la Cruz Vallejos
- Damian Vallejos
- Jose Jacobo Vallejos
- Estanislado Vallejos
- Nestor Vallejos
- Soledad Vallejos
- Margarita Vallejos
- Maria Matiana Vallejos
- Jose Mucio Vallejos
- Juan Andres Vallejos
- Maria Cleofes Vallejos
- Leonarda Nicolasa Vallejos
- Maria Soledad Vallejos

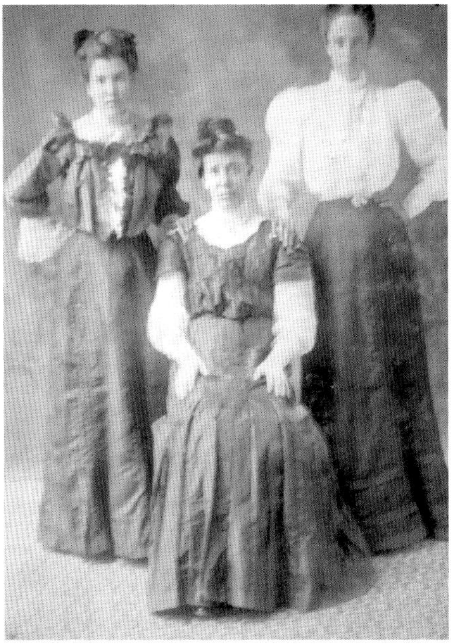

- Felix de Jesus Vallejos
- Antonio Abad Vallejos
- Teresa de Jesus Vallejos

From left: Agustina Aragon Vallejos and sisters-in-law Maria Matiana Vallejos and Teresa de Jesus Vallejos.

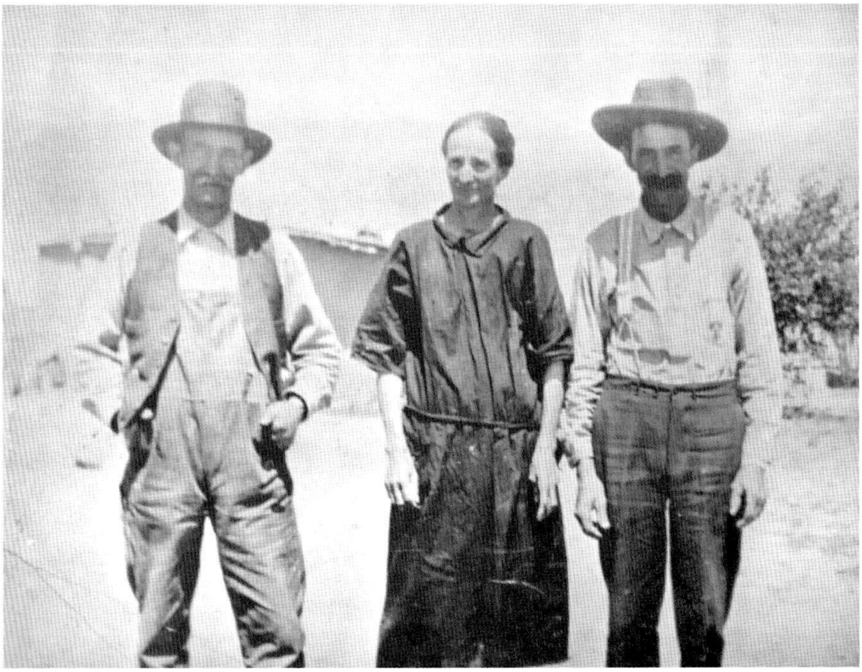

Juan Vallejos, Teresa de Jesus Vallejos and Antonio Abad Vallejos.

Appendix B

Indian Captives in Cucharas

The information in the table on the following pages details the integration of Indian captives into Hispano families in the Cucharas area.

Captive's Owners	Captive	Age	Tribe	Event/Location/Date	Captive's Spouse
Jose Rafael **Aguilar**	Francisco **Juarez**	4		Baptized at Conejos, CO, on April 4, 1870[377]	
				By August 1870 in Huerfano County[378]	
Jose Trinidad **Baca**	Rita				Francisco de Sales Vasquez[379]
Jose Ramon **Bustos** and Maria Cornelia Valdez	Jose Antonio	3	Navajo	Baptized at Arroyo Hondo, NM, on April 15, 1861[380]	
Soledad **Bustos**	Reyes	50		1870 Huerfano County Census[381]	
Jose Albino Cordova and Maria Fernanda Valdez	Jose Gregorio				Librada Espinosa[382]
Jose Rafael **Esquibel**[383] and Maria Guadalupe Avelina Borrego	Jose Antonio	6		Baptized at Costilla, CO, on April 7, 1865[384]	
				Buried in CO on November 15, 1877[385]	
Juan de Jesus **Esquibel** and Roumalda de Jesus Borrego	Manuel	10		Born in NM abt.1860[386]	
	Maria Luisa[387]	35	Navajo	Purchased from Ute Indians trading in Arizona Territory, 1860[388]	
	Maria Rita[389]	1		Baptized at Arroyo Hondo, NM, in1861[390]	Marcelino Valdez

Captive's Owners	Captive	Age	Tribe	Event/Location/Date	Captive's Spouse
Juan Evaristo **Gonzales**	Dolores	13		1870 Huerfano County Census[391]	
Manuel **Gonzales** and Maria Rosa Gomez	Gabino Chavez			Born in NM abt. 1862[392]	
	Jose Florentino			Born in NM abt. 1863[393]	Maria del Patrocinia Gomez[394]
	Jose Francisco			Baptized at Arroyo Hondo, NM, in 1856[395]	
	Juana			Born abt. 1873[396]	
	Maria Antonia			Born in NM abt.1874[397]	
	Maria de los Dolores	15 days	Ute	Baptized at Arroyo Hondo, NM, in 1860[398]	
	Maria Guadalupe	Adult	Navajo	Baptized at Arroyo Hondo, NM, in 1864[399]	
	Maria Guadalupe			Baptized at Arroyo Hondo, NM, in 1854[400]	
	Maria Rita		Navajo	Buried on November 9, 1877[401]	Perfecto Medina[402]
Jose Benito **Maes** and Maria Paula Sanchez	Antonia	23	Navajo	Baptized at Costilla, CO in 1866[403]	Jose Benito Maes[404]
	Antonio	24	Navajo	Purchased from Hispanos trading in Colorado Territory in 1864[405]	

Captive's Owners	Captive	Age	Tribe	Event/Location/Date	Captive's Spouse
Teodoro **Maes** and Maria Josefa Suazo	Juan Bautista	4	Navajo	Purchased from Hispanos trading in the San Luis Valley in 1862[406]	Maria Trinidad Baca[407]
	Juan Tomas	8	Navajo	Purchased in Arizona Territory in 1862[408]	
	Juana Librada	Adult		Baptized at Walsenburg, CO, in 1877[409]	
	Maria Rita	10	Navajo	Purchased from Ute Indians trading in the San Luis Valley[410]	Jose Antonio Jaquez[411]
Jose Antonio **Martinez** and Maria Viviana Vallejos	Margarita			Born in CO abt. 1855[412]	
Juan Bautista **Martinez** and Maria Caterina Valdez	Guadalupe[413]				
	Lupita[414]				
Jose Leonides **Valdez** and Martiana Mestas	Maria Dolores		Navajo	Born abt. 1862[415] Buried in CO in 1877[417]	Jose Ignacio Vidal Martinez[416]
Juan Benito **Valdez**[418] and Maria Estefana Vigil	Ana Maria			Born abt. 1859[419]	
	Cornelia			Born abt. 1857[420]	
	Felipe				Maria Viviana Mascarenas[421]

Captive's Owners	Captive	Age	Tribe	Event/Location/Date	Captive's Spouse
Juan Benito **Valdez**[418] and Maria Estefana Vigil *(continued)*	Guadalupe	5	Navajo	Baptized at Arroyo Hondo, NM, in 1864[422]	
	Jose	17		Born in NM abt. 1853[423]	
	Juan Antonio	13		Born in NM abt. 1857[424]	
	Maria de la Cruz			Born in NM abt. 1856[425]	
	Maria Refugio			Born abt. 1840[426]	
	Maria Ramona	6	Navajo	Baptized at Arroyo Hondo, NM, in 1864[427]	
	Soledad			Born abt. 1839[428]	
	Vicente			Born abt. 1854[429]	
Antonio Jose **Vallejos** [430] and Maria Soledad Romero	Jose Hilario[431]	2	Navajo	Baptized at Arroyo Hondo, NM, in 1860[432]	Rafaela Martinez[433]
	Maria Dolores[434]	18	Navajo	Baptized at Arroyo Hondo, NM, in 1865[435]	Antonio Jose Vallejos[436]
	Maria Isabel			Baptized at Arroyo Hondo, NM, in 1864[437]	
Jose Francisco **Vallejos** and Maria Antonia Valdez	Maria Guadalupe	2		Baptized at Arroyo Hondo, NM, in 1861[438]	
	Maria Josefa[439]	20		Baptized at Arroyo Hondo, NM, in 1861[440]	

Captive's Owners	Captive	Age	Tribe	Event/Location/Date	Captive's Spouse
Jose Maria **Vallejos** and Maria Luisa Archuleta	Rosalia[441]	18	Navajo	Purchased from Hispanos trading in Colorado Territory in 1864[442]	
Miguel Antonio **Vallejos** and Maria Paula Martinez	Dolores	30		Born in NM abt. 1850[443]	
	Josefa	8	Navajo	Purchased from Ute Indians trading in Colorado Territory in 1860[444]	
	Juan Felipe[445]	8	Navajo	Purchased from Ute Indians trading in Colorado Territory in 1863[446]	Maria de Jesus Gomez[447]
	Maria Rosalia	8		Baptized at Arroyo Hondo, NM, in 1861[448]	
	Nestor	3		Born in CO abt. 1867[449]	
	Soledad	12		Born in NM abt. 1868[450]	

Appendix C

Timeline

1821 Mexico gains its independence from Spain. Present-day Colorado is under Mexican rule. Trade exists between Missouri and Santa Fe along the Santa Fe Trail.

1843 New Mexico governor Manuel Armijo grants land in present-day Huerfano County to Cornelio Vigil and Ceran St. Vrain.

1846 United States declares war on Mexico.

1848 Hispanos in ceded area—occupying present-day Colorado, Utah, Arizona, New Mexico, Nevada, California, Texas and part of Wyoming—become citizens of the United States.

1849 First permanent settlement in present-day Colorado established at San Luis in the San Luis Valley.

1850 New Mexico Territory established. Southern Colorado becomes part of New Mexico Territory.

1859 Miners flock to Pikes Peak area in search of gold. Town of Trinidad established on the Mountain Branch of the Santa Fe Trail.

1861 U.S. Civil War begins. Colorado Territory established; Huerfano County is one of seventeen counties established.

1862 Eight Hispanos winter in the lower Cuchara Valley for the first time. Colorado Volunteers help defeat a Confederate army at Glorietta Pass in New Mexico Territory.

1864 Sand Creek Massacre: Colorado militia massacres friendly Cheyennes and Arapahos in southeastern part of territory; about two-thirds killed were women and children. Navajo Long Walk to Bosque Redondo: During the winter, Navajos were forced to walk to Bosque Redondo in New Mexico Territory; many die. Navajos were confined at Bosque Redondo for four years.

1865 U.S. Civil War ends.

1866 Badito becomes the county seat of Huerfano County. Colorado Territorial legislature includes Hispano *acequia* governance and custom in its water law. Cucharas officially established.

1867 Current boundaries of Huerfano County established.

1870 Post office established at Cucharas. Colonel William Jackson Palmer organized the D&RG Railroad.

1871 Land in Cucharas purchased for the D&RG Railroad.

1872 D&RG town of Cucharas City is incorporated. Major use of the Mountain Branch of the Santa Fe Trail ends.

1873 Name of *la Plaza de los Leones* changed to Walsenburgh, which is later spelled Walsenburg.

1874 County seat in Badito moved to Walsenburg. Utes cede mining region in the Brunot Treaty.

1876 Colorado admitted into statehood and becomes the thirty-eighth state. D&RG rails reach Cucharas.

1879 Meeker Incident: Utes at White River Agency kill agent Nathan Meeker and attack U.S. troops.

1880 Treaty of 1880 established boundaries of Southern Ute Reservation in southwestern Colorado.

1881 Ute Indians moved onto reservations.

1894 Women gain right to vote in Colorado; suffragists are not sensitive to southern Colorado Hispanos.

1899 D&RG narrow-gauge rails changed to standard-gauge rails. D&RG route removed from Cuchara Junction.

1906 Town of Cucharas Camps in the Upper Cuchara Valley established.

1911 D&RG Railroad grade moved to Walsenburg and bypasses Cucharas.

1912 Territory of New Mexico admitted into statehood.

1914 Ludlow Massacre: State militia kills several men, women and children during coal miners' strike.

1917 United States enters World War I.

1919 End of World War I.

1921 Cucharas post office closed; mail moved to Walsenburg.

1923 Native Americans gain right to vote. D&RG depot at Cuchara Junction torn down.

1924 Peak of Ku Klux Klan influence in Colorado. Citizenship Act of 1924 provides that all Native Americans born in the United States are citizens.

1930 Dust Bowl and Great Depression.

1937 D&RG rail service to Cucharas stops. Tracks removed the following year.

1950 All Cucharas schools are closed.

Notes

Preface

1. Land with an acequia was more productive in the "profitable hands of hard-working Anglos" with superior tools and farm management skills. *Huerfano Cactus*, May 10, 1884.
2. The *Huerfano Independent*, a Walsenburg weekly newspaper, was printed in English and Spanish between December 1875 and September 1876. Oehlerts, *Guide to Colorado Newspapers*, 79–80. The earliest available issue of the *Huerfano Cactus*, a weekly newspaper printed in Walsenburg, is dated May 1884. The Cuchareños likely had access to *El Progreso*, a Spanish newspaper from Trinidad. *El Progreso* was owned by Casimiro Barela. Fernandez, *The Biography of Casimiro Barela*, xxxvii. The *Anuciador*, edited by Huerfano County judge Jose Anasatacio J. Valdez, was owned by Dr. Michael Beshoar of Trinidad. Colorado Historical Society, *Portrait and Biographical Record*, 197. Spanish-language weekly papers printed in Walsenburg during a later period included: *El Imparciál* (1911–14), *El Clarín Americano* (1919–20), *El Clarín* (1934–42) and *El Clarión* (1942–51). None of these newspapers survives today. Oehlerts, *Guide to Colorado Newspapers*, 79–80. In 1904, the Public Opinion Company incorporated and purchased *La Opinión Pública* (1904–13) with the intent of publishing a Spanish newspaper. Company directors included J.D. Montez, P.L. (Pantaleon) Sanchez, A.T. (Antonio Tircio)

Bustos, Juan A. Medina, T.D. Baird, A.D. (Antonio Domingo) Valdez, J.B. (Jefferson Bouragard) Farr, J.B. Dick and Adolph Unfug. Nancy Christofferson, "Remember When," *Huerfano World*, June 20, 1991.

CUCHARAS AND ITS BEGINNING

3. Sporleder, "Description of Plaza de los Leones," 35.
4. Stoller, "Spanish-Americans," 228, footnote 14, and 230, footnote 69.
5. *Walsenburg World*, "Died at Turkey Creek, Tuesday 25th of December, Jose Mariano Valdes, Aged 88 Years," December 27, 1894.
6. Sporleder, "Description of Plaza de los Leones," 35.
7. Denver Public Library, Louis B. Sporleder Collection, WH916, Box 2, FF 7: 77–8.
8. Sporleder, "Description of Plaza de los Leones," 35.
9. Hall, *History of the State of Colorado*, 494.
10. Hunt Jackson, *Bits of Travel*, "Wa-Ha-Toy-A; or, Before the Graders," 663.
11. Slaney, *Wonders of the Weavers*, 3–4, 12.
12. Sporleder, "Description of Plaza de los Leones," 33.
13. Helen Hunt Jackson described Hispano *santos*, *retablos* and home chapels as "gaudy Roman Catholic prints and effigies and shrines." Hunt Jackson, *Bits of Travel*, "Wa-Ha-Toy-A; or, Before the Graders," 663.
14. Sporleder referred to the *araña* as a "primitive" candleholder. Denver Public Library, Louis B. Sporleder Collection, WH916, Box 2, FF 22: 229.
15. "The taste and flavor of this popular commodity [Mexican chocolate] was incomparable. Our older Mexicans had a method of preparing this fine article which has never been equaled by the American people." Denver Public Library, Louis B. Sporleder Collection, WH916, Box 2, FF 7: 88.
16. Denver Public Library, Louis B. Sporleder Collection; Sporleder, "Description of Plaza de los Leones," 31.
17. Sporleder, "Description of Plaza de los Leones," 31.
18. Huerfano County Courthouse. Public Records, Book 40. (The Archdiocese of Pueblo was formed in 1941, and Huerfano County then fell into its jurisdiction.)

19. Blocks one and four measured 150 feet by 350 feet and had seven lots; blocks two and three measured 150 feet by 250 feet with five lots. Each lot measured 50 feet by 150 feet. West of block one on lot one was a rectangular-shaped house, a large L-shaped house that straddled lots two and three and a barn north of lot one. Another rectangular-shaped house straddled Valdes Street on lot four, with the Valdes Store straddling lots five and six. In block 2, two additional rectangular-shaped houses were located on the southern ends of lots two and three. Huerfano County Courthouse, Map Book, Map of the Town of Cuchara.
20. 1885 Colorado Business Directory, 135; 1886 Colorado Business Directory, 175; 1893 Colorado Business Directory, 238; 1894 Colorado Business Directory, 233; 1896 Colorado Business Directory, 256.
21. Ibid., 1884 Colorado Business Directory, 82. By 1893, Jose Leonides Valdez and his brothers, Juan Antonio Santiago Valdez and Antonio Domingo Valdez, owned the L. Valdez and Valdez Brothers Store. 1893 Colorado Business Directory, 238; 1894 Colorado Business Directory, 233; 1896 Colorado Business Directory, 256.
22. *Pueblo Daily Chieftain*, "Huerfano County," May 13, 1874. Chavez sold the property to H.O. Rettburg.
23. By 1880, Nasario Chavez was living in Trinidad and worked as a store clerk. 1880 Las Animas County census, Trinidad, 31. Chavez enumerated with wife and two daughters.
24. First Biennial Report of the Superintendent of Public Instruction of the Territory of Colorado for the School Years Ending September 30, 1870 and September 30, 1871, 33.
25. Denver Public Library, Louis B. Sporleder Collection, WH916, Box 2, FF 22: 335 and 336.
26. Colorado Historical Society, *Portrait and Biographical Record*, 197, 198.
27. Denver Public Library, Louis B. Sporleder Collection, WH916, Box 2, FF 22: 332; Sporleder, "Description of Plaza de los Leones," 31, 38.
28. Tushar, *People of El Valle*, 64.
29. Sporleder, "Description of Plaza de los Leones," 31.
30. Tushar, *People of El Valle*, 64.
31. Hunt Jackson, *Bits of Travel*, "A New Anvil Chorus," 663.
32. Steinel and Working, "History of Agriculture in Colorado," 12, 147.
33. Slaney, *Wonders of the Weavers*, 2.
34. Stoller, "Spanish-Americans," 51.
35. De Onís, *Hispanic Contribution to the State of Colorado*, 263.

36. By 1893, Frank Bond had invested in land and sheep in southern Colorado and northern New Mexico. One transaction involved an investment in property near Walsenburg. Grubbs, "Frank Bond," 175, 180, 181; Stoller, "Spanish-Americans," 51.
37. Nancy Christofferson, interview with author, February 21, 2005.
38. Grubbs, "Frank Bond," 183.
39. Juan Evaristo Gonzales owned the first plow made with a pointed iron point pulled by oxen. Juan Evaristo Gonzales also built the first belt gristmill on the Cucharas River. Denver Public Library, Louis B. Sporleder Collection, WH916, Box 2, FF 22: 229, 233; WH916, Box 2, FF 7: 77.
40. Denver Public Library, Louis B. Sporleder Collection, WH916, Box 2, FF 22: 232. Some of Frank Bond's sheep were on partido contracts in southern Colorado and in Taos and Española, New Mexico. Bond recorded partido contracts as chattel mortgages rather than contracts. His sheep were usually run in small flocks on the public range or on land grant areas. Grubbs, "Frank Bond," 183, 299–300.
41. Ibid. "[Ute chief] Ouray and his squaw, Chepita, ran goats on [partido] shares with him." Denver Public Library, Louis B. Sporleder Collection, WH916, Box 2, FF 22: 229, 233.
42. Meketa, *Legacy of Honor*, 320.
43. Taylor and West, "Patrón Leadership at the Crossroads," 344.
44. At this time Hispanos were accustomed to using barter and trade to acquire goods and services as little cash flowed through the county. *Pueblo Daily Chieftain*, January 9, 1875.
45. United States Postal Service, Postmasters by City, San Luis Post Office, Postmaster Finder, electronic, accessed August 18, 2007; Colorado Historical Society, Fred Walsen Collection, Schrum, "An Inventory of the Papers," Box 655; Box 655, FF 16.
46. Rock, *German Footprints*, 6.
47. Denver Public Library, Louis B. Sporleder Collection, WH916, Box 2, FF 22: 265.
48. Steinel and Working, "History of Agriculture in Colorado," 147.
49. Colorado Humanities, Oral History of Frank (Jose Francisco) Cordova, July 10, 1979. Jose Francisco Cordova was a nephew of Juan Vallejos and grandson of Miguel Antonio Vallejos.
50. McNellis, "Giant of the West," 55.
51. White, "Illegal Fencing," 97.

52. In 1875, Jefferson Bouragard Farr trailed the five hundred head of two- and three-year-old steers for the Cleveland Cattle Company. He later became sheriff of Huerfano County. James Farr, recorded interview by Paul Krier and recorded by Howard Delaney, October 1963. In 1883, the D&RG constructed a stockyard at Cuchara Junction; it held enough livestock to fill eight rail cars. Marvin Davis, telephone conversation with author, November 6, 2007. His father unloaded cattle and horses shipped to Cucharas from Nebraska.
53. Walker, "The Samuel John Capps Family," 68.
54. Large cattle companies in Bent County included Beaty Brothers and Vrooman and McFife. The Arkansas Valley Company operated in both Bent and Las Animas Counties. Reynolds Cattle Company operated in Fremont County. The Livesy Brothers operated in both Fremont and Pueblo Counties. McDaniels and Davis, Routchler and Lamb, J.W. Frank, Garnett and Langford and E.C. Tane operated in Pueblo County. White, "Illegal Fencing," 98–99.
55. The Prairie Cattle Company had a ranch house at Trinidad, Colorado. The company controlled most of the region from the Arkansas River in Colorado south to the Canadian River in New Mexico, east to the Texas Panhandle and east into most of Oklahoma. McNellis. "Heat, Light, and History," 13.
56. *Colorado Magazine*, "Interview of B.A. Arnold of Walsenburg," 101; White, "Illegal Fencing," 109.
57. *Pueblo Daily Chieftain*, May 16, 1874; *Denver Daily Tribune*, "Local Advertisements," June 13, 1878.

CONFLICT AND CAPTIVITY

58. Denver Public Library, Louis B. Sporleder Collection, WH916, Box 2, FF 22: 203.
59. Ibid.; Denver Public Library, Louis B. Sporleder Collection, Box 2, FF 7: 77, 84–86; FF 40: 2; FF 42.
60. Colorado Humanities, Oral History of Patricio Maes, 1979; Denver Public Library, Louis B. Sporleder Collection, WH916, Box 2, FF 40: 3.
61. Brooks and Omohundro Institute, *Captives and Cousins*, 317.
62. Denver Public Library, Louis B. Sporleder Collection, WH916, Box 2, FF 7: 77, 86; FF 40: 2.

63. Sporleder spelled the chief's name as Kanyatcha; however, Kaniache is the preferred spelling. Denver Public Library, Louis B. Sporleder Collection, WH916, Box 2, FF 22: 202.
64. Taylor, "Ka-Ni-Ache," 287–88.
65. Colorado Humanities, Oral History of Patricio Maes, 1979.
66. Anderews and Humphry, "El Patrón de Trinidad: Don Felipe de Jesús Baca," 8.
67. Taylor, "Ka-Ni-Ache," 292.
68. Celinda R. Kaelin, e-mail message to author, December 9, 2008.
69. The meeting was held "just below the mouth of the canyon at a butte standing in the middle of the flat." Denver Public Library, Louis B. Sporleder Collection, WH916, Box 2, FF 22: 202; Taylor, "Ka-Ni-Ache," 293.
70. Denver Public Library, Louis B. Sporleder Collection, WH916, Box 2, FF 22: 203; and FF 40: 2, 3. Sporleder's uncle, Heinrich August Ludwig Teodor Sporleder, owned the Sporleder Hotel in la Plaza de los Leones.
71. *Huerfano Cactus*, May 1881; Nancy Christofferson, interview with author, October 2, 2005.
72. Colorado Humanities, Oral History of Patricio Maes, 1979.
73. Rael-Galvez, "Identifying Captivity," 50.
74. Denver Public Library, Louis B. Sporleder Collection, WH916, Box 2, FF 7: 84–86.
75. Slaney, *Wonders of the Weavers*, 2.
76. Rael-Galvez, "Identifying Captivity," 105.
77. Lafayette Head, a law enforcement officer from Missouri, served in the New Mexico Territorial legislature from 1853 to 1859. He served in the Colorado Territorial Council in 1874, representing Conejos and Costilla Counties. He was Colorado's first lieutenant governor from 1876 to 1878. Colorado Legislative Biography of Lafayette Head, electronic, accessed March 12, 2009.
78. Anglo owners of Indian captives included: G. Fulton, John Sclott, Tomas Tate Tobin, J.B. Woodson and Joseph Bounay (Bourcy). Lafayette Head's captives used the surname *Cabesa* (Spanish for head). Denver Public Library, "Letters Received by the Office of Indian Affairs," Roll 193, 1865–1866, Frame 41, Costilla County; and Frames 127 and 128, Conejos County.
79. Perkins, *Tom Tobin Frontiersman*, 187.
80. Rael-Galvez, "Identifying Captivity," 315, 364.
81. 1870 Huerfano County census. Joseph Bourcy served as a Huerfano County interpreter for several years. Denver Public Library, Louis B.

Sporleder Collection, WH916, Box 2, FF 22: 249. By 1865, Joseph Bourcy was in Culebra, Colorado, and had a twenty-year-old female Navajo servant named Resiona. Although Indian agent Lafayette Head's report states Resiona was acquired from Mexicans, Head likely meant Hispanos from southern Colorado or New Mexico as some Hispanos engaged in this type of raid commerce. She was acquired by (New) Mexicans trading in Colorado Territory in 1864. She chose to return to her tribe. Denver Public Library, "Letters Received by the Office of Indian Affairs," Roll 198, Frame 41, Line 5, Costilla County.

82. 1870 Huerfano County census. Manuel Gonzales, age sixty, farmer; Maria Rosa, age thirty, wife; Maria Rita, age twelve, (Navajo) Indian; Maria Antonia, age seven; Francisco, age ten; Florentino, age three; and Gavino Chaves, age eight, goat herder. See also Martinez, *Nuestra Señora de los Dolores*, 114, 152, 153, 162; Colorado Society of Hispanic Genealogy, "Nuestra Señora de los Siete Dolores Matrimoniales," 14; and Colorado Society of Hispanic Genealogy, "Nuestra Señora de los Siete Dolores Entierros," 13.

83. 1880 Huerfano County census, 39C, ED 6, Lines 37–40, Dwelling 307, Household 307. Maria Rosa Gonzales, age fifty, sheep raiser; Maria Antonia, age six, adopted; Florentino, age thirteen, servant, cattle herder; Juanita, age seven, servant.

84. Maria R(osa) (Gomez) Gonzales, 1885 Huerfano County Agricultural Census, Schedule 2, ED2, Sheet A1, Line 4.

85. 1900 Huerfano County census. Jose Florentino Gonzales with Maria del Patrocinia Gomez, April 1, 1884. Colorado Society of Hispanic Genealogy, "Nuestra Señora de los Siete Dolores Matrimoniales," 147.

86. Maes Creek, Maes Creek Cemetery and Maes Trail into the Greenhorn Mountains are named for Jose Benito Maes. Today, Maes Creek Cemetery is known as the Valdez Cemetery. Juan Santos Valdez donated the land for the cemetery. Maes, *Following in the Footsteps of our Ancestors from Santa Fe to Maes Creek*, 34.

87. Denver Public Library, "Letters Received by the Office of Indian Affairs," Roll 193, Frame 41, Line 7, Costilla County.

88. Martinez, "Extracts of the 1865–1881 Birth and Marriage Records," 8. "Maria Antonia Mes, twenty-three-year-old Navajo in the family of Benito Mes and Maria Paula Sanchez." Their two biological children served as godparents.

89. Colorado Society of Hispanic Genealogy, "Nuestra Señora de los Siete Dolores Registros de Matrimoniales," 114. "On 21 December 1881, Benito Maes, widower of Paula Archuleta, son of Paulin Maes and

Ignacia Varela, both deceased, with Antonia Navajosa (Navajo)." Paula Archuleta's name also appears in records as Paula Sanchez.

90. Denver Public Library, "Letters Received by the Office of Indian Affairs." Roll 198, Frame 41, Lines 1–3, Costilla County. Juan was a four-year-old Navajo when Teodoro Maes purchased him in 1862 from (New) Mexicans trading in Colorado Territory. Although Indian agent Lafayette Head's report states Antonia was acquired from Mexicans, Head likely meant Hispanos from southern Colorado or New Mexico as some Hispanos engaged in this type of raid commerce. Juan Tomas was an eight-year-old Navajo captured in Arizona Territory in 1862. Rita was a ten-year-old Navajo when Maes purchased her in 1865 from the Ute trading in Colorado Territory. All three chose not to return to their tribes.

91. Denver Public Library, Louis B. Sporleder Collection, WH916, Box 2, FF 7: 77, 80.

92. Juan Benito Valdez served in 1855, 1867 and again in 1868. Rael-Galvez, "Identifying Captivity," 313.

93. Denver Public Library, Louis B. Sporleder Collection, WH916, Box 2, FF 7: 85.

94. Brooks and Omohundro Institute, *Captives and Cousins*, 395–96.

95. Denver Public Library, Louis B. Sporleder Collection, WH916, Box 2, FF 7: 81, 85.

96. 1884 Colorado Business Directory, 82. In 1875, Jose Leonides Valdez purchased 160 acres from his father for $200.

97. Lupita Valdez was still alive in 1979 and lived in Taos, New Mexico. Colorado Humanities, Oral History of Theresa (Teresina Martinez) Armijo, July 16, 1979.

98. Sporleder, "Description of Plaza de los Leones," 35.

99. Martinez, *Nuestra Señora de los Dolores*, 1.

100. The children of Maria Dolores and Antonio Jose Vallejos were Maria Gertrudes (born about 1867), Luis Canuto (born 1877), Vicenta (born 1878), Jose Manuel (born 1880), Juan Bautista (born 1884) and Maria Soledad (born 1885); also listed as a son is his grandson Jose Encarnacion Martinez. Colorado State Archives, Huerfano Wills, vol. 1, 14–15.

101. Antonio Jose Vallejos with Maria Dolores Vallejos, August 29, 1885, Colorado Society of Hispanic Genealogy, "Nuestra Señora de los Siete Dolores Registros de Matrimoniales," 157. Antonio Jose Vallejos declared that Maria Getrudis, age fifteen; Vicenta, age eight; and Jose

Manuel, age five, were his children by Maria Dolores Vallejos. *"Antonio Jose Vallejos viudo de Ma Soledad Romero, hijo leg. de Juan* [Bautista] *Vallejos y de Gertrudis Martin, con Ma Dolores Vallejos, famiela* [sic] *del mismo. Por delante los testigos Jose Miguel Vallejos y Paula Martin, Antonio Jose Vallejos declaró ser sus hijos, Ma Gertrudis edad de quince años, Vicenta de ocho años, Jose Manuel de cinco años, hijos de la dicha Ma Dolores Vallejos, y los legitimó por el acto de este matrimonio."*

102. Pino, *Our Lady of Sorrows*, Vol. 2, Baptisms, 192. Maria Soledad Vallejos, born August 12, 1885; baptism August 30, 1885; daughter of Antonio Jose Vallejos and Dolores Vallejos of Cucharas. Godparents were Donaciano Vigil and Agapita Cisneros, also of Cucharas.
103. Antonio Jose Vallejos died July 6, 1892. Colorado Society of Hispanic Genealogy, "Nuestra Señora de los Siete Dolores Entierros," 83; Colorado State Archives, Huerfano Wills vol. 1, 14–15.
104. Martinez, *Nuestra Señora de los Dolores*, 109.
105. Denver Public Library, Louis B. Sporleder Collection, WH916, Box 2, FF 7: 84 and FF 22: 198.
106. Brooks and Omohundro Institute, *Captives and Cousins*, 4, 305.
107. Stoller, "Spanish-Americans," 228, footnote 14.
108. Sporleder, "Description of Plaza de los Leones," 35.
109. Brooks and Omohundro Institute, *Captives and Cousins*, 304–5. According to Louis B. Sporleder, Manzanares went to Crestones with Captain Charles Deus. Denver Public Library, Louis B. Sporleder Collection, WH916, Box 2, FF 42, fragment pages.
110. Brooks and Omohundro Institute, *Captives and Cousins*, 305.
111. Sisto Martinez died in 1923. Denver Public Library, Louis B. Sporleder Collection, WH916, Box 2, FF 7: 77.
112. Denver Public Library, Louis B. Sporleder Collection, WH916, Box 2, FF 22: 207, 208.
113. Colorado Humanities, Oral History of Frank (Jose Francisco) Cordova, July 10, 1979.
114. The *beher* was about twenty-seven and one-half inches long. Jefferson, et al., *Southern Utes*, 66.
115. Celinda R. Kaelin, telephone conversation with author, December 29, 2008.
116. Colorado Humanities, Oral History of Pedro Cisneros, December 24, 1979; Colorado Humanities, Oral Histories of Marcos and Benito Manzanares, July 23, 1979.
117. Harrington, "The Tewa Indian Game," 247–50, 254, 257, 264.

118. Colorado Humanities, Oral Histories of Max (Melaquias) and Lulu (Leocadia Sandoval) Valdez, December 30, 1979.
119. Colorado Humanities, Oral History of Frank (Jose Francisco) Cordova, July 10, 1979.
120. Colorado State Archives, Huerfano County District Court Record, 23 February 1899, 372. Jurors were John Quinton, F.S. Fouch, A.A. Foote, A.P. McIntyre, Roman Aguirre, John Dick, Charles Rohn, Peter Pierson, J.F. Alex Nigro, Juan de Herrera and Jose D. Quintana. The lawyers for the defendants were P.W. Sweney, Henry Hunter, James McKeough and Robert R. Ross. In 1904, Antonio Domingo Valdez went into a livestock business with Colorado state senator Juan de Dios Montez of Malachite, Colorado. Valdez entered politics and served in the House of Representatives of the Colorado General Assembly. The Valdez and Montez office was located in the Montez home on Russell Street. *Huerfano World*, January 1904.

INTO THE BEAUTIFUL CIRCULAR VALLEY

121. Beadle, *Undeveloped West*, 443, 445–46.
122. The D&RG was called a narrow-gauge railroad. Narrow-gauge rails were three feet apart; standard-gauge rails were four feet and eight and one-half inches apart. The D&RG began using standard-gauge rail in 1881. Wilson, *Denver and Rio Grande Project*, 11, 92.
123. The first narrow-gauge engine built in the United States for the D&RG was named the Montezuma. Anderson, *General William J. Palmer*, 131.
124. U.S. Department of the Interior, Scott, "Historic Trail Map," 16; Taylor, *First Mail West*, 21.
125. Alexander Zan Hicklin was associated with many New Mexico and Colorado historic men, such as Charles and William Bent, Ceran St. Vrain, Richens Lacey (Uncle Dick) Wootton, Charles Autobees, Thomas Oliver Boggs and Christopher "Kit" Carson. The Butte Valley Station was located east of the *huérfano* (orphan) butte that today stands on the east side of Interstate 25, north of the town of Walsenburg. U.S. Department of the Interior, Scott, "Historic Trail Map," 15, 34–35. There were two types of stagecoach stops: the home station and the swing, or relay, station. Home station stops provided brief stops for passenger meals and a change of drivers and teams.

They were located forty to fifty miles apart and had to meet U.S. postal requirements by providing a ticket office, post office and a stable complete with staging equipment. Home stations also provided passengers with a store, lodging and meals. Relay stations, located every ten to fifteen miles, provided brief stops to replace the teams. McCullough, "Barlow and Sanderson Stage Line," 32.

126. Beadle, *Undeveloped West*, 443, 445–46.

127. Guerminia Eugenia "Jean" Silva, interview with author, February 22, 2004.

128. A stage driver was responsible for the mail, passengers and freight delivered on his route. He was also responsible for making sure the stage reached scheduled stops on time. Taylor, *First Mail West*, 14.

129. Stagecoach companies periodically supplied their stations with freight-wagon loads of feed, blankets for the horses, staging supplies and equipment. McCullough, "Barlow and Sanderson Stage Line," 24, 31, 45.

130. John H. Beadle described his breakfast at "Cocharas" as "wheaten-cakes, fried eggs and chopped and stewed mutton." Beadle, *Undeveloped West*, 443, 445–46.

131. *Denver Rocky Mountain News*, March 6, 1876; Taylor, *First Mail West*, 142.

132. Wells Fargo and Company started a line of stagecoaches that ran north from Denver in 1858; however, no stagecoaches ran south.

133. U.S. Department of the Interior, Scott, "Historic Trail Map," 15–16.

134. Burke, *A Bumpy Ride*, 76.

135. Barlow and Sanderson's contract to deliver U.S. mail between Pueblo and Trinidad ended the following year. *Pueblo Weekly Chieftan*, "Cucharas," May 11, 1876.

136. Celedon Bustos, telephone conversation with author, October 1, 2004.

137. Anderson, *General William J. Palmer*, 34, footnote 42.

138. Wilson, *Denver and Rio Grande Project*, 11. Freighting does not appear as an occupation in the 1870 Huerfano County census. Quintana, *Pobladores*, 104.

139. Eggenhofer, *Wagons, Mules, and Men*, 92.

140. Deutsch, *No Separate Refuge*, 22.

141. Wilson, *Denver and Rio Grande Project*, 26.

142. Many *fletero* trains passed through Denver hauling ties for the Kansas Pacific Railroad. Anderson, *General William J. Palmer*, 34.

143. The Jose Manzanares freight agency used a horse and buggy or a horse and wagon to transport people or freight between Walsenburg and

Redwing. Colorado Humanities, Oral History of Benito and Marcos Manzanares, July 23, 1979. Merchant Manuel A. Sanchez likely hired fleteros to deliver goods to his customers. He began his career in San Pablo, Colorado. In 1898, he owned a general store located in the Walsen block on the west side of Walsenburg's Main Street. The store was later moved into a "double-store building known as the Chatine stone block." *Walsenburg World*, December 25, 1902. Before residing in Walsenburg, he taught school in Taos County, New Mexico. He represented Taos County in the New Mexico Territorial legislature. Manuel A. Sanchez later represented Costilla County in the Colorado House of Representatives from 1893 to 1895.

144. Simmons, *San Luis Valley*, 159.

145. Sporleder, et al., "Our Grandfather Louis Bernhardt Sporleder," 84, 88.

146. In 1877, the summer rate to freight goods from La Veta to Lake City was three to three and one-half cents per pound. From Cañon City to Lake City, the summer rate was from three and one-half to four cents per pound. From Saguache or Del Norte west to Lake City, the rate was one and one-half to two cents per pound. Williams, "Williams' Tourists' Guide," 35.

147. Harlan, *Postmarks and Places*, x.

148. "Site Location Reports of Post Offices, 1837–1950."

149. Harlan, *Postmarks and Places*, x.

150. *Colorado Springs Gazette*, August 4, 1877.

151. NARA, "Record of Appointment of Postmasters, 1832–September 30, 1971."

152. Although Joseph Adams was appointed postmaster, he did not serve his term. John Foster Read served in his place. NARA, "Record of Appointment of Postmasters," M841, R14.

153. John Grady also ran a boardinghouse at Cucharas City. Colorado Historical Society, *Business Directory and Railroad Gazetteer*, 245.

154. James Benjamin Stevens was the son of Walter V. Stevens.

155. NARA, "Record of Appointment of Postmasters," M841, R14.

156. When Gertrude arrived at the depot, conductor Donnelly told her, "You almost not made it." She responded, "What do you mean? Here's the bag. Here is the mail." Donnelly replied, "Yeah, you was almost too late." Colorado Humanities, Oral History of Gertrude (Vallejos) Farr, August 5, 1979.

157. *Huerfano Cactus*, advertisement, May 10, 1884.

158. Colorado Humanities, Oral History of Theresa (Teresina Martinez) Armijo, July 16, 1979. Also 1921 Colorado Business Directory, 276.

159. Wilson, *Denver and Rio Grande Project*, 30.

160. General Palmer was a big investor in the Maxwell Land Grant Company. He served as its president in 1872. Lamar, *The Far Southwest 1846–1912*, 243.
161. Rasmussen, *Rio Grande's La Veta Pass Route*, 43.
162. The mill was owned by a Mr. Meserve. *Pueblo Daily Chieftain*, May 14, 1873; *Pueblo Daily Chieftain*, May 20, 1873.
163. 1880 Huerfano County census. The following year, Jose Vicente Maes served as county commissioner and was a Cucharas sheriff by 1885. Nardine, *In the Shadows*, 78.
164. *Pueblo Daily Chieftain*, December 8, 1876.
165. Sporleder, "Description of Plaza de los Leones," 29.
166. Hunt Jackson, *Bits of Travel*, "Wa-ha-toy-a; or Before the Graders."
167. NARA, "Non-Mineral Affidavit," Box 1343. By 1910, his widow was living with her son, Antonio, in Bear Creek.
168. Taylor, *Colorado South of the Border*, 288–91. The 320-acre site of Walsenburg was incorporated on June 16, 1873.
169. The right of way measured fifty feet on each side of the center of track; the D&RG would "construct and maintain suitable cattle guards and crossing for roads and ditches." John G. Self to the Denver & Rio Grande Railway Company, September 4, 1874. Dotter Abstract Company, Entry 3-181.
170. *Huerfano World*, February 2, 1899. Fred Walsen was president of Walsen Banking Company; Fred O. Roof was cashier; and Fred Walsen Jr. was assistant cashier.
171. Walsen, "General Fred Walsen," 39.
172. Fred Walsen Collection. Frederick O. Roof, Frederick Walsen Jr. and William E. Renshaw were executors. Renshaw was Walsen's son-in-law. By 1910, Fred O. Roof was vice-president of the Minnequa Bank of Pueblo. That year he also served as secretary-treasurer for the Iron City Fuel Company in Pueblo. *1910 Pueblo City Directory*, 439.
173. U.S. Department of the Interior, Scott, "Historic Trail Map," 16; Taylor, *First Mail West*, 42.

FAITH, SACRIFICE AND SERVICE

174. With her parents and siblings, Gertrude Vallejos Farr daily prayed the rosary and said special prayers to *Santo Niño* ("Little Jesus"), *la Familia Sacrada* (the Holy Family), the Sacred Heart and Saint Anthony. Colorado Humanities, Oral History of Gertrude (Vallejos) Farr, August 5, 1979;

Colorado Humanities, Oral History of Theresa (Teresina Martinez) Armijo, July 16, 1979.

175. Delaney, *All Our Yesterdays*, 17. The Archdiocese of Pueblo later established churches in Cucharas, Badito, Farsita, Redwing, *Santa María* (Saint Mary), Tioga, Toltec and *Rito de Gallina* (Turkey Creek). Karen Gomez, letter to author, March 15, 1982.

176. Ibid.

177. The stained-glass windows were purchased from Benziger Brothers at a cost of $2,170.80. Delaney, *All Our Yesterdays*, 46–47, 52. Louis B. Sporleder often purchased a barrel of "mission" wine from Father Gabriel Ussel. The wine came from grapes grown in the Rio Abajo area of New Mexico (area south of Santa Fe, New Mexico). Louis B. Sporleder Collection, WH916, Box 2, FF22, 181.

178. James Farr, recorded interview with Paul Krier and recorded by Howard Delaney, October 1963.

179. Colorado Humanities, Oral History of Eleanor Cordova, August 1979.

180. Other members of the *sociedad* included Jose Leonides Valdez, Antonio Tircio Bustos, Pantaleon Sanchez, Eusebio Montez and Teofilo Bustos. *Walsenburg World*, obituary, July 21, 1927.

181. In 1899, Hispanos in Huerfano County performed the traditional procession of San Isidro through the fields. Campa, *Hispanic Culture in the Southwest*, 150.

182. Colorado Humanities, Oral History of Max (Melaquias) and Lulu (Leocadia Sandoval) Valdez, December 30, 1979.

183. Tomas Trujillo and Reynaldo Salas were two musicians from the Gardner area. "Oral History of Patricio Maes" Huerfano County Oral History Project, 1979. Juan Antonio Estevan Pacheco (born about 1920) was a musician from La Veta; Santos Trujillo (born about 1851) was a musician from Huerfano (Butte Valley). 1880 Huerfano County census.

184. Francisco Apodaca, from la Plaza de los Leones, played the guitar. Sporleder, "Description of Plaza de los Leones," 31.

185. There were various types of waltzes: the *valse despacio* (slow waltz), the *valse redondo* (danced in a circle) and the *valse del paño* (danced while holding a silk scarf or handkerchief). Popular dance tunes included *la Varsoviana*, *la Raspa*, *la Jota* and *la Jesusita*. Beadle, *Undeveloped West*, 456–57; Colorado Humanities, Oral History of Frank (Jose Francisco) Cordova, July 10, 1979; Colorado Humanities, Oral Histories of Benito and Marcos Manzanares, July 23, 1979; Tushar, *People of El Valle*, 129.

186. Jose Eluterio "Chatito" Lucero was a good *Chotís* dancer. He resembled Western movie actor George "Gabby" Hays. Conrad Lucero, interview with author, October 1, 2004.
187. Agapito Montoya (born about 1830) was a musician between 1880 and 1885. 1880 Huerfano County census.
188. 1885 Huerfano County census, 11C, Line 5, Household/Dwelling 111.
189. Jose Daniel Martinez (born about 1874) played the guitar and violin. His sons, Julian and Isador, also played the guitar. Colorado Humanities, Oral History of Theresa (Teresina Martinez) Armijo, July 16, 1979.
190. Seferino Sandoval (born about 1880) played the violin. Colorado Humanities, Oral History of Gertrude (Vallejos) Farr, August 5, 1979.
191. Huerfano County Courthouse, Public Records, Warranty Deed: Jose Leonides Valdez to Right Rev. Nicholas C. Matz, Book 40, December 18, 1894, 536. In 1890, Jose Andres Ruibal (Roybal) sold land in Cucharas for one dollar to the Right Reverend Nicholas Matz, bishop of the Catholic Church of Denver. Huerfano County Courthouse, Public Records, Waranty Deed: Jose Andres Ruibal to Right Reverend Nicholas Matz, Book 33, April 2, 1890, 247. Jose Andres Ruibal deeded one acre to the Right Reverend Nicholas Matz, Catholic bishop of the Archdiocese of Denver and trustee for the Catholic Church of Arapahoe County. J.A.J. Valdez notarized the deed. According to diocese records, no church was constructed at this location. (On same date, W.V. Stevens deeded land in Section 32 to the bishop for a Catholic cemetery.)
192. Murphy, "Architectural/Historical Component Form."
193. *Santeros* whose works were found along the Colorado Front Range were Jose Benito Ortega, Juan Ramon Velasquez, Juan Miguel Herrera, Juan Ascedro Maes, Francisco Vigil and Jose de Gracia Gonzales. Gonzales lived in Trinidad from about 1888 to 1903. His small statues were cast in molds made from hand-carved originals. Birner, "Jose Francisco Vigil," 37–41; Birner, "Juan Ysidro Maez," 86–92.
194. Colorado Humanities, Oral History of Theresa (Teresina Martinez) Armijo, July 16, 1979.
195. Delaney, *All Our Yesterdays*, 30.
196. "Smoky" Martinez drove the carriage. James Farr, recorded interview with Paul Krier and recorded by Howard Delaney, October 1963.
197. Father Liciotti was especially fond of the chile, bread and prune pies prepared by Maria del Carmel Duran Vallejos. Colorado Humanities, Oral History of Gertrude (Vallejos) Farr, August 5, 1979. Maria del

Carmel Duran Vallejos was the daughter of Miguel Antonio Vallejos and the mother of Gertrude Vallejos Farr.

198. Rene Weeks, telephone conversation with author, May 12, 2004.
199. Colorado Humanities, Oral History of Gertrude (Vallejos) Farr, August 5, 1979.
200. Ibid.
201. *The ARCO CO_2 Pipeline Archeology Project*, 85.
202. Huerfano County Courthouse, Public Records, Warranty Deed: Walter V. Stevens to Right Rev. Nicholas C. Matz, Book 33, 2 April 1890, 245.
203. Colorado Humanities, Oral History of Theresa (Teresina Martinez) Armijo, July 16, 1979.
204. Colorado Historical Society, Murphy, "Architectural/Historical Component Form."
205. Santos inside this morada included *la Virgen María* (the Virgin Mary), *San Pedro* (Saint Peter) and *Mí Señor* (My God, or Our Father). Anonymous former penitente, telephone conversation with author, July 27, 2006.
206. Ibid. Santos in this newer morada were a *Sagrado Corazón de Jesús* (Sacred Heart of Jesus), a *Virgen de Guadalupe* (Virgin of Guadalupe) and a *Santa María* (Mary, Mother of God).
207. Colorado Historical Society, Murphy, "Architectural/Historical Component Form."
208. Ibid. There was one *morada* in Turkey Creek and Bear Creek and two *moradas* in Pass Creek. One in Pass Creek was known as *la Morada de la Questa.* Colorado Humanities, Oral History of Patricio Maes, 1979.
209. Hunt Jackson, *Bits of Travel*, 663.
210. *Pueblo Daily Chieftain*, "Stage Ride to Del Norte," April 22, 1876.
211. Nuys, *Americanizing the West*, 105.
212. Colorado Humanities, Oral History of Gertrude (Vallejos) Farr, August 5, 1979.
213. Anonymous former penitente, telephone conversation with author, July 27, 2006.
214. Rene Weeks, telephone conversation with author, May 12, 2004.
215. Denver Public Library, Louis B. Sporleder Collection, WH916, Box 2, File Folder 63.
216. *Pueblo Weekly Chieftan*, October 15, 1874; 1875 Colorado Business Directory, 102–3.

217. *Pueblo Daily Chieftain*, September 23, 1874; 1870 Pueblo County census. By November, the Reverend McMains was assigned to religious duty at Saguache, Colorado, in the San Juan Mountains. *Colorado Springs Gazette*, November 21, 1874. The following year, the Reverend Oscar P. McMains ministered at Cimarron, New Mexico. Montoya, *Translating Property*, 110–11.
218. Nancy Christofferson, "This Week in Walsenburg History," *Huerfano World*, May 28, 1989; Nancy Christofferson, "This Week in Walsenburg History," *Huerfano World*, December 26, 2002.
219. McLean and Thomson, *Spanish and Mexican in Colorado*, 39. The Reverend Refugio Jaramillo also held services in a church at Huerfano Canyon at Tioga, a coal town about twenty miles from Cucharas.
220. *Hispanic Pioneers*, 36–43, 178.
221. The Theatine Order of Catholic Priests served in the San Luis Valley. *El Reino de Dios*, "La Problema Mejicano." "*Los protestantes…trabajan con gran ardor para ver de robarles la fe. Conocen sus necesidades materiales, han estudiado su modo de ser y de todo se sirven para pescarles.*"
222. Hunt Jackson, *Bits of Travel*, "Wa-Ha-Toy-A; or, Before the Graders," 663.
223. Larger missions in Rouse and Tioga offered Mass twice a month. During the 1940s, the San Antonio chapel was one of the smaller mission churches served by a parish priest and three assistant pastors. Howard Delaney, e-mail message to author, August 28, 2004.

Linked by Water, Linked by Blood

224. Sporleder, "Description of Plaza de los Leones," 29.
225. Rivera, *Acequia Culture*, 3.
226. Denver Public Library, Louis B. Sporleder Collection, WH916, Box 2, FF 7: 86.
227. Peña, "Cultural Landscapes and Biodiversity," 250–53.
228. Rivera, *Acequia Culture*, 3.
229. Holleran, "Irrigation and Water Supply Ditches," 55.
230. Meyer, *Water in the Hispanic Southwest*, 65.
231. Holleran, "Irrigation and Water Supply Ditches," 73.
232. Meyer, *Water in the Hispanic Southwest*, 184.

233. Peña, *Chicano Culture*, 261.
234. Baxter, "Measuring New Mexico's Irrigation Water," 403.
235. U.S. Forest Service, Streams Systems Technology Center, "Ask Doctor Hydro," electronic, accessed June 17, 2004.
236. Private collection, Madrid Ditch No. 2 Ledger, vol. 2, March 9, 1885, Article 6.
237. Peña, *Chicano Culture*, 261.
238. Private collection, Madrid Ditch No. 2 Ledger, vol. 2, April 7, 1915.
239. *Huerfano Cactus*, January 17, 1885.
240. 1889 Colorado Business Directory, 105.
241. Private collection, Madrid Ditch No. 2 Ledger, vol. 2, April 6, 1923.
242. Guerminia Eugenia "Jean" Silva, interview with author, March 3, 2004.
243. Private collection, Madrid Ditch No. 2 Ledger, vol. 1, 1896.
244. Conrad Lucero, interview with author, October 1, 2004.
245. Private collection, Madrid Ditch No. 2 Ledger, vol. 2, April 3, 1915.
246. NARA, "Non-Mineral Affidavit," Land Records, Patent 078147, Box 1190, Doc. 494 and Patent 075544, Box 1343, Doc. 7.
247. Smith, et al., "La Cultura de la Acequia Madre," 14, 18–27.
248. Hicks and Peña, "Community Acequias," 461; Rivera, *Acequia Culture*, 80, 178.
249. In 1864, the Colorado Territorial legislature recognized the Doctrine of Appropriation—first-in-time, first-in-right—which basically stated that during periods of limited water supply, the priority number of a water right determined when water could be diverted and delivered relative to other water rights. By Colorado Territorial law, the earliest water user had access to all the water needed before the next user in line. Under this law of prior appropriation, holders of junior ditch rights were vulnerable to the possibility of receiving no water during times of shortage. Baxter, *Dividing New Mexico's Water*, 87.
250. Ebright, "Sharing the Shortages," 11, 13, 15–17, 24, 32.
251. Private collection, Madrid Ditch No. 2 Ledger, vol. 2; Colorado Division of Water Resources, Madrid Ditch No. 2 Ledger, vol. 1.
252. Huerfano County Courthouse, Property Records, Warrantee Deed: Felix Lucero to George Mitrovics, Book 49, 26 July 1897, 441. "Priorities and water rights including grantor's interest in [the Madrid] Ditch." In March 1898, mayordomo Teofilo Bustos recorded Mitrovich as entitled to a *surco* of water. Private collection, Madrid Ditch No. 2 Ledger, vol. 1, March 15, 1898.

253. William B. Wayt was born in Iowa about 1864 and later lived in Nebraska. Arlene Johnston, e-mail message to author, January 26, 2005.

254. Private collection, Madrid Ditch No. 2 Ledger, vol. 1, August 5, 1901. "[W.B. Wayt] *Agosto 3 multa por disobedencia, tomo agua $5.00* [U.S. dollars]…[W.B. Wayt] 3 August [1901], fine for disobedience, took water $5.00."

255. Quirino Maes with Maria Viviana Sisneros, January 17, 1868. Colorado Society of Hispanic Genealogy, Salazar and Yost, *Our Lady of Guadalupe Church Marriages*, 8.

256. Denver Public Library, "Letters Received by the Office of Indian Affairs," Roll 198, Conejos County, Frame 127, Line 68; Frame 128, Lines 66, 67, 88. Maria Seferina was a twenty-eight-year-old Navajo when Quirino Maes purchased her in 1863 from "Utah" Indians trading in Colorado Territory. Jose Gregorio was an eighteen-year-old Navajo when purchased in 1853 from Hispanos trading in New Mexico Territory. Jose was fifteen years old when purchased in 1861 from Hispanos trading in New Mexico Territory. (Although Lafayette Head's report states that Antonio was acquired from Mexicans, he likely meant Hispanos from southern Colorado or New Mexico as some Hispanos engaged in this type of raid commerce.) Rafaela was fifteen years old when purchased in 1861 from "Utahs" trading in Colorado Territory. All four captives chose not to return to their tribes.

257. Quirino Maes's personal estate was valued at $4,000. Salvador, age fourteen, shepherd; Santiago, age eleven; Heriquez de Jesus, age one; Jose Gregorio, age twenty-one, Indian shepherd; Maria Seferina, age twenty-five, Indian servant; Margarita, age twenty-five, Indian servant; Jesus M., age two, Indian; and Maria Margarita, age one month, female Indian. 1870 Las Animas County census, 3, Dwelling 21, Household 21, Lines 3–11.

258. Viviana Cisneros was divorced, working as a cook in the Hilaria Osckell household. 1885 Huerfano County census, ED 2, Sheet 6B, Dwelling 54, Household 54, Line 12.

259. Huerfano County Courthouse, Public Records, Warranty Deed No. 15908: Jesus M. Cisneros to Maria Bibian(a) Maes, Book 40, February 4, 1895, 450.

260. 1900 Huerfano County census, 183A, Dwelling 401, Household 420, Line 46.

261. 1880 Huerfano County census. Maria Rosa Gonzales, age fifty, sheepherder; Maria Antonia, age six, adopted; Florentino, age thirteen, servant and cattle herder; and Juanita, age seven, servant.

262. 1885 Huerfano County Agricultural Census, Schedule 2, ED2, Sheet A1, Line 4.
263. Patentee: Maria Rosa Gonzales. U.S. Department of the Interior, Government Land Records, Document No. 3229, April 28, 1888.
264. Jose Maria Bustos, September 18, 1881. Colorado Society of Hispanic Genealogy, "Nuestra Señora de los Siete Dolores Registros de Entierros," 34.
265. Huerfano County Courthouse, Public Records, Warranty Deed: Juan B. Bustos to Manuelita (Maes) Bustos, Book 33, No. 12244, March 26, 1892, 392. Maria Manuela Maes y Bustos paid $100 "together with the interest in the Madril [sic] Ditch for irrigating this land."
266. "*…que Dn Crispin Lucero reuzo [rehuso] trabajar.*" "…that *Don* Crispin Lucero refused to work." Private collection, Madrid Ditch No. 2 Ledger, vol. 1, March 23, 1896.
267. Gabriel Madril with Marcelina Martin, Colorado Society of Hispanic Genealogy, "Nuestra Señora de los Siete Dolores Matrimoniales," 73.
268. Huerfano County Courthouse, Public Records, Warranty Deed: Jesus M. Cisneros to Maria Bibian(a) Maes, Book 40, No. 15908, February 4, 1895, 450. "To the Gabriel Madrid ditch No 2."
269. Colorado State Archives, Huerfano Wills, 20198-M, vol. 1, 151–52.
270. Martinez, "Nuestra Señora de los Dolores," 1.
271. Antonio Jose Vallejos with Maria Dolores Vallejos, August 29, 1885. Colorado Society of Hispanic Genealogy, "Nuestra Señora de los Siete Dolores Registros de Matrimoniales," 157.
272. Colorado Society of Hispanic Genealogy, "Nuestra Señora de los Siete Dolores Registros de Entierros," 83.
273. Included in his will were Maria Viviana Vallejos, a daughter from his first marriage, and Jose Hilario Vallejos, a Navajo captive who had been with the Vallejos family since age two. Other named biological children from Maria Dolores were Maria Gertrudis, Luis Canuto, Vicenta, Jose Manuel and Maria Soledad. Colorado State Archives, Huerfano Wills, 20198-M, vol. 1, 14–15.
274. Ibid. His only debt was $150 for a trust deed on his Huerfano County property. This debt was covered by the sale of his horses and cattle.
275. Private collection, Madrid Ditch No. 2 Ledger, vol. 1, 1896.
276. Meyer, *Water in the Hispanic Southwest*, 70. Reference to an 1823 Bexar County, Texas document.
277. The Old Time Ditch irrigated fifty acres. Water Right, historical information.

278. The Sanchez Ditch was claimed by Pablo Sanchez and his mother, Maria Magdalena (Martin de) Sanchez, the widow of Manuel de Jesus Sanchez. The Sanchez Ditch irrigated two hundred acres. Colorado Division of Water, Map and Filing Statements 62–64, 196–97; Joe Flory, telephone conversation with author, January 3, 2008. Priority 25 allowed irrigation of thirty acres of land; Priority 54 allowed irrigation of an additional seventy acres of land; and Priority 65 allowed irrigation of one hundred acres of land. Maria Magdalena (Martin de) Sanchez's farm was valued at $1,200. 1880 Huerfano County census.
279. Patentee: Jose Ylario Vallejos. U.S. Department of the Interior, Government Land Records, Document No. 2776, March 17, 1892; Reed Decree, June 12, 1869. Huerfano County Records, No. 7, Ballejos Ditch Decree: 56 and 57; Colorado Division of Water Resources, Map and Filing Statement No. 7: 189, 190; Ballejos Ditch Decree, Huerfano County Records, No. 7, 20 June 1890. Copy with author.
280. In 1874, the subsidiary of the D&RG "contracted" the Duran Ditch for its railroad town and for D&RG company lands. *Colorado Springs Gazette*, November 21, 1874.
281. Steinel and Working, "History of Agriculture in Colorado," 230.
282. Colorado Division of Water Resources, Stevens Reservoir and Feeder Map and Filing Statement, December 18, 1890.
283. Huerfano County Courthouse, *Walter V. Stevens v. Jose Hilario Vallejos et al.*, Reed Exception Decree, Grand Docket 582, Book 3, 16 February 1894, 295; Colorado Division of Water Resources, Map and Filing Statements for Lucero and Duran Ditches and Stevens Reservoir.
284. By 1906, the D&RG obtained supplementary water for a pump house south where D&RG land crossed the Cucharas River. "Cuchara, Station and Misc. Buildings—Pump House," Building and Bridges Book, 314.
285. Colorado Division of Water Resources, Map and Filing Statements, McCaskill Ditch, No. 10, 191; Huerfano County District Court case CA1963.
286. The eighteen parciantes represented by this claim were (Maria) Manuelita Maes and her sons Antonio Tircio Bustos, Juan Basilio Bustos and Teofilo Bustos; Jose Federico Chavez; Jose Concepcion Cisneros and his siblings Jesus Maria Cisneros, Jose Antonio Cisneros and Viviana Cisneros; Juan Tomas Espinoza; Ramon Gonzales; Feliz Lucero and his brother, Manuel Antonio Lucero; Juan Jesus Lucero; Gabriel Madril (Madrid); Antonio A. Martinez; (Jose) Eulogio Martinez; and Maria Dolores Vallejos. Colorado Division of Water Resources,

Killian Water Decree. Madrid Ditch No. 2, ditch No. 22, ID 601, 327; Huerfano County District Court Law Record Book, vol. 2, Madrid Ditch No. 2, 221.

287. It was almost a year and a half later before the association subsequently received an additional 7.4 cubic feet of water for irrigation under Priority 63. Colorado Division of Water Resources, Reed Water Decree. Madrid Ditch No. 2, Ditch No. 53, ID 601, 213–14.

288. Colorado Division of Water Resources, Mexican Ditch Decree, No. 12, 13 June 1871, Killian Decree: 59, Huerfano County Records, Mexican Ditch Map and Filing Statements.

289. The parciantes of the Mexican Ditch were Felipe Abeyta, Jose Abundo Bustos, Jose de Gracia Bustos, Jose Ramon Bustos, Marcelo Bustos, Jesus Juan Nepomuceno Chavez, Maria Cisneros, Juan Manuel Espinoza, Nestor Guerrero, Jose Vicente Maes, Juan Andres Maes, Jose Andres Ruibal, Antonio Esteban Sanchez and Martin Tafoya. Map of Mexican Ditch in private possession.

290. Colorado Division of Water Resources, Reed Decree; Sanchez Ditch Map and Filing Statements; Joe Flory, telephone conversation with author, January 3, 2008. Priority 25 allowed irrigation of thirty acres of land; Priority 54 allowed irrigation of an additional seventy acres of land; and Priority 65 allowed irrigation of one hundred acres of land.

291. 1880 Huerfano County census, Production of Agriculture, Schedule 2, Precinct 8, Line 5.

292. *Huerfano Cactus*, May 10, 1884.

293. Between 1881 and 1903, the D&RG's water services included two wooden water tanks, three wells and one cistern. Building and Bridges Book, 308, 314, 315, 317.

FROM A DUSTY ROAD TO A RAILROAD

294. At the time, the U.S. government granted railroads rights of way through public land. Wilson, *Denver and Rio Grande Project*, 81.

295. Brayer, *William Blackmore*, 195.

296. *Pueblo Weekly Chieftan*, May 14, 1873. Permanent officers of the Kansas Colony were professor and musician George Walter Morton, president; Cassimer Williams, vice-president; Smith Faris, treasurer; and Judge William A. Offenbacker, secretary. At this time, Offenbacker was

president of the People's Bank in Pueblo. Colony residents included J.P. Carither, John Chappel, J.A. Coffelt from Tennessee, J. Henry L. Lewis from Pennsylvania, Prior B. Mayo, Thomas Miller from West Virginia, George Walter Morton, Seymour Newton, Jonathan L. Pettyjohn, P. Smith, Robert. B. Stanley and Thomas Wilkin. *Pueblo Weekly Chieftan*, "The Cucharas," June 3, 1874. George Walter Morton owned a grocery and provisions store and became a town trustee in 1876. *Colorado Springs Gazette*, February 26, 1876.

297. Of five town trustees, only Thomas Miller and William A. Offenbacker obtained land patents for land at Cucharas City. Of the thirty-two businessmen listed in the 1875 Colorado Business Directory, only six men obtained land patents for land in Cucharas. Land deed records, Dotter Abstract Company; Homestead Patents, Government Land Records.

298. Members of the clergy likely included Catholic parish priest Father Gabriel Ussel and C.H. Kirkbride, an itinerant Methodist minister from Pueblo who contracted laborers for work on the D&RG in 1875. *Pueblo Weekly Chieftan*, October 15, 1874; 1875 Colorado Business Directory, 102–3.

299. These street names cannot be confirmed. Known streets named at Cucharas City were First Street, Second Street, Third Street, Miller Avenue, Main Street and Marshall Avenue. Miller Avenue was likely named for Thomas Miller, who replaced George W. Brown as route agent for the D&RG. *Colorado Springs Gazette*, "Round About the State," September 30, 1876.

300. By 1889, Union Depot at Cucharas City was a single-story frame building that measured twenty-four feet by seventy-four feet. Colorado Railroad Museum, *Building and Bridges Book*, 308.

301. Montezuma Masonic Lodge no. 109 was chartered on May 8, 1851, at Santa Fe, New Mexico Territory. It is said to be the oldest lodge west of the Rocky Mountains. Elder and Weber, *Trading in Santa Fe*, 106, footnote 27.

302. *Colorado Springs Gazette*, September 30, 1876.

303. Prior B. Mayo led the cornet band. 1874, 1875, 1876 Colorado Business Directory.

304. John Walker was the train engineer, and Robert Glascott was the train conductor who received the ticket punchers. The newspaper erroneously printed that E. Thompson was a Colorado Territory Constitutional Convention delegate from Rio Grande County. *Pueblo Weekly Chieftan*, "Cucharas," May 11, 1876. According to Colorado

Legislative Council records, Thompson did not represent Rio Grande County in the constitutional convention. Huerfano County representatives to the convention were Robert A. Quillian and Agapito Vigil, both Democrats. Vigil, of Las Animas County, represented both Huerfano and Las Animas Counties. (The only other Hispanos to the constitutional convention were Casimiro Barela and Jesus Maria Garcia, who represented Las Animas County as Democrats.) Thompson may have substituted for an official delegate while the convention was in session. Colorado Legislative Biographies of Casimiro Barela, Jesus Maria Garcia, Robert A. Quillian and Agapito Vigil, electronic, accessed March 12, 2009.

305. *Pueblo Weekly Chieftan*, February 24, 1876. J.A. Gibson served as committee chair. Also named on the committee were P. Ducey, secretary; Samuel Todd, assistant secretary; Sam Gates, superintendent of waterworks; J.W. Powell, chief of the fire department; and E.P. Snydam, justice of the peace. Chairman Gibson appointed P. Craig as parade marshal. Mr. Ruibal, D&RG civil engineer captain Howard Schuyler and Cucharas City town trustee John Shank served on the committee to borrow the cannon. *Colorado Springs Gazette*, February 26, 1876. Schuyler was one of the civil engineers who directed the railroad's track-laying gang in 1876. *Pueblo Weekly Chieftan*, March 30, 1876. Schuyler was a former partner of William Jackson Palmer when Palmer helped construct the Kansas Pacific Railroad. Wilson, *Denver and Rio Grande Project*, 7. Samuel Todd was formerly from Trinidad. In 1874, he managed the Cucharas stage station, and by 1876, he ran the hotel. By 1800, he was in La Veta and ran its hotel. By 1885, he was a justice of the peace and a notary at La Veta. *Huerfano Cactus*, May 10, 1884; *Pueblo Weekly Chieftan*, May 11, 1876. Other committee members included Mr. Dunn, Mr. Lafremiere, Thomas Miller, B.K. Simpson and S.S. Adams. Adams became a Cucharas City town trustee in 1876.

306. Although the town name in the directory was listed as Cucharas, the listing actually referred to Cucharas City. The 1875 directory published the population of the Cucharas community and not of Cucharas City. According to one directory, it had a population of four hundred. 1875 Colorado Business Directory, 102–3; 1885 Colorado Business Directory, 47.

307. *Pueblo Daily Chieftain*, "Cucharas," May 12, 1874.

308. *Pueblo Weekly Chieftan*, "Cucharas," November 1, 1874.

309. Colorado Historical Society, Canon and Parsons, "Huerfano County History."

310. Waranty Deed: Juan Jose de Aguero to John F. Read and Charles D. Hayt of the firm of Read and Hayt, August 20, 1874, Entry 3-168: 30. Dotter Abstract Company.
311. Land Patent: Juan Jose de Aguero. Government Land Records, Certificate 1250, 1 October 1874.
312. Fred Walsen paid $450, or $3.75 an acre, for the land. According to the deed, the D&RG was "to construct and maintain suitable cattle guards and crossings for roads and ditches." Waranty Deed: John F. Read and Charles D. Hayt of the firm of Read and Hayt to Fred Walsen. Entry 3-173, 21 August 1874: 31. Dotter Abstract Company.
313. Fred Walsen also purchased land on the north side of the Cucharas River just south of Cucharas City, which later became the right of way for D&RG rails leading to Walsenburg. Colorado Railroad Museum, *Railroad Land Book*, Valuation Section Colo. 5-D, Map #S-4, Huerfano County, Parcel No. 1.
314. John Foster Read and Charles D. Hayt purchased land south of the Cucharas River. Walter V. Stevens purchased land along the right of way east of the D&RG tracks. Read Quit Claim Deed No. 949; Hayt Quit Claim Deed No. 948; Fred Walsen Quit Claim Deed No. 959. Railroad Land Book,
315. Taylor, *First Mail West*, 167.
316. Vallejo, "Early Settlements and Settlers," 4.
317. *Pueblo Weekly Chieftan*, February 24, 1876; *Pueblo Weekly Chieftan*, "Cucharas," May 11, 1876.
318. J.M. Murphy and Co. also had a store in Pueblo. *Pueblo Daily Chieftain*, August 20, 1875.
319. *Walsenburg World Independent*, "Obituary of Jesus Maria Manzanares," April 7, 1933.
320. *Pueblo Daily Chieftain*, November 4, 1874; *Pueblo Weekly Chieftan*, May 11, 1876. Brick for the "commodious new hotel" arrived by rail.
321. 1900 Huerfano County census, Precinct 8, ED 142, Sheet 17B, Line 55, Household 403, Dwelling 418; Lines 65–68, Households 408–410, Dwellings 423–425.
322. Tom Rogers, telephone conversation with author, April 16, 2004.
323. Colorado Humanities, Oral History of Gertrude (Vallejos) Farr, August 5, 1979.
324. Denver Public Library, Louis B. Sporleder Collection, WH916, Box 2, FF7, 81.
325. Jonney Minou also appears in the census as Jenney Miwon. 1900 Huerfano County census, Precinct 8, ED 142, Sheet 17B, Line 69, Household 403, Dwelling 418.

326. Wilson, *Denver and Rio Grande Project*, 68.
327. Winslow, *Loggers and Railroad Workers*, 31.
328. E.P. Snydam owned a billiard hall at Cucharas City in 1876. *Pueblo Weekly Chieftan*, May 11, 1876.
329. Field and Hill also had a forwarding house in Pueblo and a feed store in Alamosa. *Pueblo Daily Chieftain*, July 28, 1875; U.S. Department of the Interior, Scott, "Historic Trail Map," 39; *Pueblo Weekly Chieftan*, March 30, 1876.
330. *Pueblo Weekly Chieftan*, May 11, 1876.
331. Hunt Jackson, *Bits of Travel*, "A New Anvil Chorus."
332. Samuel Todd and George Walter Morton became La Veta town trustees. Morton also taught school, ran the Placer Hotel and owned a grocery and dry goods store. Thomas Miller was appointed La Veta route agent for the D&RG and later became involved in a mining business. John Shank and Thomas Wilkins also moved to La Veta, where Wilkins ran a hardware store. Robert B. Stanley moved west to the mines.
333. Hunt Jackson, *Bits of Travel*, "A New Anvil Chorus."
334. Hunt Jackson, *Bits of Travel*, "Wa-Ha-Toy-A; or Before the Graders," 663.
335. Colorado Railroad Museum, *Building and Bridges Book*, 315; Colorado Railroad Museum, D&RG ICC Valuation Forms, 35–37.
336. Delaney, *All Our Yesterdays*, 25–26.

EDUCATION IN CUCHARAS

337. Colorado Historical Society, *Portrait and Biographical Record*, 197–98; Colorado Department of Education, Biennial Report of the Superintendent of Public Instruction, 1907–8, 15; Colorado Department of Education, Report of the State Superintendent of Public Instruction of the State of Colorado, 1907–8, 15.
338. Colorado Department of Education, Biennial Report of the Superintendent of Public Instruction, 1870–71, 33.
339. Colorado Department of Education, Biennial Report of the Superintendent of Public Instruction, 1907–8, 15, 36.
340. Pueblo Library District, Dodds, "Cucharas School." The 1980 report states the school was built in 1874. Colorado Historical Society, Murphy, "Architectural/Historical Component Form," Inventory Resource No. 5-HF-732.

341. The Cucharas school district was erroneously associated with District 42, which was in Sandy (Arroyo). District 42 was established about 1917. Sandy was located north of Walsenburg.
342. Nancy Christofferson, "County History: Huerfano Annals, Cucharas," *Huerfano World*, March 26, 1998; Nancy Christofferson, "This Week in Walsenburg History," *Huerfano World*, February 20, 2003.
343. *Walsenburg World Independent*, September 2, 1927.
344. Guerminia Eugenia "Jean" Silva, telephone conversation with author, October 2, 2008.
345. Tom Rogers, telephone conversation with author, December 13, 2006.
346. *Huerfano World*, September 30, 1896. The school was incorrectly referred to as the Cucharas School. Nancy Christofferson, "County History: Huerfano Annals, Cucharas," *Huerfano World*, March 26, 1998; *Huerfano World*, November 22, 1900; Nancy Christofferson, interview with author, April 6, 2006.
347. Spanish Peaks Library District, "Voices of the Past."
348. *Walsenburg World Independent*, "Grandma Cruz, 92, Tells Her Story," August 20, 1929.
349. Colorado Society of Hispanic Genealogy, "Nuestra Señora de los Siete Dolores Registros de Matrimoniales," 311.
350. 1910 Las Animas County census, Trinidad Ward 3, 1A, ED117, Line 26, Household 404; 1920 Las Animas County census, Trinidad, 1A, ED142, Line 1, Household 501.
351. Colorado Historical Society, Murphy, "Architectural/Historical Component Form," Inventory Resource No. 5-HF-731. The report states that the school was originally built north of what is now Highway 10. The report also states that until about 1920, classes were held in Spanish; there is no documented proof to substantiate that this statement was true.
352. Gene Morris, e-mail message to author, February 2, 2007.
353. Lee Saunders was the WPA zone supervisor for Huerfano County. *Walsenburg World-Independent*, November 7, 1938; Tom Rogers, telephone conversation with author, December 13, 2006; Guerminia Eugenia "Jean" Silva, telephone conversation with author, April 6, 2004.
354. Colorado Historical Society, Murphy, "Architectural/Historical Component Form," Inventory Resource No. 5-HF-732.
355. Pueblo Library District, Dodds, "Bustos School."
356. *Walsenburg World Independent*, November 7, 1938.
357. Tom Rogers, telephone conversation with author, December 13, 2006.
358. Guerminia Eugenia "Jean" Silva, interview with author, April 6, 2004; Sanchez, "Cucharas, Colorado," 36–37.

359. Colorado Preservation, Inc., "Colorado's Most Endangered Places," nominations submitted by author on July 12, 2004, and July 15, 2007.
360. Guerminia Eugenia "Jean" Silva, telephone conversation with author, February 21, 2007; *Walsenburg Independent*, April 29, 1941; Nancy Christofferson, interview with author, April 6, 2006.

THE END OF CUCHARAS

361. Hall, *History of the State of Colorado*, 494.
362. Vallejos and his first wife, Maria Soledad Romero, served as godparents to Frieda Marie Gertrude Walsen, Fred Walsen's daughter. She was baptized Gertrudis Walsen. Denver Public Library, Louis B. Sporleder Collection, WH916, Box 2, FF 22: 284; Pino, *Our Lady of Sorrows*, vol. 1, *Baptisms*, 198.
363. Denver Public Library, Louis B. Sporleder Collection, WH916, Box 2, FF 22: 284; Colorado Historical Society, Fred Walsen Collection, Manuscript 655, FF4.
364. Nardine, *In the Shadows*, 45. Maes was the son of Felipe Santiago Maes and Maria Dolores Velasquez, who settled in the Lower Cuchara Valley before 1870.
365. George M. Chilcott served in the Colorado Territorial Council in 1861, 1862, 1872 and 1874. From 1867 to 1869, he served as a Colorado Territorial representative to the U.S. House of Representatives. After his return to the territory, he served as council president in 1872. He represented El Paso and Pueblo Counties. Jerome B. Chaffee had interests in banking and mining. He served in the Colorado Territorial Council in 1861, 1862 and 1864. In 1864, he became speaker of the Territorial House. He served as Colorado Territorial representative to the U.S. House of Representatives from 1872 to 1875. From 1877 to 1879, he represented the territory as U.S. senator representing Gilpin County. Chaffee County is named for him. Colorado Legislative Biographies of George M. Chilcott and Jerome B. Chaffee, electronic, accessed March 12, 2009.
366. Through the efforts of Charles O. Unfug and Fred Walsen, the county seat at Badito was moved to la Plaza de los Leones. Pisarczyk, "August Sporleder," 32.

367. Fred Walsen became postmaster of Walsenburg on December 14, 1873. United States Postal Service, Postmasters by City, Walsenburg Post Office. Postmaster Finder, accessed July 17, 2000.
368. *Pueblo Daily Chieftain*, May 20, 1873.
369. Deutsch, *No Separate Refuge*, 31.
370. *Pueblo Weekly Chieftan*, March 30, 1876.
371. "1935: Reyes Casias, 74, of Malachite died. He first settled at the site of the Walsen mine in 1869 on land then owned by Evaristo Gonzales." Nancy Christofferson, "This Week in Walsenburg History," *Huerfano World*, November 11, 1993.
372. Walsen, "General Fred Walsen," 38.
373. In 1893, Alexander Levy was in Crested Butte, Colorado, attempting to secure a D&RG contract. *Huerfano World*, June 8, 1893.
374. Hunt Jackson. *Bits of Travel*, "Wa-Ha-Toy-A; or, Before the Graders," 663.
375. Schrum, "An Inventory of the Papers of Henry Anton Frederick Walsen (1841–1906)." Colorado Historical Society, Fred Walsen Collection, Box 655, FF 16.
376. Fred Walsen was buried at Fairmont Cemetery, Lot 4/5, Block 4, Denver, CO.

APPENDIX B: INDIAN CAPTIVES IN CUCHARAS

377. Salazar and Yost, *Our Lady of Guadalupe Church, Baptisms*, 1.
378. 1870 Huerfano County census, 14, Household/Dwelling 120, Line 20.
379. Colorado Society of Hispanic Genealogy, "Nuestra Señora de los Siete Dolores Registros de Matrimoniales," 79.
380. Martinez, *Nuestra Señora de los Dolores*, 127.
381. 1870 Huerfano County census, 2, Household/Dwelling 10, Lines 5.
382. Colorado Society of Hispanic Genealogy, "Nuestra Señora de los Siete Dolores Registros de Matrimoniales," 65.
383. In 1874, Jose Rafael Esquibel became a Walsenburg town officer at its second election and elected one of four trustees. *Pueblo Daily Chieftain*, May 13, 1874. The following men were elected during the second election of Walsenburg town officers: Cornelius D. Hendren, president; John Albert, A.R. Campbell, Jose Rafael Esquibel and Juan Evaristo Gonzales, trustees; Charles O. Unfug, secretary; Henry Daigre, town marshal; and Jas. F. McMahon, assessor. "The present population of the town numbers

about 150; three-fourths Mexican. The registered voters at this precinct, which includes the citizens in and near the town, number 240." Jose Rafael Esquibel and John Albert were brothers-in-law.

384. Martinez, *Extracts of 1865–1881 Birth and Marriage Records*, 2.

385. Colorado Society of Hispanic Genealogy, "Nuestra Señora de los Siete Dolores Registros de Entierros," 13.

386. 1870 Huerfano County census, 1, Household/Dwelling 8, Lines 36–38. Luisa, age forty, Indian; Rita, age nine, Indian; Manuel, age ten, Indian. All born in New Mexico.

387. Ibid.

388. Rael-Galvez, "Identifying Captivity," 347.

389. 1870 Huerfano County census, 1, Household/Dwelling 8, Lines 36–38.

390. Martinez, *Nuestra Señora de los Dolores*, 129. Maria Rita, one-year-old Indian child adopted by Juan Esquivel and Maria Romaldo Borrego.

391. 1870 Huerfano County census, 29, Household 249, Dwelling 253, Line 18.

392. 1870 Huerfano County census, Schedule 1, 28, Lines 23–29, Household 242, Dwelling 247. Maria Rita, twelve, Indian, born in New Mexico; Maria Antonia, seven; Francisco, ten; Florentino, three; and Gavino Chaves, eight, herds goats. All born in New Mexico.

393. Ibid., 1880 Huerfano County census, ED 6, 39C, Household/Dwelling 307, Lines 37–40. Maria Antonia, six, adopted, born in New Mexico, parents born in New Mexico; Florentino, thirteen, servant, cattle herder, born in New Mexico, parents born in New Mexico; and Juanita, seven, servant, born in Colorado, parents born in New Mexico.

394. Colorado Society of Hispanic Genealogy, "Nuestra Señora de los Siete Dolores Registros de Matrimoniales," 147.

395. Jose Francisco was seven years old when baptized into the Manuel Gonzales family. Martinez, *Nuestra Señora de los Dolores*, 153.

396. 1870 Huerfano County census, Schedule 1, 28, Lines 23–29, Household 242, Dwelling 247. Maria Rita, twelve, Indian, born in New Mexico; Maria Antonia, seven; Francisco, ten; Florentino, three; and Gavino Chaves, eight, herds goats. All born in New Mexico. 1880 Huerfano County census, ED 6, 39C, Household/Dwelling 307, Lines 37–40. Maria Antonia, six, adopted, born in New Mexico, parents born in New Mexico; Florentino, thirteen, servant, cattle herder, born in New Mexico, parents born in New Mexico; and Juanita, seven, servant, born in Colorado, parents born in New Mexico.

397. Ibid.

398. Martinez, *Nuestra Señora de los Dolores*, 114. Maria de los Dolores, fifteen-day-old Ute Indian child adopted by Manuel Gonzales and Maria Rosa Gomez.
399. Ibid., 162. Maria Guadalupe, adult Navajo, family of Manuel Gonzales and Maria Rosa de los Reyes Gomes.
400. Ibid., 152. Maria Guadalupe Gonzales was nine years old when baptized into the Manuel Gonzales family.
401. Maria Rita Gonzales was fifteen years old when she died. Colorado Society of Hispanic Genealogy, "Nuestra Señora de los Siete Dolores Registros de Entierros," 13.
402. Colorado Society of Hispanic Genealogy, "Nuestra Señora de los Siete Dolores Registros de Matrimoniales," 14.
403. Martinez, *Extracts of 1865–1881 Birth and Marriage Records*, 8. Maria Antonia Maes, twenty-three years old, Navajo, family of Benito Maes and Maria Paula Sanchez.
404. Colorado Society of Hispanic Genealogy, "Nuestra Señora de los Siete Dolores Registros de Matrimoniales," 114.
405. Although Indian agent Lafayette Head's report states Antonia was acquired from Mexicans, Head likely meant Hispanos from southern Colorado or New Mexico as some Hispanos engaged in this type of raid commerce. When Jose Benito Maes purchased Antonia from (New) Mexicans in Colorado Territory, Antonia was twenty-four years old. By 1864, Antonia had one child. Denver Public Library, "Letters Received by the Office of Indian Affairs," Roll 193, Frame 41, Line 7, Costilla County. Benito Mes from Culebra, Colorado.
406. Ibid., Roll 193, Frame 41, Line 3, Costilla County.
407. Colorado Society of Hispanic Genealogy, "Nuestra Señora de los Siete Dolores Registros de Martrimoniales," 172.
408. Whether Teodoro Maes captured Juan Tomas cannot be determined from the records. Juan Tomas, age eight, was captured in Arizona Territory in 1862. Denver Public Library, "Letters Received by the Office of Indian Affairs," Roll 193, Frame 41, Lines 1–3, Costilla County.
409. Pino, *Our Lady of Sorrows*, vol. 1, *Baptisms*, 66.
410. When interviewed by Indian agent Lafayette Head, Maria Rita stated that she wished to remain with the Maes family. Denver Public Library, "Letters Received by the Office of Indian Affairs," Roll 193, Frame 41, Lines 1–3, Costilla County.
411. Colorado Society of Hispanic Genealogy, "Nuestra Señora de los Siete Dolores Registros de Martrimoniales," 4.

412. 1870 Huerfano County census, 26, Household 225, Dwelling, 230, Line 14.
413. The gender of Guadalupe is unknown. Colorado Humanities, Oral History of Theresa (Teresina Martinez) Armijo, July 16, 1979.
414. Ibid.
415. 1870 Huerfano County census, 26, Household 225, Dwelling, 230, Line 14.
416. Colorado Society of Hispanic Genealogy, "Nuestra Señora de los Siete Dolores Registros de Martrimoniales," 28. "Vidal Martinez, from Cucharas, single legitimate son of Juan Santos Martinez and Maria Rafaela Romero, with Maria Dolores Valdez (Navajoe [*sic*] woman), single, adopted by Leonires Valdes and Maria Martina Mestas." Cucharas captive owners Manuel Gonzales and Maria Rosa Gomez served as godparents.
417. Maria Dolores Valdez, burial November 2, 1877. Colorado Society of Hispanic Genealogy, "Nuestra Señora de los Siete Dolores Registros de Entierros," 10.
418. According to the 1870 census enumerations, Juan Benito Valdez established dual residencies in Huerfano and Taos Counties. His patent for land in Huerfano County was approved on 19 December 1870. Land Claim: Juan Benito Valdez. Huerfano County Records, Precinct #6, Book 4: 86, 105; Book 27, Doc. VC-36-37, 9.
419. 1860 Taos County census, Territory of New Mexico, Household 1179. Juan Benito Valdez, forty-seven; Maria Estefana Vigil, thirty-two; Jose Leonides, eleven; Maria Tomasa, nine; Bibiana, seven; Juan Antonio Santiago, four; Antonio D., two; Jose Vicente, Indian, six; Cornelia, Indian, four; Maria de la Cruz, Indian, four, born in Rio Colorado (Questa), New Mexico. In 1860, his real estate was valued at $4,000 and his personal property valued at $6,000. He owned "one hundred-eighteen acres of unimproved land, sixty acres improved, cash value of farm $3,000, $100 value of farming machinery, seven horses, nineteen asses, ten milk cows, sixteen oxen, twenty other cows, one thousand sheep, fifteen swine, with total value of livestock at $4,150, three hundred fifty bushels of wheat, two hundred acres Indian corn, one thousand (bags of) wool."
420. 1860 Taos County census, Territory of New Mexico, Household 1179.
421. Colorado Society of Hispanic Genealogy, Salazar and Yost, *Our Lady of Guadalupe Church Marriages*, 29. Felipe Valdez listed as adopted.

422. Maria Guadalupe, age five, and Maria Ramona, age six. Navajo children in the family of Juan Benito Valdes and Maria Estefana Vigil. Both children were baptized August 1864. Martinez, *Nuestra Señora de los Dolores*, 166.
423. 1870 Huerfano County census, Schedule 1, 9, Household/Dwelling 81, Lines 37–39. Jose, seventeen, Indian, shepherd; Juan Antonio, thirteen, Indian, shepherd. Both born in New Mexico.
424. Ibid.
425. 1860 Taos County census, Territory of New Mexico, Household 1179.
426. 1880 New Mexico census, Rio Colorado, Fernando de Taos, Territory of New Mexico, 12, Household 117, Dwelling 103.
427. Martinez, *Nuestra Señora de los Dolores*, 166.
428. 1880 New Mexico census, Rio Colorado, Fernando de Taos, Territory of New Mexico, 12, Household 117, Dwelling 103.
429. 1860 Taos County census, Territory of New Mexico, Household 1179.
430. Colorado State Archives, Huerfano Wills, Will Record 20198-M, vol. 1, 14–15.
431. Based on her long association with Jose Hilario, Navajo captive Maria Dolores was the only connection to his Navajo heritage.
432. Martinez, *Nuestra Señora de los Dolores*, 109.
433. Colorado Society of Hispanic Genealogy, "Nuestra Señora de los Siete Dolores Registros de Matrimoniales," 156.
434. By 1900, widow Maria Dolores took in boarders and resided with captive Jose Hilario Vallejos and his family. 1900 Huerfano County census. Dolores Vallejos is listed as mother.
435. Martinez, *Nuestra Señora de los Dolores*, 1. M. Dolores Ballejo, baptized April 7, 1865, sixteen-year-old Navajo adopted by Antonio Jose Vallejo and Maria Soledad Romero.
436. Colorado Society of Hispanic Genealogy, "Nuestra Señora de los Siete Dolores Registros de Matrimoniales," 157; Colorado Society of Hispanic Genealogy, "Nuestra Señora de los Siete Dolores Registros de Entierros," 83.
437. Salazar and Yost, *Our Lady of Guadalupe Church, Baptisms*, 73–74. Maria Isabel Vallegos, six years old, servant of Antonio Jose Vallejos and Maria Soledad Romero.
438. Maria Guadalupe, two-year-old Indian (*Indita*) of Francisco Ballejos and Maria Antonia Valdez. Martinez, *Nuestra Señora de los Dolores*, 126.
439. 1870 Huerfano County census, 11, Lines 5–17, Household/Dwelling 92.

440. Maria Josefa, twenty-year-old Indian adopted by Francisco Ballejos and Maria Antonia Valdez. Martinez, *Nuestra Señora de los Dolores*, 126.

441. Maria Juliana Vallejos was the daughter of Rosalia Vallejos. Martinez, *Extracts of 1865–1881 Birth and Marriage Records*, 1.

442. Although Indian agent Lafayette Head's report states Antonia was acquired from Mexicans, Head likely meant Hispanos from southern Colorado or New Mexico as some Hispanos engaged in this type of raid commerce. In 1864, Jose Maria Vallejos purchased eighteen-year-old Rosalia from (New) Mexican traders in Colorado Territory. Denver Public Library, "Letters Received by the Office of Indian Affairs," Roll 193, Frame 42, Line 44, Costilla County.

443. 1870 Huerfano County census, 11, Lines 5–17, Household/Dwelling 92. Dolores, thirty, Indian, house servant, born in New Mexico; Josefa, fifteen, Indian, house servant, born in New Mexico; Felipe, fourteen, Indian, herds sheep, born in New Mexico; and Nestor, three, Indian, born in Colorado.

444. Denver Public Library, "Letters Received by the Office of Indian Affairs," Roll 193, Frame 42, Line 40, Costilla County. Josefa, eight-year-old Navajo purchased in 1860 from Ute Indians trading in Colorado Territory.

445. 1870 Huerfano County census, 11, Lines 5–17, Household/Dwelling 92. Dolores, thirty, Indian, house servant, born in New Mexico; Josefa, fifteen, Indian, house servant, born in New Mexico; Felipe, fourteen, Indian, herds sheep, born in New Mexico; and Nestor, three, Indian, born in Colorado. Maria de los Reyes Vallejos, daughter of Juan Felipe Vallejos and Maria de Jesus Gomez, was baptized at Arroyo Hondo, New Mexico, on January 6, 1874. Their son, Pablo Antonio Vallejos, was also baptized at Arroyo Hondo on April 4, 1876. Martinez, *Nuestra Señora de los Dolores*, 41, 61; Denver Public Library, Louis Sporleder Collection, WH916, Box 2, FF 7: 78.

446. Denver Public Library, "Letters Received by the Office of Indian Affairs." Roll 193, Frame 42, Line 41, Costilla County. Felipe, eight-year-old Navajo purchased by Miguel Antonio Vallejos in 1863 from Ute Indians trading in Colorado Territory.

447. Daughter of Diego Antonio Gomez and Maria Antonia de la Cruz Lopez. Martinez, *Nuestra Señora de los Dolores*, 41, 61. By 1874, Juan Felipe Vallejos and his wife, Maria de Jesus Gomez, lived in Costilla County.

448. Maria Rosalia was eight years old when baptized into the Miguel Antonio Vallejos family. Martinez, *Nuestra Señora de los Dolores*, 126.

449. 1870 Huerfano County census, 11, Lines 5–17, Household/Dwelling 92. Dolores, thirty, Indian, house servant, born in New Mexico; Josefa, fifteen, Indian, house servant, born in New Mexico; Felipe, fourteen, Indian, herds sheep, born in New Mexico; and Nestor, three, Indian, born in Colorado.

450. Soledad is the only servant enumerated in the Vallejos household in 1880; she worked as a cook and is presumed to be an Indian captive. 1880 Huerfano County census, 3, ED 60, Lines 22–31 Precinct 8, Household/Dwelling 22. Soledad, twelve, servant, cook, born in New Mexico.

Bibliography

Archives and Manuscripts

Colorado Department of Education, Denver

Biennial Reports of the Superintendent of Public Instruction of the State of Colorado. Years Ending August 31, 1879, and August 31, 1880; August 31, 1883, and August 31, 1884; August 31, 1885, and August 31, 1886; and Term Ending June 30, 1888, and 1907–8.

Report of the State Superintendent of Public Instruction of the State of Colorado, 1907–8, 15.

Colorado Division of Water Resources, Division 2, District 16, Denver

Colorado Water Right, historical information database, http://cdss.state.co.us/DNN/WaterRights/tabid/76/Default.aspx.

Killian Water Decree.

Map and Filing Statements: Ballejos Ditch, Duran Ditch, Lucero Ditch, Madrid Ditch No. 2, Old Time Ditch, McCaskill Ditch, Mexican Ditch, Sanchez Ditch and the Stevens Reservoir.

Reed Water Decree.

Colorado Historical Society, Stephen H. Hart Library, Denver

Business Directory and Railroad Gazetteer, "Walsenburg," 1879.

Canon, Benton, and Eugene Parsons. "Huerfano County History." In *History of Huerfano County, Colorado*. N.p., 1922.

Colorado Business Directories. 1875–82, 1883–93, 1894–5, 1896–1935.

Fred Walsen Collection, Box 655, Estate file folder.

———. Schrum, Keith. "An Inventory of the Papers of Henry Anton Frederick Walsen (1841–1906)."

———. Walsen Family file folder.

Murphy, Sara. "Architectural/Historical Component Form," Inventory Resource No. 5-HF-727, -728, -731, -732 and -735. Office of Archaeology and Historic Preservation (OAHP).

1910 Pueblo City Directory.

Portrait and Biographical Record of the State of Colorado, Containing Portraits and Biographies of Many Well-Known Citizens of the Past and Present. Chicago, IL: Chapman Pub. Co., 1898.

Colorado Humanities, "Huerfano County Oral History Project," 1979, Denver

Oral History of Theresa (Teresina Martinez) Armijo. Documented by Frances Cruz.

Oral History of Pedro Cisneros. Interviewed by Gloria Campbell.

Oral History of Eleanor Cordova. Translated by Lorraine Vargas.

Oral History of Frank (Jose Francisco) Cordova.

Oral History of Gertrude (Vallejos) Farr.

Oral History of Patricio Maes. Interviewed by Gloria Campbell.

Oral Histories of Marcos and Benito Manzanares. Documented by Cleo Bellah.

Oral Histories of Max (Melaquias) and Lulu (Leocadia Sandoval) Valdez.

Colorado Land Office, Reading Room, Denver

Railroad Maps," D&RG Map, La Veta to Cuchara Junction, Mile Post 169-100, RR-2.

"Tax Evaluation Maps of Railroad Facilities."

Colorado Preservation, Inc., Denver

Colorado's Most Endangered Places nominations. Submitted July 12, 2004, and July 15, 2007.

Colorado Railroad Museum, Robert W. Richardson Railroad Library, Golden

Building and Bridges Book.

D&RG ICC Valuation Maps.

Railroad Land Book.

Colorado Society of Hispanic Genealogy, Denver

"Nuestra Señora de los Siete Dolores Registros de Entierros (Burials), September 4, 1876 to July 25, 1895." Saint Mary Catholic Parish Church, Walsenburg, Colorado. Photocopied by Eileen Bankson, indexed by Brenndan Patrick Torres.

"Nuestra Señora de los Siete Dolores Registros de Matrimoniales (Marriages), July 12, 1871 to August 31, 1899." Saint Mary Catholic Parish Church, Walsenburg, Colorado. Photocopied by Eileen Bankson, indexed by Brenndan Patrick Torres.

Salazar, David, extractor, and Hope Yost, compiler. *Our Lady of Guadalupe Church Baptisms, 1868–1871, Marriages 1860–1881 and Deaths 1860–1896, Conejos, Colorado*, self-published.

Colorado State Archives, Denver

District Court Law Record Book.

Huerfano County Grand Docket, Vol. 4, 1890–1901.

Huerfano County Tax Roll, 8080D.

Huerfano Wills, 1874–1911 "Will Record," 20198-M, Vol. 1, 14–15; "Will Record," 20198-M, Vol. 1, 151–52.

Colorado State University, Morgan Library, Special Collections Department, Fort Collins

Parshall, Ralph L. "Irrigation in Colorado," Fort Collins: Colorado Experiment Station, June 1927.

Steinel, Alvin T., and D.W. Working. "History of Agriculture in Colorado, 1868–1926." 1926.

Denver Public Library Western History Department, Denver

"Letters Received by the Office of Indian Affairs, 1824–1880," Colorado Superintendency, 1865–1866, Microcopy 24, Roll 193, Frame 41, Costilla County.

———. Roll 198, Frames 127 and 128, Conejos County.

Louis B. Sporleder Collection, WH916, Box 2, File Folders 7, 22, 40 and 42.

Dotter Abstract Company, Walsenburg

Warranty Deeds No. 5–32, August 30, 1874, to December 13, 1894. Copies with author.

Huerfano County Courthouse, Walsenburg

District Court Law Record Book, Vol. 2, February 12, 1898, No. 22.

Grand Docket 582, Book 3, Reed Exception Decree, 16 February 1894.

Map Book, "Map of the Town of Cuchara," Survey Plat Map 3, 1891. "Map of Cuchara City," Survey Plat Map 30, 1922.

McCaskill Ditch, No. 10, Huerfano County District Court case CA1963.

Public Records, Book 33.

National Archives and Records Administration, (NARA), Rocky Mountain Region, Lakewood

"Non-Mineral Affidavit and Timber-Culture Proof-Testimony of Claimant of John F. Read," January 4, 1896, Box 1343.

"Record of Appointment of Postmasters, 1832-September 30, 1971," M841, Roll 14.

"Site Location Reports of Post Offices, 1837–1950," Cucharas Post Office, Microfilm 1126, Roll 76.

"Township Survey Plat," Book 80, Map 36, Township 27 South Range 65 West, 6th Prime Meridian.

Pueblo Library District, Special Collections Department, Pueblo

Dodds, Joanne. "Bustos School." 1980. Huerfano County Country Schools Folder, Historic Site Form.

———."Cucharas School." 1980. Huerfano County Country Schools Folder, Historic Site Form.

Spanish Peaks Library District, Walsenburg

"Voices of the Past: Historical Study of Huerfano County, Teacher's Edition 1891–1950."

University of New Mexico, Office of Contract Archeology, Albuquerque, New Mexico

"Prehistoric and Historic Adaptations in Eastern New Mexico and Southeastern Colorado," Vol. II, Section VI by James O. Piggott, and Section VII by Dan Scurlock in *The ARCO CO_2 Pipeline Archeology Project*, edited by Joseph C. Winter.

MISCELLANEOUS DOCUMENTS

Cucharas Warranty Deeds 1890–1917 associated with Huerfano County District Court Civil Action No. 3783. Private collection. Copies with author.

Madrid Ditch No. 2. Ledgers Vol. 1, 1884–1912, and Vol. 2, 1913–1923. Unpublished, private collections. Copies with author.

Rael-Galvez, Estevan. "Identifying Captivity and Capturing Identity: Narratives of American Indian Slavery in Colorado and New Mexico, 1776–1934." Doctoral dissertation, University of Michigan, 2002.

Government Publications

Colorado Legislative Biographies of Casimiro Barela, Jerome B. Chaffee, George M. Chilcott, Jesus Maria Garcia, Lafayette Head, Robert A. Quillian and Agapito Vigil. Colorado Legislative Council. http://www.leg.state.co.us/lcs/leghist.nsf?OpenDatabase.

U.S. Department of the Interior, Bureau of Land Management, Government Land Records, Huerfano County, Colorado, Townships 27 and 28 South, Range 65 and 66 West, 6th Prime Meridian. http://www.glorecords.blm.gov/PatentSearch/Default.asp?.

———. National Park Service, National Register of Historic Places. Holleran, Michael. "Irrigation and Water Supply Ditches and Canals in Colorado."

———. U.S. Geological Survey. Scott, Glenn R. "Historic Trail Map of the Trinidad 1° x 2° Quadrangle, Southern Colorado." Geologic Investigations Series I-2745, 2001.

U.S. Forest Service, Streams Systems Technology Center, "Ask Doctor Hydro." http://www.stream.fs.fed.us/news/streamnt/jan97/jan97a2.htm#anchortop.

U.S. Postal Service. Postmasters by City, San Luis Post Office. Postmaster Finder. http://webpmt.usps.gov/pmt003.cfm.

Colorado Census Records

1870, 1880, 1885, 1900, 1910, 1920 and 1930 censuses, Huerfano County.

1880 census, Las Animas County.

1870 census, Pueblo County.

1860 census, Taos County, New Mexico Territory.

Newspapers

Colorado Springs Gazette.

Denver Daily Tribune.

Denver Rocky Mountain News.

El Reino de Dios (Spanish edition of the *Catholic Register*).

Pueblo Daily Chieftain.

Pueblo Weekly Chieftan.

Trinidad Enterprise.

Walsenburg Huerfano Cactus.

Walsenburg Huerfano World.

Walsenburg World Independent.

Books and Pamphlets

Anderson, George L. *General William J. Palmer: A Decade of Colorado Railroad Building 1870–1880.* General Series No. 209, Colorado Springs: Colorado College, 1936.

Baxter, John O. *Dividing New Mexico's Waters 1700–1912.* Albuquerque: University of New Mexico Press, 1997.

Beadle, J.H. *The Undeveloped West or Five Years in the Territories, 1872*. Philadelphia and Chicago: National Pub. Co., 1873.

Brayer, Herbert O. *William Blackmore: Early Financing of the Denver and Rio Grande Railway and Ancillary Land Companies, 1871–1878*. Vol 2. Denver, CO: Bradford-Robinson, 1949.

Brooks, James E., and Omohundro Institute of Early American History and Culture. *Captives and Cousins: Slavery, Kinship and Community in the Southwest Borderlands.* Chapel Hill: University of North Carolina Press, 2002.

Burke, Marrill Lee. *A Bumpy Ride: A History of Stagecoaching in Colorado*. Lake City, CO: Western Reflections Publishing Company, 2007.

Campa, Arthur L. *Hispanic Culture in the Southwest.* Norman and London: University of Oklahoma Press, 1979.

Delaney, Howard L. *All Our Yesterdays: The Story of St. Mary Parish, Walsenburg, Colorado*. N.p.: Consolidated Pub. Co., 1944.

De Oñis, Jose. *The Hispanic Contribution to the State of Colorado*. Boulder, CO: Westview Press, 1976.

Deutsch, Sarah. *No Separate Refuge: Culture, Class, and Gender on an Anglo-Hispanic Frontier in the American Southwest, 1880–1940*. New York and Oxford: Oxford University Press, 1987.

Ebright, Malcolm. *Spanish and Mexican Land Grants and the Law*. Manhattan, KS: Sunflower University Press, 1989.

Eggenhofer, Nicholas. *Wagons, Mules, and Men*. New York: Hastings House, 1961.

Elder, Jane Lenz, and David J. Weber. *Trading in Santa Fe: John M. Kingsbury's Correspondence with James Josiah Webb, 1853–1861*. Dallas, TX: Southern Methodist University Press, 1996.

Fernandez, Jose Emilio. *The Biography of Casimiro Barela.* Albuquerque: University of New Mexico Press, 2003.

Hall, Frank. *History of the State of Colorado.* Chicago: Blackely Printing Company, 1891.

Harlan, George. *Postmarks and Places*. Alamosa, CO: Ye Olde Print Shoppe, 1976.

Hispanic Pioneers in Colorado and New Mexico. Denver, CO: Alliance Press, 2006.

Hunt Jackson, Helen. "A New Anvil Chorus" and "Wa-ha-toy-a; or Before the Graders." In *Bits of Travel at Home, 1878*. Vol. 39, no. 236. Boston: Roberts Brothers, 1878.

Jefferson, James, Robert W. Delaney and Gregory C. Thompson. *The Southern Utes: A Tribal History*. Ignacio, CO: Southern Ute Tribe, 1972.

Lamar, Howard Roberts. *The Far Southwest 1846–1912: A Territorial History*. Albuquerque: University of New Mexico Press, 2000.

Maes, Arthur F. *Following in the Footsteps of our Ancestors from Santa Fe to Maes Creek*. N.p.: self-published, 1995.

Martinez, Maria Clara. *Extracts of the 1865–1881 Birth and Marriage Records of Parroquia de San Miguel, Costilla, New Mexico*. N.p.: self-published, n.d.

———. *Nuestra Señora de los Dolores, Arroyo Hondo, New Mexico*. N.p.: self-published, n.d.

McLean, Robert N., and Charles A. Thomson. *Spanish and Mexican in Colorado: A Survey of the Spanish Americans and Mexicans in the State of Colorado*. N.p.: Board of National Missions of the Presbyterian Church in the USA, 1924.

Meketa, Jacqueline Dorgan. *Legacy of Honor: The Life of Rafael Chacon: A Nineteenth-Century New Mexican*. Albuquerque: University of New Mexico Press, 1986.

Meyer, Michael C. *Water in the Hispanic Southwest: A Society and Legal History, 1550–1850*. Tucson: University of Arizona Press, 1996.

Montoya, Maria E. *Translating Property: The Maxwell Land Grant and the Conflict over Land in the American West, 1840–1900*. Berkeley and Los Angeles: University of California Press, 2002.

Nardine, Henry. In the Shadows of the Spanish Peaks. Revised. Walsenburg, CO: self-published, 1988.

Oehlerts, Donald E. *Guide to Colorado Newspapers, 1859–1963*. Denver, CO: Bibliographical Center for Research, Rocky Mountain Region, 1964.

Peña, Devon G. *Chicano Culture, Ecology, Politics: Subversive Kin*. Tucson: University of Arizona Press, n.d.

Perkins, James E. *Tom Tobin Frontiersman*. Pueblo West, CO: Herodotus Press, 1999.

Pino, Theresa L. *Our Lady of Sorrows/St. Mary Church, Walsenburg, CO*. Vols. 1 and 2. *Baptism*. N.p.: self-published, 2002.

Quintana, Frances Leon. *Pobladores: Hispanic Americans of the Ute Frontier*. 2nd ed. Notre Dame, IN: University of Notre Dame Press, 1991.

Rasmussen, Stephen. *The Rio Grande's La Veta Pass Route: Gateway to the San Luis Valley*. Burlington, VT: Evergreen Press, 2000.

Rivera, Jose A. *Acequia Culture: Water, Land, & Community in the Southwest*. Albuquerque: University of New Mexico Press, 1998.

Rock, Kenneth W. *German Footprints in Colorado*. Denver, CO: Committee for the German Heritage Festival, 1983.

Simmons, Virginia McConnell. *The San Luis Valley: Land of the Six-Armed Cross*. Niwot: University Press of Colorado, 1999.

Slaney, Deborah C. *Wonders of the Weavers, Maravillas de los Tejedores: Nineteenth-Century Río Grande Weavings from the Collection of The Albuquerque Museum*. Albuquerque: Albuquerque Museum, New Mexico, 2005.

Taylor, Morris F. *Colorado South of the Border*. Denver, CO: Sage Books, 1963.

———. *First Mail West: Stagecoach Lines on the Santa Fe Trail*. Albuquerque: University of New Mexico Press. 1971.

Tushar, Olibama. *The People of El Valle: A History of the Spanish Colonials in the San Luis Valley*. 3rd ed. Pueblo, CO: El Escritorio, 1997.

Van Nuys, Frank. *Americanizing the West: Race, Immigrants, and Citizenship, 1890–1930*. Lawrence: University Press of Kansas, 2002.

Williams, Henry T. *Williams' Tourists' Guide and Map of the San Juan Mines of Colorado*. N.p.: 1877.

Wilson, O. Meredith. *The Denver and Rio Grande Project, 1870–1901*. Salt Lake City, UT: Howe Brothers Publishers, 1982.

Winslow, Mimi. *Loggers and Railroad Workers*, New York: Twenty-First Century Books, 1995.

ARTICLES, CHAPTERS AND SERIES

Andrews, Paul D., and Nandy L. Humphry. "El Patrón de Trinidad: Don Felipe de Jesús Baca." *Colorado Heritage* (Winter 2004).

Baxter, John O. "Measuring New Mexico's Irrigation Water: How Big Is a *Surco*?" *New Mexico Historical Review* 75, no. 3 (July 2000).

Birner, Fred. "Jose Francisco Vigil: Southern Colorado Santero (1855–1928)." *Tradicion Revista* 5 (Winter 2000).

———. "Juan Ysidro Maez: The Last Traditional Santero." *Tradicion Revista* 6 (Summer 2001).

Ebright, Malcolm. "Sharing the Shortages: Water Litigation and Regulation in Hispanic New Mexico, 1600–1850." *New Mexico Historical Review* 76, no. 1 (January 2001).

Grubbs, Frank H. "Frank Bond: Gentleman Sheepherder of Northern New Mexico 1883–1915." *New Mexico Historical Review* 35, no. 3 (July 1960).

Hall, Frank. "History of Huerfano County." In *History of the State of Colorado.* Chicago: Blakely Printing Company, 1889–95.

Harrington, John P. "The Tewa Indian Game of Cañute." *American Anthropologist* 14 (1912).

Hicks, Gregory A., and Devon G. Peña. "Community Acequias in Colorado's Rio Culebra Watershed: A Customary Commons in the Domain of Prior Appropriation." *University of Colorado Law Review* 74, no. 2 (Spring 2003).

"Interview of B.A. Arnold of Walsenburg." *Colorado Magazine* 2, no. 2 (1975).

McCullough, Frances. "Barlow and Sanderson Stage Line in the San Luis Valley." *San Luis Valley Historian* 30, no. 3 (1998).

McNellis, Dan. "The First Hundred Years." *Co-Operative Century: Colorado Cattlemen's Association 100th Anniversary Issue* (1967).

———. "Giant of the West." *Co-Operative Century: Colorado Cattlemen's Association 100th Anniversary Issue* (1967).

———. "Heat, Light, and History." *Co-Operative Century: Colorado Cattlemen's Association 100th Anniversary Issue* (1967).

Peña, Devon G. "Cultural Landscapes and Biodiversity: The Ethnoecology of an Upper Rio Grande Watershed Commons." In *La Gente: Hispano History and Life in Colorado*. N.p.: Colorado Historical Society, 1998.

Pisarczyk, Louise Sporleder. "August Sporleder." In *Pioneers of the Territory of Southern Colorado*, Vol. 5. Monte Vista, CO: CBI Offset Printers, 1980.

Sanchez, Virginia. "Colorado Indian Acquisitions." *Colorado Hispanic Genealogist* 5 (Fall 2008).

———. "Cucharas, Colorado: School Days and Spiritual Life in Huerfano County." *Colorado Heritage* (Winter 2007).

Smith, Jeffrey S., Matthew R. Engle, Douglas A. Hurt, Jeffery E. Roth and James M. Stevens. "La Cultura de la Acequia Madre: Cleaning a Community Irrigation Ditch." *North American Geographer* 3, no. 1 (2001).

Sporleder, Amelia, Freda Sporleder Haney, Virginia Sporleder Anderson and Geraldine Sporleder. "Our Grandfather Louis Bernhardt Sporleder." In *Pioneers of the Territory of Southern Colorado*, Vol. 2. Monte Vista, CO: CBI Offset Printers, 1980.

Sporleder, Louis B. "Description of Plaza de los Leones." *Colorado Magazine* 10, no. 1 (January 1933).

Stoller, Marianne L. "Spanish-Americans, Their Servants and Sheep: A Culture History of Weaving in Southern Colorado." In *Spanish Textile Tradition of New Mexico and Colorado*. Santa Fe: Museum of New Mexico Press, 1979.

Taylor, Morris F. "Ka-Ni-Ache." *Colorado Magazine* 43, no. 4 (Fall 1966).

Taylor, William B., and Elliott West. "Patron Leadership at the Crossroads: Southern Colorado in the Late Nineteenth Century." *Pacific Historical Review* 42, no. 3 (August 1973).

Vallejo, Frances Nelson. "Early Settlements and Settlers in Huerfano County." In *Pioneers of the Territory of Southern Colorado*, Vol. 2. Monte Vista, CO: CBI Offset Printers, 1980.

Walker, Evalyn Capps. "The Samuel John Capps Family." In *Pioneers of the Territory of Southern Colorado*, Vol. 2. Monte Vista, CO: CBI Offset Printers, 1980.

Walsen, Augusta Virginia. "General Fred Walsen." In *Pioneers of the Territory of Southern Colorado*, Vol. 2. Monte Vista, CO: CBI Offset Printers, 1980.

White, William R. "Illegal Fencing on the Colorado Range." *Colorado Magazine* 2, no. 2 (1975).

Interviews and Personal Correspondence

Anonymous former penitente.

Bustos, Celedon. Albuquerque, New Mexico.

Christofferson, Nancy, Huerfano County historian, La Veta.

Davis, Marvin. Walsenburg.

Delaney, Howard. Pueblo.

Farr, James. Interviewed by Paul Krier; Howard Delaney, recorder. Sound cassettes tape two of two, Side B.

Flory, Joe. Colorado Division of Water Resources, Division 2, Pueblo.

Gomez, Karen. Genealogical historian for the Huerfano County parishes, Catholic Diocese of Pueblo.

Johnston, Arlene.

Kaelin, Celinda R. Pikes Peak Historical Society, Florrisant.

Lucero, Conrad. Pueblo.

Morris, Gene. National Archives and Records Administration, Civil Records, Washington, D.C.

Rogers, Tom. Walsenburg.

Silva, Guerminia Eugenia "Jean." Pueblo.

Weeks, Rene.

Index

D

M

N

O

P

W

Y

About the Author

Virginia Sanchez is an independent historian who enjoys research. Her articles have appeared in the *New Mexico Magazine*, *La Herencia* and in historical, cultural and genealogical journals such as *Colorado History*, the *New Mexico Genealogist* and the *Colorado Hispanic Genealogist*. Virginia has presented her research to historical and genealogical societies in New Mexico, Colorado and Wyoming. In 2008, she was recognized in Denver, Colorado, by the Hispanic Annual Salute for her contributions to the Hispanic community in the area of history. She worked for a *Fortune* 500 telecommunications company for twenty years and received a master's degree in technical communication from the University of Colorado at Denver in 1988 and a bachelor's degree in music from the University of Wyoming in 1976. Her ancestors were among the first soldiers/colonists to settle the Spanish Province of New Mexico in 1598.

Virginia is a member of the Colorado Historical Society, the New Mexico Historical Society, the Huerfano County Historical Society and the Colorado Society of Hispanic Genealogy.